TEA LOVE AND WAR

TEA
LOVE AND
WAR

SEARCHING FOR
ENGLISH ROOTS
IN ASSAM

DAVID MITCHELL

Matador
9 Priory Business Park,
Wistow Road, Kibworth Beauchamp,
Leicestershire. LE8 0RX
Tel: (+44) 116 279 2299
Fax: (+44) 116 279 2277
Email: books@troubador.co.uk
Web: www.troubador.co.uk/matador

ISBN 978 1780880 891

British Library Cataloguing in Publication Data.
A catalogue record for this book is available from the British Library.

Typeset in 11pt Bembo by Troubador Publishing Ltd, Leicester, UK
Printed and bound in the UK by TJ International, Padstow, Cornwall

Matador is an imprint of Troubador Publishing Ltd

INTRODUCTION

This is a patchwork of a book – a book conceived as a novel based on the experiences of the dramatis personae it describes – but a book finally born as mixed race with non-fiction the dominant gene.

The embryo of the book was formed by the discovery of long-forgotten correspondence from my uncle Stuart, fertilized first by curiosity and then by my researches concerning the specifics of the war years. This, combined with the vivid memories of the survivors, my mother Mary and Ann herself, across their separate generations enabled the embryo to develop until the child was ready for full-term delivery. It should be said that the descriptions by Mary and by Ann are moulded from their respective personal recollections and it is only in passages of Stuart's life story that some poetic licence has been used to merge the text of his long letters with knowledge gleaned from other contemporary documents and records of the time.

Rather than interpose myself as narrator it has been an easy decision to appoint my mother to that role. Much of the text is already taken from the many exercise books that she filled with her memories, and whilst my investigations have expanded and updated her story, the history of the relevant elements of the Second World War, the Blitz and public perception of the Malayan campaign leading to the fall of Singapore are more eloquently seen from her individual viewpoint. For those interested in the Malayan campaign a more detailed description of that theatre of war and Stuart's particular exploits will be found in Book Two.

I will conclude this introduction by saying that the first five years of Stuart's time in India were meticulously recorded in his weekly letters home. Sadly, my mother loaned the letters to an aunt on my father's side of the family who had determined to write a novel based on Stuart's tea planting experience. The aunt died, and it can only be surmised that the letters were destroyed. My mother's recollections of what Stuart wrote to her and told her, together with other records, photographs and stories, have been combined with memories from those in Assam at the time and have thus enabled the story of his first posting to be told; but it is to my huge regret that the first-hand description, with all its individuality, is lost.

The letters from Stuart's return to India after his first leave remain intact, and the narrative of his subsequent adventures is taken from them and from contemporary histories of the Malayan campaign.

David Mitchell

PREFACE

This book is completed in my 97th year – and would not have reached fruition save for the industry of my son in assembling the various disparate elements, and massively expanding the handwritten scribblings on which my side of the story is based. I have told him that I do not think my part in the events described was abnormal and he knows that I am far from convinced that my involvement will be of interest to other than members of the family, but his determination that there is a wider audience has carried the day.

I am conscious that my mind is narrowing, excessively concerned with the minutiae of day-to-day survival, at the expense of my constant concerns at the state of the nation that measured the progress of earlier years. Not that my present daily perusal of the newspapers does not arouse indignation and fuel an enthusiasm – fortunately rarely indulged – for penning an appropriate diatribe for the correspondence columns, but more immediate problems of day-to-day existence tend to gain precedence.

Having said all that, as one reaches my time of life, the mind seems to focus more clearly on the past, and one spends – one could say wastes – many hours recalling and reliving the events of the past. Sometimes the memories are painful, sometimes they are joyful, but they define what we were and what we are – and one dares to hope that those events have made some mark on future generations, and contributed to a better world. If so, then that might be a sufficient epitaph for those who are no longer with us.

Mary Mitchell

CONTENTS

BOOK ONE

Stuart Poyser with his sister Mary on holiday in September 1931,
eight months before Stuart's departure for Assam

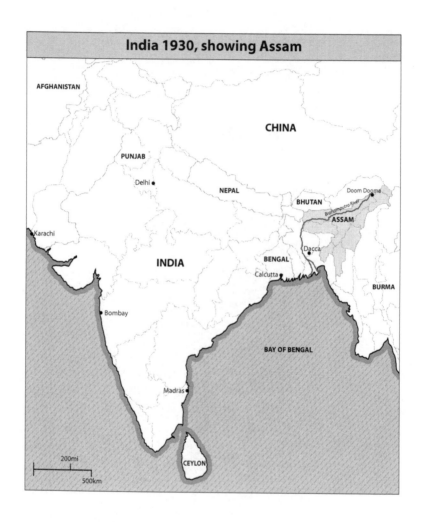

India 1930, showing Assam

AFGHANISTAN

CHINA

PUNJAB

NEPAL

Delhi

BHUTAN

Doom Dooma

ASSAM

Brahmaputra River

Karachi

INDIA

BENGAL

Dacca

Calcutta

BURMA

Bombay

BAY OF BENGAL

Madras

200mi

500km

CEYLON

CHAPTER ONE

The mist of the early morning began to lift as the cluster of mourners slowly made their way to the small grave that had been carved out of the sun-baked earth of the isolated cemetery. The three nuns were in their usual white, two of them whispering in Italian whilst the third held the little Asian girl firmly by the hand. The girl wore the simple cotton dress in which her sister would carefully dress her on Sundays at the convent school. It was the dress given to her by her mother when the two girls had left her to start their long journey from the tea plantation in distant Assam so many months ago. Her sister would dress her and comb her hair and try so hard to make up for the longing she knew the four-year-old had for her mother and the faraway village in which they had both grown up.

Now the small wooden casket was lowered into the grave and the native gravediggers replaced the earth as the priest murmured his long liturgy. Sister Maria, the nun whose native Italian accent mixed so badly with her broken Hindi, let go of the little girl's hand and handed to her the wreath of wild flowers that she had carried during the journey from the school. Hesitatingly, holding the wreath tightly in her small hands, the child went forward and gently placed the flowers on the mound of bare earth. The tears glistened as she turned back to the white folds of the nun's habit and the disapproving murmurs of the other sisters.

It was a lovely May morning when I joined my parents in taking my brother Stuart down to catch the boat for India from Tilbury Docks on 11th May 1932. I was wearing a new green dress with a matching hat of which I was very proud. We went on board to see Stuart's cabin and then said our farewells.

Stuart's passage on SS *Rajputana* had been arranged by Shaw

Wallace & Co. Ltd with whom his new employment as junior assistant manager on the Budla Beta tea estate in Assam had been arranged. I recall my brother's small but sturdy figure standing on the upper deck, waving at the three of us on the quayside, his figure receding as the ship moved further from the shore. We were a close family, and at my young age the thought that my brother was going to be away for at least five years was dreadful. My father Vernon Poyser, a doctor who in his spare time was an amateur philatelist of some repute with a speciality in postmarks, had tried to conceal his sadness by constantly reminding Stuart of the need to post 'covers' from every carefully chosen post office in every port, so that his stamp collection could be suitably enhanced. I could tell that my mother Millicent was completely grief stricken, but on the way down the gangway my nose had started to bleed and her concern to staunch the flow before my new dress was stained helped her to concentrate on more mundane matters.

My own distress at my brother's departure, not knowing when I would see him again, had been increased by embarrassment at the nosebleed which had rather spoiled the dignified way in which I had planned to say my farewells. Through my own tears, as we stood waving on the quay, I had barely been able to make out the impassive features of my father beside me. He was always a man to suppress emotion, partly derived from his time as a surgeon in the bloodbath of the First World War trenches and partly from his generation's instinctive determination to appear calm in all situations; and my teenage mind failed to sense the desolation he felt. As we left the ship his swift parting grasp of Stuart's shoulder, a clumsy clutch and a repeated exhortation to remember to post his wretched 'covers' had annoyed me, but with hindsight this seeming detachment must have served to conceal his considerable anguish.

No such concealment from my mother, her dark and depressive nature very much in evidence that day. During the long journey down in the family Austin 10 she had striven to be normal, talking of Stuart's good fortune in obtaining work, speculating as to the excellence of the quality of life he would find. Finding employment in the depressed years of the early 1930s had not been easy, even for an engineer trained by the renowned Tangye company, but the persuasive powers of Stuart's aunt Kitty and her husband David, formerly a doctor on the tea plantations, had succeeded in pulling the necessary strings.

I know that Stuart had talked to Aunt Kitty and Uncle David in an attempt to discover the conditions he might expect – they had not been as expansive as he had hoped and he had told me that constant reference to the weather and to 'the coolies' had not impressed him. He told me he knew it was going to be hot; and as to servants he regarded himself as well used to that concept since our parents now had a maid, Daisy being the current incumbent, and this was common amongst our other middle-class friends. Stuart said he could not see that the Indian equivalent was likely to represent any great change. Uncle David, in an unguarded moment, had talked to him of 'inner strength' apparently in the context of the remoteness of the tea estates, but Stuart assured me that he could not see that this would be a problem that could not be overcome with local transport.

I now suspect that Stuart's main sympathies lay with me on that day of departure. For the past three years we had been allies against the inevitable parental disapproval of his adolescence. Not that I had seen myself as having stepped out of line: I was young and rather innocent, full of life and enthusiasm with my love of sport and I rarely outstayed the unofficial curfew hours that the parents imposed.

My brother's extrovert character had been another matter. It was not unknown for him to call on me for a suitable alibi for his extensive network of liaisons. I recall one occasion the previous summer at Shoreham where I had sat in lonely and rather cold vigil on the pebbled beach whilst Stuart and a big-breasted girl called Pauline concealed themselves behind one of the fishing boats drawn up on the shingle. I also remembered Beth, Stuart's last-but-one girlfriend; and then there was Grace, to whom Stuart had told me of a tearful farewell during the week prior to his departure, hinting at some fever of their departing lovemaking, but as ever appreciative of the way in which his faithful sister had covered for his absence.

Not that I had ever wished to know the detail of those particular activities, perhaps out of embarrassment or the coyness of my lesser years, but in all other respects I liked to think that we had no secrets. Stuart would never say so, but I believe he was proud of my developing sporting abilities, bearing in mind that I was four years younger so at that time they did not come close to matching his own skills at tennis, hockey and cricket. We still competed against each other as far as we could, and many were the evenings when father would join us in cricket catching practice, and I learned not to complain when my nails were broken by mistiming a hard-flung ball.

On his departure Stuart was just twenty-one years of age. I speculate now, looking back to the vision etched in my mind of the twin-funnelled ship moving away from shore, whether he would have had a flashback to the time when he was left by our parents at his boarding school, Epsom College in Surrey. Whilst a common destination for the children of the medical profession, made more certain in his case by the fact that father had himself been there, it is probable that none of this would have diminished the welling up of homesickness in my then thirteen-year-old brother. Now, only eight years but seemingly a lifetime later, Stuart was departing from all that he knew for a term of what was expected to be at least five years. I still wonder whether his eager anticipation of the new adventure ahead of him, which had so lifted him in the previous weeks, would have been as suddenly extinguished by apprehension. Anyway, my parents' emotions on the quay and on the long journey home mirrored the devastation that I felt at the time.

CHAPTER TWO

The nuns had given Mary's dress, the lemon-coloured one with the tiny red flowers, to Pantoo because it was her size. Ann wondered if her fists had hurt Sister Maria as she hammered them into the nun's plump waist and whether it was her sobbing or her shouts of rage that had caused the dress to be returned. Crumpled now it was held tightly between Ann's arms and legs under the thin blanket. In the morning she would put it back into the cardboard box where it lived with Mary's big brown shoes in which Ann had tried so hard to walk without tripping. It had probably been Sister Teresa who had made them return the dress. Ann loved Sister Teresa who was so kind to her and Aileen, the youngest children in the convent school.

An atlas will show the familiar triangle of the Indian subcontinent with Bombay (or Mumbai as it is now called) at the middle left and Calcutta (today known as Kolkata), the then capital city, at the top right where the many tributaries of the vast Ganges river system flow into the sea from the heights of Nepal. Bangladesh, the former Bengal, now a separate country having formed the eastern wing of Pakistan following the 1947 partition from India, flanks Calcutta upwards from the right and makes it easy to forget the almost detached north-eastern part of India as it climbs up into the foothills of the Himalaya range and touches China and Burma. That vast area of eastern India is bisected by the Great River, as the mighty Brahmaputra is often called. It runs for a thousand miles from its source in Arunachal Pradesh and drains the whole of the valley of Assam and about a third of the Himalayan mountain range. It is hard to comprehend that the river will have expanded to a width of around twelve miles by the time it finally meets the Ganges following its long journey from the distant mountains.

Assam is five hundred miles to the north-east of Calcutta between Bhutan and the north of Burma and has a landscape totally unlike the remainder of the country. It is an isolated place, living in the shadow of the eastern Himalayas and facing west towards the distant blur of Kanchenjunga. Heavy monsoons fall on the Naga Hills and provide a vegetation of teak and bamboo and dense evergreen forests. It is a land of thick jungle, the legendary haunt of tigers, and peopled by warlike hill tribes.

At the turn of the century the expansionist empire of the British Raj had extended its control over much of this wild and unknown country. In this sense Assam became part of British India, but it remained subdivided into four Indian states each of which led an uneasy but semi-independent existence within its own limited boundaries. These states included the native state of Manipur, populated by mild-natured Hindu Methei in the Manipur river valley and by less peaceful Nagas and Kukis in the nearby hills. The Naga Hills were traditionally the home to headhunting tribesmen and there was bitter rivalry between the remote villages. In some areas it was said that a girl would only marry a man who could prove the number of enemies he had slain and that the killing of women and children could even be regarded as more laudable, theoretically demonstrating that the warrior had penetrated enemy territory rather than simply chancing on a stray adversary.

The lawlessness of the area in the days of the British Raj is perhaps demonstrated by the fact that three Political Agents, effectively the local British Governors, met violent deaths in the late 1880s. The fifty years from then until Stuart's planned arrival in 1930 had seen much progress in terms of both access and politics; railway lines had pumped technological lifeblood into the area; coal had been mined to fuel the imported machinery; and the presence of the British had put an end to the headhunting and village raiding parties. Notwithstanding this small degree of modernization it remained a huge, inaccessible and largely isolated part of India, still inherently wild and with a diversity of tribal inhabitants intermixed with imported labour from other parts of the country, mainly to populate the isolated tea estates. Overall, the jungle remained dominant.

This was to be Stuart's home.

Stuart revelled in the journey on the 16,600-ton SS *Rajputana*. He was looking forward to meeting his fellow travelling companions. He had always prided himself on being able to converse at all social levels. He supposed that his middle-class upbringing as the son of a doctor and the grandson of a headmaster endowed him with the status of the professional middle classes, seen by some as a cut above those in retail and similar commercial activities. At the same time his engineering apprenticeship in Birmingham had brought him into day-to-day contact and indeed friendship with both manual and 'blue collar' workers. Although he had not been privileged enough to attain university his many sporting activities, particularly in team games such as rugger and hockey, had brought him comradeship across a wide social range. He was not tall nor considered particularly handsome but he had been blessed with a quick wit, always able to throw an amusing comment into a conversation; and his infectious laugh made him good company. He intended to make the most of his new life and the starting adventure of the long journey.

As the ship sailed towards the open sea an announcement over the tannoy identified the *Empress of Britain*'s white hull and two other liners, *Homeric* and *Berengaries*. A few hours later, when Stuart had been down below to unpack, further news came, this time of a sighting of the *Mauritania*. He went back on deck as the four funnels of the big liner passed by.

Stuart's cabin was on the second lower deck and just below the area set aside for deck tennis. This lower deck had a promenade running around it and as the days passed his customary pose, when not involved in the daily programme of sporting and social activities, was to lean on the rail watching the sea. Westwards down the channel and then turning south he began to settle into the routine of the voyage. The trip across the Bay of Biscay was calm and three days after leaving England they docked in Gibraltar. Remembering to post the envelopes given to him by his father Stuart took the opportunity to go ashore. He was beginning to acclimatize to the warmer weather, and he took the obligatory trip to see the monkeys on the Rock and had his first taste of native hawkers trying to sell their primitive wares. He wandered along the narrow streets, still redolent with naval history, and enjoyed watching the activities of the port. Back on board he photographed the distant Atlas mountains, realizing that his simple camera was never going to capture the grandeur of the landscapes that he would witness, and resolving to confine his efforts to people rather than places.

The second landfall was at Marseilles, reached on 20th May: an occasion for Stuart to explore the streets of the town and practise his schoolboy French. He began to appreciate that each port had its own smell and flavour – this one was spicily pungent. As the ship sailed on he competed in the deck tennis and table tennis competitions, savoured the increasingly different food in the dining room and watched the world flow by. The diverse company on board included military men joining or returning to their regiments; East India company staff taking up posts or finishing their leave; and a cross-section of other political and commercial personnel. There was the occasional wife or fiancée eagerly awaiting an appropriate reunion but, sadly in Stuart's eyes, a marked shortage of single women. He was already beginning to miss the girlfriends he had left behind, Grace in particular. She was inconsolable at his departure, not helped by his encouragement that she should do her best to forget him, his explanation that five years away was a lifetime and she must close her mind to any future with him being badly received. Would she be able to do so?

Malta was reached on 22nd May. Now the heat intensified: Stuart felt ground down by the languor it induced. If Gibraltar had a touch of naval history, this small island was overwhelming. He watched the small boats that clustered round the ship on arrival, photographing their colourful cargoes of fruit and flowers. Again he went ashore to walk the streets, admiring the tall houses on steep narrow roads that represented the dramatic architecture of Valetta. He joined other passengers to take a boat trip around the great harbour, learning the history of past battles from the boatman's accented commentary.

Back at sea a welcome breeze brought some relief but on 25th May Port Said was reached and Stuart felt the full glare of the North

African sun. As an engineer, he enjoyed much time on deck observing the passage through the Suez Canal and admiring the mechanics of the lock system.

After considerable delay in the passage through the canal came Aden. Watching the shore activity as the ship made port Stuart realized it was a full eighteen days since his departure from England. Aden seemed a strange mixture of the Arab world mingled with the hauteur of European military and commercial characters, but again he found that the high temperatures tended to limit his explorations.

Onwards once more, now knowing more of his fellow passengers; friendly with John MacDonald and his wife Mary, meeting others at the bar and enjoying their company. Life on board was suddenly varied by the exuberance of the ceremonial of 'crossing the line' on 30th May. Stuart took in good heart the rituals of his being variously covered in foam, pretending to be shaved with a huge sword and then being doused with buckets of sea water. There were games in which he raced others to crawl under a net stretched across the deck. Now he was properly blooded in the traditions of sea travel as the ship ploughed on towards India.

For three leisurely weeks Stuart had been able to acclimatize himself to the warmth of the Mediterranean and the heat of the Middle East. In parallel with this he had gradually absorbed the sights and sounds of foreign lands totally outside his narrow experience of the world. He had begun to appreciate that heat was not of itself the enemy, but when combined with humidity it became unbearable. Before long he would realize that nothing in these short weeks had adequately prepared him for either the climate or the experience of that most extraordinary country, a land the size of Europe, a land containing unimaginable numbers of people – India.

Would the words of his uncle come back to haunt him?

CHAPTER THREE

Ann slept fitfully, tossing and turning on the sleeping mat in the narrow dormitory. She had cried so much earlier that evening when Angela, Mary's best friend, had lain down in Mary's dress on the mat that her sister used to sleep on. How the others had all laughed when Ann had excitedly called out to her sister, thinking that she was alive – and it was Angela and not Mary who jumped up.

Bombay, 2nd June: Ballard Pier, the triumphal arch of the Gateway to India. The docks were only a first taste of what was to come but already a sickly sweet and sour smell was blowing off the shore as the mooring lines were caught by scrawny, turbaned figures in white dhoti garments – Stuart's first vision of the universal garb of the male population.

He fought his way down one of the three gangways through swarms of gesticulating coolies, the front line clad in ragged khaki shirts with red markings on the back. Saluted by a European policeman (and Stuart quickly found that all whites were called European) smart in his khaki uniform and topi, he was then guided towards the customs shed by two native policemen in loose blue cotton uniforms piped with yellow and matching yellow turbans. Wet through with sweat he emerged on the heels of four shouting coolies carrying his baggage. Half trotting, half striding, Stuart anxiously followed the men precariously balancing his precious luggage on their heads as they weaved through the seething crowds towards a rank of ancient taxis. Choosing one of the clustering drivers he mouthed 'Victoria Terminus' and was duly installed in the back seat craning his neck to check that his cases had joined him and passing the lead porter a tip, probably excessive, through the lowered window.

Now through unimaginable traffic he was disgorged at the railway station and more porters guided him towards the waiting train, the Imperial Mail, the word CALCUTTA emblazoned on boards along the side, clouds of steam from the engine heralding its imminent departure.

His ticket inspected by an official in crumpled dark blue uniform at the carriage door, Stuart slumped thankfully into the seat of his compartment, thinking to himself that it was good that he had left the ship refreshed by the leisurely sea passage. He was perspiring heavily and he suppressed his initial feelings of exhilaration, knowing it was rather pathetic that he should already be exhausted after achieving such a small step of the journey that would now take him across India and up to Assam in order to reach his new job. Whilst relieved that by disembarking in Bombay he had avoided the long sea journey around the bottom of India and up to Calcutta on the eastern side, he was daunted by the prospect of the long train journeys that now lay ahead. Still, he had certainly given himself the opportunity to see the sights of central India.

Not just sights but smells, and hot smells, he thought to himself. More of a stench perhaps: sweat mingled with oil, ammonia mixing with the ozone of the sea, fish and the sharpness of chemicals, undertones of faecal waste.

Thanks to the generosity of his aunt Kitty the tickets were for a coupe, a first-class sleeper with a cabin to himself which converted to a bed. Stuart found a switch for the fan and felt the sweat begin to dry as he gazed out of the window. Scenery shifted with the slow movement of the train pulling out of the station, the life of Bombay's millions beginning to expose itself: low brick shacks, rudimentary shops, open casement houses, cotton mills, small factories. A multitude of vehicles: cars, lorries, buses, bicycles, carts, rickshaws. An equal array of animals: donkeys, mangy horses, buffalo carts, the occasional elephant, a haughty camel, sacred cows wandering unchecked. And everywhere yet more people: walking, standing, squatting, talking in groups, washing themselves at street hydrants, men carrying loads across their shoulders, women with water jars on their heads, closed palaquins; sedan chairs carried shoulder high by teams of natives;

thousands of naked – or nearly naked – children playing in the dust and dirt. The whole life of the city seemed to unfold before his eyes.

As the train moved across the causeway crossing the mud flats that joined Bombay to the mainland Stuart saw that the telegraph wires alongside the track were lined with multi-coloured birds. He recognized none of them and found it hard to comprehend how they could sit so happily in the glare of the intense sun. The ramshackle suburbs seemed endless: shanty towns, the sharp tang of excrement catching the back of Stuart's throat in passing. Now moving into the country the scenery again began to change: primitive buildings clustered together in the dust; wandering animals; women carrying water towards far horizons; huge areas of emptiness. Stuart's natural prudery was offended to see men defecating beside stagnant waterholes at the side of the tracks, his traditional preconceptions of privacy and proper sanitation shifting as he tried not to watch. And as each cluster of housing came into view there were more people, hundreds upon hundreds of people.

Much of the land now seemed more fertile: mango groves and ancient banyan trees, coconut and banana palms across the lush and tropical landscape. The train crossed high gorges with the river far below, the carriages rattled over viaducts and through rocky cuttings. At Kalyan Stuart had to gather his possessions and follow the carriage attendant to a new train, the gauge of the railway having altered and the engine being substituted for the larger shape of a huge red locomotive of the Great Indian Peninsular Railway. Sitting in his new compartment he felt lonely and isolated as evening fell, passing villages with smoke from cooking fires rising in the evening air and then seeing nothing but the flicker of fires and the light of a million fireflies.

Shaking himself out of his solitude Stuart changed his shirt and went along the train to the drawing room car where he was delighted to find a bar and some companions to talk to; then dinner, and finally back to his cabin now converted into a sleeper with surprisingly silky sheets. Stuart was not surprised that blankets did not feature, the continuous heat making them redundant. His uniformed attendant or servant – Stuart did not know what to call him – warned him to keep the windows closed: there was a plate-glass sheet, a sheet of bluish glass and a metal mesh. He was told that train thieves or terrorists often boarded the train and crept along carriage roofs to find a means of entry. Despite the heat and humidity Stuart decided that wisdom demanded he heed the warning.

Breakfasting in the dining car, Stuart returned to his watchful vigil as the carriages swept across the plains of central India. Halting at only a handful of stations they roared through smaller stops, seeming to brush against the crowds of people crammed on to the primitive platforms. There were just two first-class sleeper carriages, with a dining car between them, and Stuart was able to lunch on mulligatawny soup followed by curried mutton, washing it down with beer against the fear that the cloudy water on the table would cause unimaginable ills. The curry was an unfamiliar dish to someone used to the more traditional diet of 1920s Birmingham; the beer was more recognizable, if lighter in colour and texture than he was used to, but he was grateful for it. A flow of hot air struggled through the windows of the dining compartment and eddied around the three Indian businessmen at the next table, who seemed reluctant to converse despite their spicy-smelling proximity.

Stuart slept a little during the afternoon but then had to change carriages yet again to accommodate another gauge of track. He was suddenly weary of the thirteen hundred mile journey. At last, in the early evening of a second long day, and now pulled by a black locomotive of the Bengal Nagpur Railway, the train rumbled over the Howrah Bridge spanning the Hugli River and into the brilliantly lit cavern of Calcutta's Howrah Station.

If Bombay had seemed frantic this was bedlam. The enormous crush was reminiscent of crowds leaving a football stadium, with the addition of huge numbers of others lying and sitting on every available part of each platform, whole families seemingly settling in for the night. It was an unforgettable scene. As the train approached, a set of steel doors at the entrance to the platform was flung open and a horde of local people poured out, pushing the waiting Europeans, clerks and agents forward towards the carriages.

Suddenly a short white-suited figure materialized at the carriage doorway and salaamed in greeting.

'Sir, you are Poyser Sahib, the new junior assistant for the Budla Beta tea estate?'

'Yes, that's so,' Stuart replied, relieved to be identified.

'The agent's car is here, sir, and I will take you to the Bengal Club, where we have reserved a room for you.'

So, thought Stuart, this was the agent of Shaw Wallace: a fat Indian man in a stained suit. In a short space of time Stuart's luggage had been identified and borne aloft by two natives and he and his new companion were propelled by the moving crowd towards the exits. Stuart could not imagine how it was that his suitcases, seemingly lost for ever in the multitude, emerged at the side of the waiting taxi which was ready to launch itself into the seething traffic, rickshaws competing with bullock carts, elephants, bicycles and a million people all conspiring to block their vehicle's way.

The cacophony of hooting, shouting and babble diminished as the taxi door closed.

'You are billeted at the Bengal Club for the next two nights, then off by train to Assam. I will pick you up at 10 a.m. tomorrow and take you to the company offices to sort everything out.'

Further conversation was minimal as the vehicle carrying Stuart and his guide plunged into the mass of animals, vehicles and humanity that filled the darkened roads from side to side. The crush of people was overwhelming and Stuart's senses were numbed by the heat, the noise and the sweet sweat-based spicy smells that were overlaid by the faint stench of sewage.

A short exchange of further pleasantries and Stuart found himself under the portico of a square stuccoed edifice, turbaned porters sweeping away his suitcases and an assistant manager introducing himself. Signing the register in the small hall he glimpsed a high-ceilinged lounge through double doors ahead of him. As he looked around Stuart was reminded of Epsom College – an aroma redolent of a boarding school, stuffed animal heads looking down on the echoing corridors. Stuart followed the slippered feet of the uniformed porter along the polished floorboards to his room, the heat stirred by the beating of the brass ceiling fan.

The last to dine that night following his late arrival, waited upon by shuffling staff under the chandeliers of the empty dining room, its French doors now open to the comparative cool of the evening, Stuart began to relax. The long upstairs bar was deserted so after dinner he escaped into the small garden, conscious of the cacophony of noise from the street outside, and smoked a cigarette before retiring to his shuttered room to sleep off the effects of the second leg of his long journey.

CHAPTER FOUR

The offices of Shaw Wallace & Co. Ltd were large and imposing; Stuart had done his research and recognized the substantial white edifice of Wallace House in Bankshall Street from the photograph in the company brochure. It reminded him of a Whitehall ministry save that either side of the frontage was populated by stalls selling a multitude of goods and foodstuffs to the passing population. He knew that R. G. Shaw & Company and Shaw Wallace & Co. Ltd were closely linked, the latter with strong ties to the tea industry in Ceylon, and that the former was fast diversifying into the import of motor cars and was even involved in Imperial Airlines. He understood that they had a total of six tea estates in Assam and felt confident that there would be opportunities for advancement as the years went by.

Stuart's guide of yesterday held his elbow as he took him through the crowds towards a rather grand entrance guarded by uniformed doorkeepers. Passing into a marbled reception hall and up a sweeping staircase Stuart was conducted into the offices of the director managing the tea estates.

'Poyser – my name is Adams. Good to see you. How was the journey?'

A tall man, authoritative but helpful, Adams spelled out the duties that Stuart would fulfil. Stuart already knew that the post of junior assistant was directly below that of the estate manager and that his function was to run the manufacturing side of the estate under such supervision as was needed. It was explained that he would not need to concern himself with fieldwork as there was a field manager to deal with the planting and cultivation side, but that the smooth running of the factory was crucial and that his engineering skills would be fully tested. Adams questioned him closely on the machinery he would be working with and then gave him a selection of manuals and books and told to study them as soon as he could.

After half an hour, tea was brought. The bearer poured the cups with great care and Stuart watched cautiously as Adams tasted the brew with silent concentration before, seemingly satisfied, he relaxed and continued with the briefing.

'So, what knowledge do you have of the weather and its impact on how you are going to spend the rest of your life?'

Stuart sensed it was not wise to imply any doubt on his lifetime commitment. 'Sir, very little save to know of the monsoon season.'

'Traditional planters will tell you there are two principal seasons in Assam: the Rains, lasting from the middle of May until the middle of October, and the Cold Weather, lasting from the beginning of November until the middle of March. The remaining months, from March until May, are called Chota Barsat – Small Rains. I fear you are going to be arriving as the Rains begin but this is also the time of our summer, so you will have the heat as well as the rain which is the most difficult time for those not used to our climate. I hope you enjoy the experience!

'As for the journey, this will all be by rail: there is an alternative route which involves a train to Goalundo in Bengal and then a steamer up the Brahmaputra to Dibrugah, but that would take nearly three weeks in all which is too long. I'm afraid you will be heartily sick of the railway by the time the Assam Mail and its smaller cousins have transported you to the little station at Doom Dooma but at least you will be there slightly sooner.'

And what a journey it was: north from Calcutta and skirting Bengal, then at Gumani a sharp move to the south-east via the Boag loop and then north again through Malda Town, Kumedpur and up to New Jalpaiguiri Junction. Stuart liked to sit facing the engine and on the occasions that he looked up from the books that he was studying he saw how the everlasting miles of farmland were becoming more overgrown and less cultivated as the vistas passed by, interrupted by constant stops at tiny stations.

Nearly two long days before the train turned east across the top of Bengal, Stuart was bored and tired but at least feeling he was at last pointed in the direction of his final destination. He now realized what an immense distance he had come from faraway Birmingham and all his family and friends and how isolated he was going to be for the next five years until his first leave, seemingly a lifetime away.

As the hours passed Stuart saw that on his left-hand side a continuous line of mountains began to build, standing as a mighty backdrop to the unfolding scenes of the plains. This was the beginning of the Himalaya range, the railway always tracing the line of the huge Brahmaputra River. The plains across which the train passed were green and lush, the Indian winter had given way to summer and humidity was building up. Stuart realized that as the month advanced the start of the monsoons would come. At present the heat was tempered by a refreshing breeze as the train moved onwards, stopping at every station, mostly only a cluster of huts but always thronged with people.

An overnight stop at Cooch Behar Junction and then down to the northern shore of the Brahmaputra at Agthori. Here the train halted since it had as yet proved too difficult to build a bridge over the wide river with its banks constantly changing in the floods. With his fellow passengers Stuart now embarked on to a steam ferry, a ghat as he would learn to call it, and saw at first hand the enormous pale white expanse of the empty river. During the long crossing he watched the far black line of the southern side grow into a range of buildings stretching into the distance either side of the ferry dock, revealing itself as Gauhati, the capital city of Assam. Here Stuart had another overnight stop before boarding his penultimate train destined for Lumding and then onwards to Tinsukia.

The carriages were more primitive now, the horizontal bars at the windows segmenting the view, and Stuart's fellow passengers were more numerous. He was disappointed to learn that this line did not pass through Dibrugah itself. He knew from his studies that Dibrugah was known as the Tea City of India and was the gateway to the three tea-producing districts of Tinsukia, Jorhat and Dibrugah itself, areas that his researches told him accounted for fifty per cent of the tea production of the whole of India.

Suddenly he realized that he was seeing tea beside the road: green bushes stretching into the distance with trees to shade the crop growing out of the flat expanse of green. He worked out that these must belong to either the Khanjikowa or Kharjan estates. The train travelled on towards Tinsukia, the unfenced rails running on the very edge of the dusty highway flanked with flimsy shacks.

Next Tinsukia itself, a shanty-town sprawl of single-storey huts between which the narrow road surged with traffic, people and animals. Although nearly at his final destination Stuart knew he had to change trains yet again. Urged on by the conductor, porters transferred his luggage to the waiting train on the single branch line leading to Doom Dooma. As usual Stuart felt himself the centre of attention, guessing that few Europeans travelled this far into Assam, and again he suffered the stares of the population as he settled himself into the last train he hoped he would have to endure for many months to come.

Now the chaos of Makum Junction where the line divided, the train imperiously forcing its way across the very centre of the T-junction which was the only serviceable road link between the east and west of that part of the country, clattering its way north in the direction of Doom Dooma rather than taking the line south-east towards Digboi and Marguerita. Stuart remembered the history of Digboi, one of his books describing the scene at the beginning of the century when primitive oil derricks heralded the site of the first oil refinery in Asia. He had read that oil had first been struck near Digboi nearly fifty years earlier in 1882, and had followed the stories of black mud smelling of oil coating the legs of working elephants used by the Assam Railways and Trading Company. This was the company that had completed the mammoth task of building the railway on which he was travelling, enabling the manufactured tea to travel to Calcutta by train rather than on river steamer.

The train travelled more slowly now as it moved north-east towards Doom Dooma, the nearest station to the Bokpara and Budla Beta tea estates, the lush green landscape of the wide plains giving way to distant views of dense vegetation, the encroaching jungle now a line towards the horizon. The station was barely a touch of civilization, with the ugliness of patched-together buildings standing alongside the shanty-type outskirts of the small halt as the train finally reached Stuart's destination.

The humidity was much greater than before and the heat of the day was uncomfortable. Stuart felt soiled and battered as he stepped off the train and looked anxiously around to find a friendly face.

'Mackie's my name. I'm the manager of the Budla Beta estate. You must be Poyser.'

It was a statement, not a question, but the logic was obvious since he was the only European figure to emerge from the train on to the small platform. Shaking hands he eyed up the much older stocky figure in regulation shorts and a white topi hat. He was guided to a battered Bedford lorry and they both climbed up to join the driver in the cab. Stuart's luggage had already made its way into the back where it sat with various bits of equipment and other packages; also sharing the open loading space were four or five other Indians – Stuart could not work out their seniority or capacity.

Mackie shouted information over the noise of the engine. He told Stuart that Budla Beta and nearby Bokpara together formed one of the biggest estates in the area, in excess of a thousand hectares and so one of the largest in Assam. Then there were the estates of Kharjan and Khanjikowa, all part of the Shaw Wallace group. Stuart learned that there was a planters' club in Doom Dooma and a larger one back down the road near the Kharjan estate at Panitola, although the Panitola estate itself was part of the rival Jokai tea company. As the truck crashed and bumped along the mud road carved through the jungle he realized that a visit would be a major expedition and not a gentle stroll, and wondered how transport could be arranged.

Stuart's companion emphasized that in addition to the managers for each of the estates, there was a superintendent in overall charge of the district. He went on to say that there were just five British on the Budla Beta estate itself, including Mackie's wife who was the only European woman there.

Stuart's sense of geographical isolation increased during the lurching ten mile journey and he was relieved when the truck began to travel down a track with tea bushes on either side and realized that he was now travelling into the estate itself. What at a distance resembled a raised carpet of green lawn was revealed as the smooth top surface of endless rows of tea bushes, planted closely together and stretching into the distance, the line of the jungle appearing as a far perimeter. The shade trees were planted at regular intervals, almost like lamp standards on a domestic street, and the paths for the pluckers between each area of bushes gave symmetry to the vast area of emerald leaf.

They came to a halt next to an untidy jumble of factory buildings one of which Stuart quickly identified as the engine room. He knew the others would include the sorting room, the rolling room and other places of production. In the other direction, a hundred paces from the factory area, were individual thatched two-storey buildings, each at least fifty yards from the next. These, with their mesh-enclosed outside verandahs under the projection of the thatch, were the bungalows in which the managers and other officers of the estate lived.

Workers from the factory and estate had already gathered round the lorry and started to unload under the shouted direction of the Indian foremen, who Stuart knew were called sirdars. From the various buildings emerged three more Europeans to whom he was introduced: Petrie, Ross and Swannell. Mackie had already explained to Stuart that he was to share a bungalow and he learned that he was sharing with Petrie who would now take him there. The others went back to work, Stuart being told that he was to meet Mrs Mackie at dinner that evening – he was invited to their bungalow for a welcome meal.

Petrie was a big man, fifty years of age and sweating heavily in the humidity. He explained that he was the field manager. 'So you and I are the two buggers who run the whole shooting match!'

Stuart's bags were taken to an elderly jeep by a driver who then drove them the short distance to the house. As they came closer Stuart thought it looked vast, standing some distance from the factory complex with views over the estate and the other bungalows each in their own area of cultivated garden land. High wrought-iron gates were opened by a servant and they went up the outside steps into a huge verandah area, windows enclosed by mesh where a shy and wiry Indian with a striped turban put his hands together and bowed to Stuart. 'Welcome, Sahib' was the greeting in English.

Petrie introduced the man as Daniel, and said that he was the personal bearer to himself and Stuart. Stuart was soon to find that not only did his bungalow have a bearer but there was also a cook, a sweeper, a paniwalla, two malis and a night watchman, so that his personal staff, albeit shared with Petrie, already numbered seven. By the end of the day and following a guided tour of the factory complex he was to discover that as junior assistant he had a sirdar and four mechanics under his control. 'And I'm only twenty-one,' Stuart thought to himself, realizing how quickly he was going to need to learn rudimentary management skills.

The bungalow was as large as it had appeared from the car; the verandah was the coolest room, perhaps ten metres square with a vast fan in the vaulted ceiling creating a welcome current of air. Rattan sofas and tables furnished the area from which double doors led into an equally large lounge with more sofas and a long dining table towards the rear. Doors on either side led to the bedrooms, each with a dressing area and a bathroom. The back of the lounge had a door to the servants' area from which a stone outside staircase descended to the single-storey kitchen.

CHAPTER FIVE

'Do you play bridge?' Nodding by way of confirmation, Stuart mentally thanked his parents for teaching him and Mary in their early teenage years. His hostess, Margaret Mackie, was a tall, angular woman with an outdoor, rather leathery complexion. They were sitting around the dining table in the Mackies' bungalow that first evening as Stuart fought to stay awake after the long journey and the strain of absorbing so many new experiences. He was very much the youngest amongst the Europeans on the estate and was quickly realizing the isolation of this small community in its acreage carved out of the surrounding jungle.

He thought back to the conversation with his uncle David and the words 'inner strength' began to have more meaning as he surveyed the small group that was to represent his social life for an immeasurable time to come. Still, the Mackies seemed a pleasant couple and the others were clearly welcoming. Ross was a stocky Scotsman only a few years older than Stuart, short on words but friendly; Swannell rather elegant with a cigarette holder and beautifully pressed linen suit, incongruous in this tiny gathering; Petrie more the archetypal Scot abroad, bluff and, at first judgement, something of a drinker.

The first few days passed in a blur. Stuart began to settle into life in the bungalow, which he still found an odd description for a two-storey building. He learned that they lived on the upper floor because snakes and other wildlife were discouraged by the iron girders that formed the stilts on which the property was built. The ground floor area was used mainly for storage, and he would have no reason to go there. The separation of the two bedrooms, each with its own bathroom, made it delightfully private and to Stuart's surprise, considering what he had seen of the primitive nature of the country thus far, each bathroom was plumbed in and had both hot and cold water, the former provided by an outside coal-fuelled boiler and a convoluted system of pipework. The rear of the bungalow was where Daniel held sway and was not a place to which either Stuart or Petrie was expected to go. There the servants came and went, and the cooking and washing and other duties were directed.

Stuart was also becoming more familiar with the activities and pace of the estate. He realized that his tasks were continuous at this time of year, keeping the machinery running, organizing the factory and being on duty well into the night. Mackie was in overall command, and was a point of reference if any questions arose, but he expected Stuart to run things as far as possible and particularly to look after the night-shift production.

The main engine room housed the massive Tangye engine which powered the machinery including the tea dryers. As a Tangye-trained engineer Stuart was entirely familiar with every aspect of the great machine, but it needed constant attention and continuous stoking, fed with coal from the Ledo coal mines near the border between Assam and Burma. The engine was old: Stuart knew that Tangye had ceased to make steam engines like this in 1896 and the modern equivalent would be powered by diesel fuel, so the Budla Beta engine was over thirty years old but still going strong.

Although Stuart had devoured every book he had been given on tea planting and manufacture, it was salutary to view the plant and equipment at first hand and to see how they all came together. It was Petrie who took him out to see the plucking process in operation. Plucking took place between March and the end of November. He explained that the bushes needed to be plucked dead level, which meant that the skilled women pluckers took the leaves off so evenly that it looked as if each bush had been sheared by a machine. The rule was 'two leaves and a bud' which meant that each young shoot to be plucked must have only two leaves and the opening small bud at the apex removed. Failure to do this by taking more than the prescribed length was called 'coarse plucking' and whilst that would increase the woman's basket for the day, the season's yield would suffer as would the quality of the tea.

The plucking of the young growth or 'flush' was continuous during the growing season since, if the plucking was good, another flush would grow within ten days or so. Stuart marvelled at the number of women involved but also at their jealousy in seeking to guard the rows of bushes that they had themselves plucked previously – because they knew that if they plucked well and consistently the yield from their rows would be maintained. However, the allocation of rows was ultimately down to the sirdars in charge so certainty could not always be achieved. Each woman plucked three rows of tea 240 yards long – half a mile of bushes – each day, fingers working with immense speed. When the factory hooter sounded they carried the picked leaf in baskets on their heads, had them weighed and the weights, over twenty kilograms each, marked up against their names on a blackboard, the plucking register. They then climbed the sloping walkways on the outside of the open factory structure to empty the green leaf on to vast withering racks where small boys with long thin bamboos spread it out evenly. Stuart learned that withering was necessary because the leaves were too brittle to roll until they had softened and this process took between eight and eighteen hours, depending upon temperature and humidity, which meant that manufacture could be started if they wished at any time between midnight and dawn. He quickly realized that when that occurred he would effectively become a night-shift worker for the duration of that session.

Mackie had continued Stuart's education at the production end of the process.

'Wait till the leaf feels like fine-quality kid leather and it will be ready for rolling – but it's more scientific than that and you have to become used to tasting the infusion of the withered leaf in boiling water. Later in the season, when the Rains break, you will get under-withered leaf but it still has to be processed although the taste will be harsher.'

Stuart pulled a face at the taste of the infusions, but noted the large number of tasting cups, the scales for weighing out the leaf and the board for recording the results, realizing that his required skills were not going to be confined to engineering. He was shown how the leaf was then run across to the rolling room and put into rollers, raised circular metal containers fitted with battens and rotating in an opposite direction to the table beneath, thus crushing and twisting the leaf. He knew from his studies that the crushing of the cells in the leaf released enzymes and essential oils which would later prove essential in the fermentation process. The fermentation took place on beds of smooth polished concrete in a specially cooled room but not until the leaf had endured two or three rollings and sievings. Mackie explained that the speed of fermentation partly depended upon weather and took around three hours, by which time the fermented leaf was copper coloured; again the timing of the process depended upon preparing and tasting further infusions.

As they continued through the heat of the day, Stuart saw how the fermented leaf was lifted into large bowls and tipped on to the chain of trays that passed through the great firing or drying machines, moving through a continuous blast of hot air until it became the finished product. The aroma of the tea was intense as he moved into the sorting room where further machinery shook and funnelled the tea through different-sized sieves into the different grades and qualities, assisted by rows of girls with trays. Finally the grades passed over conveyors where older women and children stooped to remove stalks and other impurities before a final firing to further dry the tea and then the packing into chests lined with tin foil. Now the tea was ready for its long journey to the Mincing Lane tea market in London.

It was not helpful that, as predicted, the advancement into June had brought the start of the monsoon season. The first roar of the rain had been a revelation to Stuart: it was as if some huge container had burst and shed its load in a solid wall of water, stunning the senses with its force. He became used to carrying out all his work to the accompaniment of the thunder of rain on the corrugated roofs of the buildings. The bungalow was less than two hundred yards on foot and his frequent commute to the factory buildings, and his retreat to the bungalow for food and rest, required a muddy run under umbrellas which rarely protected fully from the downpour that bounced up from the earth as well as down from the skies. It was quite a distance to some of the neighbouring bungalows so a car was preferred unless the weather was kind.

As for social life, Stuart got on well with Ross and also developed a good relationship with Petrie – the laconic Scotsman had a developed sense of humour and a love of whisky. The humidity was such that they tended to use what he called the jalicumra or mosquito verandah as their sitting area, and on free evenings they would sit into the night sharing a peg of whisky, as he had learned to call it, and talking over the sounds of the jungle and the constant crash of the rain on the thatched roof. He realized that the mesh was a crucial defence against the invading insects, and that the mosquito net enveloping his bed was a similar protection – but he was still bitten on an almost continuous basis.

Seeing his bites, one evening Petrie gave Stuart a recitation of the joys of what he called the creepy crawlies of Assam.

'In the hot months of May and June the insect world really gets going.

'First – mosquitoes. No need for me to tell you much about them as you've been bitten enough already. Bearing no comparison to the English gnat, these are bloodthirsty beasts with low cunning, particularly in their ability to lurk unseen in the inside fold of a mosquito curtain awaiting the return of the sleeper. Malaria is not an option: you will succumb. We are all used to it and know how to treat it when the time comes. I divide my own symptoms between Low Fever and High Fever. Low Fever tends to come on at regular intervals, sometimes for only a few hours a day; High Fever lasts about a week and you may experience some interesting hallucinations when you're burning up with it! The hospital here is good and will look after you and as a last resort the School of Tropical Medicine in Calcutta cures all known ills. Just be as careful as you can.

'Second – ants. As the sun goes down you'll see that the white ants with their white wings come out of hiding and make our lives a misery until about nine in the evening when they disappear – the sweepers whisk the dead ones off the floor each morning. Be happy with the ants: not only do they provide the evening meal for the bird population, but before they grow their wings and sacrifice themselves for bird feed they eat the dead wood on the tea plants which would otherwise be diseased. Only snag is that they also find any trace of weakening timber in any of the buildings or posts, and despite creosote, bowls of old engine oil and other deterrents the woodwork soon collapses into a heap of dust!

'Third – snakes. Whilst there are lots of non-poisonous snakes that are valuable in keeping down rats and other pests there are others which will do you a power of no good such as the Banded Krait and the Bamboo Snake. Then there's the famous King Cobra or Hamadryad, not to be confused with the ordinary Cobra or Nag Samp. Avoid snakes when they have moulted or cast their skins; remember most are short sighted and sluggish and if in doubt it's wiser to kill them than not. You can break a snake's back with a blow with a stick and then finish it off when it can't move. By the way, I quite like pythons but in India they often come in twenty-foot sizes – at least that means you can see them coming!

'Then there are the rest: spiders can be enormous – you might think some of them have a six-inch stride – and their bite, or lick as it's termed, can incapacitate you from active work for some days. Fortunately not much in the way of tarantulas, and scorpions likewise. Cockroaches of course, and they love leather goods. Centipedes – four to six inches in length not unusual and with an unfortunate turn of speed. Their bites are highly toxic and particularly painful as I can verify! Moths – not a problem healthwise, but when you've seen the giant Atlas with a ten-inch wingspan you may think you're living in a world of monsters.

'But it's the mosquito that rules India, and Assam in particular!'

As the days passed, Stuart settled into the summer ritual which was dominated by the tea production season; the winter months would be very different. He was at the factory till the small hours, supervising every process leading up to the final packing of the tea, watching over the night shift and ensuring continued maintenance of the machinery so that the following day's productive process would not be delayed. A few hours' sleep and then an early start helped by

Daniel having arranged for a bath to be run and laundered clothes laid out. After bathing and shaving, breakfast on the verandah: porridge, boiled eggs and toast, even some marmalade; then across to the factory to check on the engines, then other tasks before the noon hooter when the pluckers would bring their leaf back to the factory.

In the late morning there was a need to check that the sirdars were properly supervising the manufacturing process and then the walk back to the bungalow for a scratch sandwich lunch – too hot for a main meal and clothes by then so wet with sweat that Stuart would throw them off and jump into a cold bath. After lunch an essential siesta for a couple of hours, but it was virtually impossible to sleep, lying on the bed trying to find a cool portion of the covering sheet. Back into the clothes of the morning, Daniel having put them out to dry on the verandah rail during lunch, and then to the factory again. Dinner in the evening, but Stuart still needing to ensure that production was progressing smoothly, necessitating visits back and forth to his office, partitioned off in a corner of the factory, until early morning.

It was not a good time to have arrived, straight into the busiest time of the year, and not until September did the pace start to slow. Communication was a major problem: Stuart had started to study Urdu but he soon found that the tea estate seemed to have its own language, or baht, derived from the many different races that populated the 'Lines' where the native workers lived their lives. The Lines surrounded the estate, some on the far edge near to the jungle and others nearer the road. They comprised muddy streets of living huts, lean-to shops, eating stalls under awnings and even open air offices where letter writers and other more semi-literate individuals helped those less able for an appropriate fee or a bartered item. Here also were the moneylenders or kayahs. There were some clusters of houses comprising tiny villages nearby in the jungle itself but the majority of those working on the estate lodged in the Lines where the womenfolk brought up their children, most of whom would come to work on the estate when they grew up.

The differences between the groupings of people working on the estate were huge. Recruitment of workers for the tea estates of Assam had traditionally come from areas as widely separated as Jubbulpore in Central India, Midnaput in Bengal, Gorakhpur in the Himalayan foothills and Coconda on the Madras coast. Most had been employed through the sidari system whereby sirdars who started work on the estate were paid to return to their original homes to persuade relatives and fellow former villagers to return with them to Assam. This worked well since the sirdars rarely misrepresented the working conditions, knowing that they would suffer if they exaggerated. Many of the Indian labourers recruited were suitably awed by what they saw as palatial coolie Lines and the convenience of being eligible for modern hospital and medical treatment.

The downside was that this method of recruitment produced a babble of languages and dialects – the tea estate baht was mainly a mixture of Assamese, Hindustani and Bengali. Also, not everyone was prepared to live in peace and harmony with their neighbours: some elements such as the Dom and the Kurdi seemed traditionally unhappy at living in close proximity to each other. Then again, almost all the different groups were insular and would only seek a partner for their son or daughter of marriageable age amongst their own kind. It would be at least two years before Stuart was able to sort out all these differences in his mind, and many months before his attempts at achieving some level of verbal dialogue began to succeed.

As for the more local population, many came from the Cachar District which divided between those from the hills and those from the plains. In the plains was the Surma valley, a nearby and very picturesque area of subtropical evergreen forest and bamboo jungle, the plains dotted with rice fields, rivers, woods and swamps. The hills were two to five thousand feet high and the natives from there tended to be more isolated and warlike.

Stuart quickly realized that both region and caste were all important. The Assamese saw themselves as quite different from the other groups whom they viewed as visitors to the area rather than indigenous. The Assamese would only perform certain carefully defined tasks but then that was equally true of some of the other races and religions. The jobs that each geographical group of natives performed tended to define their caste, and since a change of occupation could result in a loss of caste, great care needed to be taken when asking anyone to perform any duty different from normal.

As for religion, it was the Hindus whose social organization most used – Stuart might have said abused – the caste system, combining as it did religion, parentage and country. In terms of other religions the Jains were also strongly represented, the two principal sects being Digambara and Swetambara: both close to Buddhism in their belief in reincarnation. There were some Muslims but a higher proportion of Sikhs with their own disciples and system of Gurdwara.

All in all it was a heady mix and Stuart could do no more than listen to his fellow Europeans and try not to cause conflict by saying the wrong thing to the wrong native person.

Stuart found the climate stupefyingly oppressive. He had known that the monsoon season brought high humidity but this was beyond all his fearful expectations. Appreciating that his arrival had coincided with the hottest months, June to September, he still found it totally exhausting. Whilst at present he remained healthy he had taken in what Petrie had told him about malaria being endemic amongst the planters and managers and realized there was little he could do to prevent following suit in due course. He took all precautions he could against mosquito bites but the conditions were against him.

The natives suffered from malaria too, but also from hookworm, cholera, yaws and blackwater fever, and they often acquired a variety of sores and abrasions that flourished in the conditions. The tea estate management was in charge of health care, and since it was in their interests to ensure as healthy a workforce as possible Stuart was told he must watch out for illnesses and be quick to refer patients to the estate hospital as soon as he suspected that symptoms had appeared. He was also to try to ensure that the coolies preserved as sanitary conditions as possible, not always easy with such a variety of primitive peoples unused to the modern world and its perception of basic hygiene.

There was little to do on the estate outside the working environment. Letters from home took a month to arrive but were his lifeline to normality. He wrote to his parents every week, sometimes separate letters to Mary and letters to his friends such as Arthur Mitchell. He worked on the principle that if he did not write regularly to them, they would not write regularly to him. His mother's letters were warm and loving, his father's more formal and descriptive; Mary's were full of news of her progress at school in Edgbaston and her myriad sporting activities. The waiting time between the delivery of each batch of letters seemed interminable.

CHAPTER SIX

I missed Stuart enormously but I was very busy once school restarted so I tried to put his absence out of my mind.

It had been four years earlier, in 1928, that father had been promoted from Deputy Regional Medical Officer for Yorkshire to Regional Medical Officer in Birmingham so we had all gone back to live in Birmingham, the city we had left only a few years before. Thus I was to return briefly, this time as a boarder, to Edgbaston Church of England College where I had spent a year as a day pupil in 1924.

Stuart had then been away at boarding school at Epsom College which was a typical public school for boys only, so I was left to go to school in Birmingham. I wasn't a proper boarder as Edgbaston was really a day school with just one boarding house but there was no spare bed there so I had to stay in the vicarage. This was a huge old Gothic house. The property was said to be haunted and, what was perhaps worse, I was frightened of the vicar and his wife who nonetheless acted as my proxy parents. I was only thirteen and very homesick but fortunately I was only there for a term and we then moved to a house in Acocks Green.

I loved my mother very much, she was warm and caring and possessed of a lovely personality, but before Stuart left for India there came a time when she suddenly succumbed to a melancholic depression – I suppose that nowadays it would be called a nervous breakdown. She became very excitable and was taken to St Andrew's mental hospital in Northampton. She was to be there for about six months and my aunt Janet came to live with us in Acocks Green to look after my father, Stuart and me until that September. We then moved to a house in the suburb of Four Oaks owned by a wealthy old school friend of my mother rejoicing in the name of Daisy Crump.

When my mother was able to return from St Andrew's she seemed much better in herself and it was not until many years later, in 1936, that she was to suffer a relapse. We were short of money: my father was funding Stuart's school fees and had to pay for my mother's treatment at St Andrew's. Civil servant doctors did not earn a great deal and I recall that when the Depression was at its worst all state employees were required to take a pay cut – not something that would be popular nowadays.

In any event, my father managed to find a house to rent at 13 Calthorpe Road, near to Five Ways in Birmingham, and close to my school. It was a Georgian house with a lovely bay window in the drawing room. We lived there for eight happy years; there were plenty of rooms for us all, and a large garden where my father set up a tennis practice game and clock golf in order to keep us entertained. Eventually Stuart bought a motorbike and would bring his friends back to the house; he played rugger at weekends and had a number of girlfriends including his favourite, a girl called Grace. He explained to me that he could not bring Grace home because she would be out of her 'class' with my parents.

One of Stuart's friends who came to the house was Arthur Mitchell, the son of another doctor; his father Charles Martin Mitchell was a very much larger-than-life figure with something of a reputation as an expert in Shakespeare. Arthur was four years older than me and a school friend of Stuart's from Epsom College. They had played rugger together and were great pals.

Before Stuart's departure we had all joined the Harborne Tennis Club as a family and spent weekends playing tennis together both in tournaments and with friends. My father was a very good player, cutting and spinning the ball at will, and I remember playing in mixed doubles tournaments with him.

Once I was back living at home I enjoyed the school experience much more and became heavily involved in games. I must have been assisted by my sporting heritage, in the shape of my father who had won a 'half blue' at Cambridge for his tennis, had also played soccer for his college and on occasions was even selected to play for the Corinthian Casuals amateur football side which had a national reputation. As time passed I became more senior at school which gave more opportunity for me to choose specific sporting activities.

I was not particularly aware of how bad the Depression was in the early 1930s. Certainly my father referred to problems on an almost daily basis, but I was so used to his negative view of life that I probably took less notice for that reason. I knew that money was very tight and that there was a lot of unemployment. Looking back, it is remarkable that my father managed to fund my school fees and, later, to pay for my training whilst maintaining a household with all the expenses that went with it.

I longed for Stuart's letters. He was very good at writing; I suppose he missed us as much as we missed him and this was the only way to keep in touch. Most of the letters were addressed to my parents as well as to myself so I only received them second hand, but occasionally to my great delight he would write to me alone. We were very close and often called each other names as illustrated by his first postcard to me from the ship at Marseilles:

Old spud yourself! Only got two letters so far, yours and mummies and Margarets. The others may come by the mail tonight. Post this on quay, leave at midnight. Arrived this morning, taxi all round the Boulevards and Cathedral on the hill. Topping views – blue Mediterranean, Palms, Isle de Monte Cristo. Taxi driver did not understand English but DID understand my French!

Stuart's first letters had enclosed photographs of the voyage, small black and white pictures but pored over by all of us. Later pictures showed the tea estate. We found his lurid descriptions of life on the estate fascinating but difficult to imagine. He would tell us of the expeditions to the 'club' and the games he played there.

Stuart was good at sending photographs: we treasured the pictures of the bungalow in which he was living, groups of seemingly shy natives with names written on the back of each photo, Stuart holding a monkey, riding a horse, on a boat on a river; evocative labels such as 'weighment', 'baby carried by tea plucker', 'garden pani-wallah', 'Coolie hoeing'. Then there were the pictures of the buildings: sorting room, rolling room, Tangye engine room.

Every one gave us some small flavour of his remote existence and each of us formed our own mental picture of what life in India was like. We later realized that none of us had been able to properly imagine the extremes of weather, and when he talked dramatically of the rains and of the humidity this rather passed us by.

CHAPTER SEVEN

Stuart's first year in Upper Assam passed swiftly. The energy-sapping heat and humidity; the disruption of the monsoon rains; the constant pressure of keeping the factory running; the learning of new skills; and particularly the need to learn a different language to communicate – all added their own burden and quickly occupied the passing months.

As the weeks passed and the slacker days of winter took their place Stuart began to relax and find life more enjoyable. His existence to that point had been a steep learning curve in so many ways: not just in terms of culture, geography and weather conditions, but more in the absorbing of a completely new social structure.

It was a strange life: there he was, waited on hand and foot by a huge team of helpers orchestrated by the ever-present Daniel, pandering to his every need. Granted all the helpers had their own idiosyncracies, and a seemingly inevitable ability to malfunction in some irritating way. These would become a regular topic of conversation, each European vying to tell of some particular failing of those serving them. Stuart thought back to the naivety of his reaction to those conversations in England with his aunt and uncle, when he had mentally likened his parents' maid to the situation he would find in India. Whilst he would not have seen Daisy as of his own social class, she would have seemed positively aristocratic in the world in which he now lived.

Stuart had plenty of time to think and he would often let his mind wander during the long watches of the night when keeping the factory running. He supposed that poverty was the great class distinction. Here even the sirdars were pathetically poor by English standards, and unless granted accommodation within the factory area they simply lived in larger wooden huts on the coolie Lines than those under them. Those with an army background had some knowledge of the world and how the 'other half' lived and had their being, but the experience of the remainder was very limited and their horizons small.

On the other hand much of Indian society seemed driven as much by position as by money, and the quality of the position was in relation to the service of the 'sahib'. Thus the man who served the sahib most closely gained the greater prestige, and advancement was to that end, rather than to the gaining of some sort of release from service or independence. In England, thought Stuart, Daniel would be seen as a personal valet, and regarded as important only in the servants' quarters. Here Daniel was Stuart's bearer, and therefore of greater influence than the senior factory sirdars whose skills were in reality much more valuable to Shaw Wallace in particular and the world in general.

As for life outside the factory it was fortunate that Stuart had been taught by his parents to play bridge, since that was the main summer evening activity amongst the few of them at Budla Beta: the Mackies both played, as did Ross, so Stuart could make up the four in the evenings when his duties permitted.

Bridge was also part of the life of the Doom Dooma Club but Stuart far preferred more strenuous activity, although in the first few months the humidity was against him. Once November came the 'Cold Weather' turned out to be delightful: warm and sunny, dry, much lower humidity – and much less work. The frenetic activity of the growing season slowed as the winter months advanced and visits to the club became a pleasure. There were also opportunities for journeys into the vast complex of the rivers and mountains of Assam.

There was golf at Doom Dooma and Stuart was proud to see that his uncle Dr David Williams had been the first captain of the club. His manager John Mackie was the current captain and he and Stuart often played together. The small boys from the nearby Lines were desperate to caddy for a few coins and it was a welcome diversion from tea production duties.

Stuart was good at tennis and at table tennis, able to turn out at cricket when there were sufficient numbers to raise a team, and game for any other sport that might be going. He was talented at hockey, his first love in sporting terms, and he started the first ever hockey team in the area. Until sticks had been requisitioned from Calcutta a degree of improvisation was necessary, but before long a workmanlike team was developed and challenges against other clubs were made. The club had an odd sort of atmosphere, probably closer to an officers' mess or perhaps a small rugger club, but it was the one social beacon in his life and he threw himself into every activity.

Stuart would go to the Doom Dooma Club whenever he could find transport. On occasions there would be only a handful of people there, but on the weekly Club Night and at most weekends it would seethe with life. There were some local Europeans from the town, mainly working for the Assam Railways and Trading Company as it was the biggest employer in the area, but most members were drawn from the tea trade and the majority were from the individual tea estates in the area. The Doom Dooma tea estate itself was large and only a few miles from the cluster of club buildings, so their resident core of members knew each other well; but they were welcoming to the fresh faces of those from other estates, particularly those with sporting skills, and the social life was good.

The snag was that the distance from Budla Beta was significant and it would take well over an hour crashing over the unmade track to reach this haven of sociability. Only Mackie as manager had a personal car so although he would sometimes attend Club Nights there needed to be some considerable persuasion from Stuart to encourage more frequent visits. The return journey, fuelled with beer and whisky as was usually the case, seemed swifter but there was little doubt in Stuart's mind that this was owing to the insulating effect of what had been consumed. Keeping the car on the road was vital – the jungle was not a hospitable place if a vehicle left the road.

Then there was the much larger Panitola Club: a huge low thatched clubhouse, an outdoor swimming pool, a squash court, grass tennis courts and an area which doubled up for both hockey and cricket. There was a monthly film show in the big hall adjacent to the bar and it was a delight for Stuart to be able to obtain transport to visit there, but it was a long journey through the chaos of Makum Junction and past Tinsukia.

Apart from club life, when the manufacturing season was over there were outings with friends to explore the area, usually involving hunting, and these were magnificent. In his letters home Stuart described the Dehing River picnic where he and Ross together with bearers, cooks and porters set off for a long weekend under canvas to explore the river and its rapids. They soon learned that Assam abounded with leopards, tigers, bears and other beasts of prey not to mention the occasional rhinoceros. Of course elephants were common and used in garden service in the same way that a tractor might be used back in England. Ross told Stuart that the presence of a leopard or tiger galvanized the natives into action and they would immediately turn up at one of the bungalows and either seek to have the sahibs loan them guns and bullets or invite them to go out and shoot the creature themselves. It was not uncommon for either beast to make its presence felt by seeking out cattle belonging to local villages, or on occasions even ponies and dogs belonging to the Europeans.

Stuart was persuaded to join the Assam Valley Light Horse which was a mounted group rather similar to the Combined Cadet Corps, or CCF, in an English boarding school. Mackie and Ross were already involved and it was Mackie who encouraged Stuart to take part. He quickly learned to ride and as his skills increased he was able to join in the various military activities, a legacy of the era of the Raj and the need at that time to maintain discipline in each geographical area. There were also the leisure competitions such as pig sticking and other mounted pursuits. Each year a camp was held at which there was much competition and camaraderie, under the guise of learning military necessities such as map reading and other such joys. Days at camp counted towards the qualifying 'drill days' needed during the year – sixteen was the average and Stuart managed to achieve that number. He was fortunate in having learned a lot of the rudimentary military skills at Epsom College, and he was able to relax and thoroughly enjoy the break from the isolation and monotony of

Budla Beta that such gatherings involved. It also enabled him to meet others of his age from different tea estates: he counted over twenty different estate addresses amongst his fellow subalterns in his enrolment year of 1932.

Nothing was the same as at home but Stuart felt that he had coped well with his loneliness and was rather proud of what he had achieved. One major downside was that Ross was the only British person of his own age at Budla Beta; and although he had some good friends at the club he constantly felt particularly cut off in the small estate. Also he missed his family – letters were one thing but no real substitute for the warmth of being at home – and the thought that years would pass before his first leave was daunting.

He visited some of the other estates including the Pengaree estate which was smaller and with limited factory facilities. This was the most isolated of all the estates: theoretically it was accessible from Budla Beta but there was no easy road for vehicles in that direction, simply a walking track stretching more than ten miles through the jungle. The main route was back to Makum Junction and thence to Digboi where there was a road passable by vehicles up to the Pengaree estate.

The first Christmas Day away from home was spent at the Doom Dooma Club: much drinking and merriment and wearing of magnificently designed paper hats but with the constant underlying sadness of missing his parents and Mary. Stuart counted sixteen of his European friends as he photographed the merry group – and that was the largest gathering of the year.

But above all a huge void in his life was women. Since his early teenage years Stuart had always had a girlfriend, or two or three he thought to himself. Over six months had passed since he had last kissed a girl, and he could not see how the deprivation was to be addressed. Apart from Mrs Mackie, who was pleasant but rather senior and hardly an object of adoration from Stuart's point of view, there were two or three other wives and the only additional European girls were occasional visitors to the club. There were two secretaries who lived in the town and came to the club from time to time but one was engaged and other 'spoken for' in her relationship with an assistant manager from Khanjikowa. Those planters whose wives were with them were capable of being counted on the fingers of one hand, and the wives clearly inaccessible to Stuart: he judged that the confines of the tea estate community were not a healthy place to consider conducting an affair even if the opportunity were to present itself.

Stuart had gone into the situation with his eyes open. He knew that finding an English girl to marry in India was rare. He had been advised that in his position 'you should not marry until you have five years' service'. Indeed, his terms of employment had made it clear that he would need to seek permission to marry during the first ten years with the company, and he had not questioned this at the time. He had read that civilians who did not find the right girl in India usually waited until their first period of leave, or furlough, before making an intensive, indeed feverish, search for a wife. At the time he had thought this rather sad, but now he could understand.

Stuart appreciated that he was still under twenty-five and should not be impatient, but at the same time he had thought there would be opportunities for flirtation and dalliance but these had not materialized. He found his abstinence dictated by lack of opportunity, not prudence, and was becoming increasingly desperate.

Stuart raised the issue with Petrie one night, over their customary peg of whisky.

'Was married once,' Petrie replied. 'Never worked out, and rather lost interest in that sort of thing as a result. Came out here a few years later and not got involved since. Can't say I miss it in particular.'

Stuart made what he hoped were the right sympathetic noises, whilst secretly marvelling at how his colleague could have cut himself off from what he regarded as one of the main essentials of life.

'Still – lot of chaps over here go native, if you know what I mean? Lots of pretty girls about and age is no barrier to the Indian girl. Never fancied that side of it myself but no doubt Daniel could fix you up if you're interested.'

'Very funny. But to be serious for a moment, who else that I would know has followed that route?' Stuart was at once inquisitive whilst privately a little intrigued by the way the conversation was going.

'McAllister from Kharajan for one – two bastard children there; then there's Prior from Pengaree – only one coffee-coloured little one to date; and I reckon even Swannell has a twinkle in his eye most mornings – but far be it from me to suggest anyone has done anything out of line. One problem is that the memsahibs are likely to cut dead those who step out of line, so dalliance can play havoc with the bridge fours!'

From the time of that conversation Stuart began to keep his eyes and ears open. When visiting other estates he noted mixed-race children in the vicinity of some of the bungalows and began to draw conclusions.

One night when he was playing bridge at the Mackies' the topic came up again, Margaret Mackie commenting that one of the servant girls on the Kharajan estate had suffered a miscarriage and that a certain field manager seemed rather concerned.

'Yes, I had heard rumours,' said Mackie to no one in particular. 'These things happen – not enough women to go round, more's the pity.'

Silenced by a fierce glance from his wife, Mackie winked at Stuart and carefully counted out the tricks before gathering up the cards to deal the next hand.

CHAPTER EIGHT

I still missed Stuart enormously. Not having my madcap brother around took the edge off many things, but life had to go on and my life both at home and at school continued to develop. My earlier sporting promise seemed to have blossomed and as I came towards the end of my schooldays I found myself captain of cricket, captain of hockey, captain of netball and playing 'first couple' in the tennis team. I hasten to add that it was quite a small school.

Then in my final year, much to my surprise, I was appointed head of house. I was nervous about how I would manage as I seemed to be feverishly busy already but fortunately it was not as onerous as I had feared. Came the summer and, in addition to my school certificate exams, I managed to pass the entrance exam to Bedford Physical Education College, and was due to start there in September 1933 coinciding with my eighteenth birthday.

So off I went to Bedford. It would be lovely to record undiluted enjoyment there but I hated the first term. I was thoroughly homesick and seemed to do badly in everything save hockey and academic work. I was very much below average in dancing – and there was a lot of dancing associated with PE training in those days – and not much good at swimming; also the standard of gymnastics was much higher than I had anticipated. All in all it was damned hard work. We had to study anatomy, physiology, pathology, first aid and the theory of gymnastics and dancing. We also had to get up early to act as 'bodies' for the seniors who had to practise 'general massage' as part of their training. This meant lying on a cold plinth in an icy medical room at about seven in the morning. Not much fun… but the seniors were about to take their physiotherapy exams and needed practice on real bodies.

After a suitable period we were sent out to teach Physical Training in the elementary schools, cycling all over Bedford from school to school taking mixed classes of youngsters in their school playgrounds for their PT lessons.

Gradually I began to enjoy life and make friends, but on the whole I look back on those three years at Bedford as 'hard labour'. It must have been totally unlike today's university and college courses since we were not allowed to fraternize with young men and life consisted of work, games and how to coach them, and little else.

Throughout this time Stuart's letters to my parents continued to arrive and each time I went home I would sit down and read them through. My father was a great letter writer and wrote to Stuart every week without fail; Stuart wrote back at almost equally frequent intervals. My mother would also write; my own letters were rather more sporadic.

I duly passed all my exams at Bedford, gained colours in hockey and cricket, and captained the first cricket XI. My swimming was now good and I had my Life Saving Diplomas in bronze and silver and also as an instructor. I had managed to qualify as a Member of the Chartered Society of Massage and Medical Gymnastics (now called Physiotherapy).

All this training had been funded by my father with considerable sacrifice – there were no grants for that sort of thing in those days – but I think he was proud that I had a qualification and some letters after my name. This enabled me to apply for a job and after a number of interviews I was appointed in September 1936 as the games mistress at Derby High School.

I found digs to live in and would travel home to Birmingham on occasional weekends, sometimes by bicycle. I made good friends amongst the staff and also with a number of the older girls and their parents. The music mistress was called Dorothy Dean and in 1937 she and I decided to share a flat; that was a happy time and my first real taste of independence. I was selected to play hockey for Derby County, the first sport at which I was to be capped, and I enjoyed that tremendously.

It was with Dorothy that I shared some of the letters from Stuart since these were often laboriously copied out by my mother so that I could have my own version. Dorothy and I would talk happily about the extraordinary world that he occupied.

CHAPTER NINE

Another season, enduring the rains, exhausting himself in the production process but occasionally visiting other estates and other clubs, so life went on. As the second year came Stuart again particularly enjoyed the time of the Cold Weather, the respite until March when the plucking season resumed. This had proved to be a time for consolidation and some relaxation. In working terms the cutting back of the jungle, the planting of new tea bushes and the thousand needs of general maintenance and repair would start. Tropical weather took its toll on plants and buildings alike. Machinery needed to be repaired and often rebuilt, bungalows had to be patched up and maintained, and above all the land must be hoed and prepared to enable the bushes to flourish.

These were the months when outings, particularly to the planters' club at Doom Dooma but also to Panitola and others further afield, could be enjoyed rather than simply squeezed into the frenetic race for production. Stuart continued his quest for social life accompanied by his seemingly hypothetical but constant hope that one day a girlfriend might be found. If one of the others was going to Doom Dooma or elsewhere then Stuart was always keen to accompany them. Ross had now acquired a car so both he and Mackie were potential sources of transport but the tracks were so bad that they were understandably reluctant to use their cars for the journey too often. Sometimes a truck had to go that way and Stuart could take a lift, but then the return journey had to be organized and this could be frustrating. Ross allowed Stuart to borrow his car every now and then, but he found that the excursions to the clubs, outside the mandatory Club Nights, were far too few and far between for his social needs. Club Nights were usually only once a week. When there were free weekends those able to get away would customarily go to one of the clubs for a day and possibly stay overnight, playing tennis and bowls and generally socializing; but the days in between tended to drag excessively.

Not that his world was totally without women. Stuart could not help observing that many of the pluckers and other garden girls were exceedingly shapely, and there was a good deal of flirtatious banter which enlivened the day. Any response Stuart made would provoke a riposte in dialect so rapid that he could only guess at the detail, although the accompanying laughter and giggles often left the meaning in little doubt.

There were also the women and girls helping with domestic tasks, tending to be hidden away in the staff quarters but quick to flash a smile when encountered. One such was a young girl who Stuart worked out was related to Daniel, probably his niece. At first he was not sure of her name but a few weeks after she arrived to help in the bungalow he found her sweeping up when he came back for his lunch and asked who she was.

'Salam – Hum Monglee hai – Daniel ka phagni.'

So: Monglee, related to Daniel, Stuart translated, congratulating himself on his correct assumption.

It was 19th August 1933. Stuart acknowledged the glasses raised to celebrate his twenty-third birthday, the toast proposed by Mackie to the assembled company at the club. 'Thank you – to think I shall be as old as thirty in only seven years' time!'

And to think that I am the most sexually frustrated twenty-three-year-old in India, Stuart thought to himself as he drained his glass and waited for the bearer to fill it up again.

Daniel never slept, or if he did, Stuart had never detected an hour when this phenomenon might have taken place. It mattered not whether Stuart returned from the factory at 10 p.m. or 3 a.m., Daniel would shimmer out from the back of the bungalow to check whether any refreshment was wanted. Stuart used the word 'shimmer' having recently been introduced to the writings of P. G. Wodehouse, detecting in his bearer a striking similarity to the self-effacing Jeeves.

Came midnight and Petrie had retired for the night, being about to depart on a two-week-long tour of other tea estates in the area. Stuart was looking forward to being on his own, free from their mundane conversation which rarely strayed beyond the routines of their tea-dominated world. Lying back in the basket-weave armchair he closed his eyes, rampant in the sexual fantasies that increasingly seethed in his young brain.

'Anything further tonight, sir?'

Unsettled by Daniel's silent approach, Stuart gave a short and cynical laugh:

'Just three beautiful girls – or even one would do. Sorry, Daniel, forget I spoke. I expect you find that life gets to even you sometimes!'

'I fully understand, Sahib. Think no more about it. Although perhaps I might be bold enough to say that my niece, Monglee, is one of your great admirers. But I fully understand that you will be seeking a lady from your own kind.'

Stuart was taken aback. Somehow he had not anticipated that Daniel would cast himself in the role of family matchmaker. Whilst he was still working out how to respond Daniel placed the whisky decanter on the side table and moved away.

'Good night, sir. It will be another warm day tomorrow.'

In the days that followed Stuart found that Daniel's niece Monglee was often in his thoughts and surprisingly often in his living quarters, seemingly always being about to clean, sweep up or bring in fresh towels as he arrived home. He would ask how she was and she would answer in a shy but encouraging manner. She was small in stature but quite pretty and he found himself attracted to her.

Stuart's responsibilities were not helped by Petrie's absence. Whilst Petrie was away Mackie had asked him to supervise some of the planting that was taking place on the furthest part of the estate and whilst this made a change from the constant noise of the factory, Stuart was not yet confident that his scant knowledge of cultivation equipped him for the task.

He did the best he could, but there was then a minor factory breakdown which led to a stoppage of the winnowing process and his engineering skills were in demand. It was a wearing time, backwards and forwards between the machines and the fields, and he was glad to be back at the bungalow for his early evening meal, often having missed out on lunch altogether.

One night during the second week of Petrie's absence Daniel was clucking about Stuart, mixing the customary whisky and water, running the bath and setting out a change of clothes. Stuart thought his bearer unduly solicitous when he suggested an early night:

'Poyser Sahib, everything is running very smoothly in the factory tonight. It is time you had some rest.'

'Don't fuss, Daniel. But I will turn in after one more drink, thank you.'

Stuart allowed his mind to drift across the experiences of the day, closing his eyes against the slats of moonlight which lay across the verandah. Suddenly he became aware of someone in the room.

Opening his eyes he saw Monglee standing beside him with a fresh jug of water for his whisky.

Later he would recall asking her to sit down and talk to him; he remembered the limitations of their conversation, she speaking no English. Looking back much later he would remember their kissing, and the taste of her. Quite how this had happened and how they had subsequently found themselves in his bedroom was less clear. Time had seemed to accelerate in the grip of their mutual attraction and then their combined passion.

Stuart was in no doubt that his mind had telegraphed the moral protest of his upbringing just as he had been caught in a hot embrace from which his will to escape was instantly abandoned. The frustrations of the last two masturbatory years were swept aside by the flooding ache of sexual tension. Neither the girl's gasp nor the constriction as he moved inwards registered in the overwhelming fever of his excitement; he was lost, pounding, in the tangle of limbs.

Eventually, gradually, Stuart's breathing had begun to slow as awareness emerged.

'I should never – shouldn't – so sorry but …'

Monglee's finger reached his lips as he remembered the girl's ignorance of his language. He kissed her gently, cradling her in the crook of his arm as the wetness on their bodies began to dry.

'Monglee – you are marvellous – let me look at you properly.'

Stuart reached over for his matches to light the lamp beside the bed. The girl blinked against the sudden light and pulled the sheet to her chin. He saw her large brown eyes and attractive face. But how young she now seemed. Gently he pulled the sheet from her fingers, drawing it down the bed as she shyly tried to cover the buds of her small breasts. Traces of blood were on the sheets and as his eyes ran back over her body realization of her youth came to him.

'How old are you?'

She seemed not to understand.

'How many years?'

He thought she now understood but he could not make out what she was whispering. She lifted her hand and carefully counted her fingers: once; twice; and then again but stopping at her thumb. He now realized she had been using the word 'chouda'.

'Fourteen?'

Stuart's head swam. If he was right the girl in his bed was a fourteen-year-old virgin. Somehow he knew that in Indian culture this was neither illegal nor unusual, but was he really a part of that culture? What had he been thinking? What was he doing?

She smiled at him and reached across to turn off the lamp. Once more he let excitement take him away into the humidity of the night.

CHAPTER TEN

Stuart hadn't known what to say to Daniel but, Jeeves-like, his bearer resolved the problem without embarrassment.

'I believe you like my niece, Monglee?' Daniel enquired, impassively, at breakfast the next morning.

'Her father, my uncle, is a blacksmith by trade, working for the Assam Railway and Trading Company. He is, like me, of the Adivasis community and lives in the village near Pengaree tea estate. He knows that Monglee is visiting here, helping with the cooking and the cleaning. Her mother also knows that she is here. My niece says she is very happy to have made your acquaintance and trusts that she may continue to be of assistance?'

'Of course, delighted, please send her parents my compliments.' Stuart was conscious of the weakness of his reply as Daniel glided from the verandah, acutely aware that none of the staff who had remained backstage in the bungalow that previous night could have been ignorant of the liaison. During the day he looked carefully at the faces of those servants he encountered for any sign of disapproval or disrespect, but their features remained as impassive as always. The fearful apprehension which had dominated his wakening moments in the bed of which he was by then the sole occupant began to fade.

Stuart's fears reasserted themselves as the days until Petrie's return swiftly passed. Each night the slight figure of his childlike lover slid into his bed, and each night he sought to minimize the sounds of passion as he delighted in her body. He found himself smiling involuntarily during the day, humming to himself as he went about his duties, and giving praise and thanks to those working with him when none was due. If Mackie and the others had noticed any change they said nothing; but Petrie was a different problem and Stuart did not know how to deal with it.

In the end he decided to grasp the nettle. In the first break in conversation during dinner on the night of his colleague's return, Stuart spoke out.

'You remember our conversation about women and going native? Well, rather out of the blue Daniel seems to have entered me into that category.'

After a pause:

'Looking for my blessing, old chap? Not really up to giving you the sign of the cross but youthful sap rising and all that sort of thing I suppose. Anyone I know?'

'Niece of Daniel – calls herself Monglee, you may have seen her back of house?'

'Better keep my eyes open then. Anyway, have another beer whilst I tell you how badly those buggers at Kharajan estate have planted the new bushes we gave them last year.'

Three months later Mackie announced that Mr Adams, the managing director of the company, was making a visit. Feverish preparations were the order of the day: the tea bushes themselves were in good order but the surrounding cultivated areas were to be tidied, the bungalows were to be made presentable, and the factory spaces had to be perfectly organized to demonstrate the efficiency of the unit.

Fortunately there had been three days' notice of the visitation, so by the time the great man's car had drawn up everything was ready for inspection. Adams was accompanied by two other senior officials from Calcutta and all three fired questions as they checked records and took stock of the whole operation. They were put up in the various bungalows overnight, Stuart escaping that duty, and then conducted interviews the following day, first with Mackie and then with the others in order of seniority. When it came to Stuart's turn to be invited into the factory office, which had been taken over for the purpose, he was in a state of some anxiety – would his performance be regarded as satisfactory?

'You have done very well.'

The opening words relaxed Stuart, as he noted that his hard work in his first job had been recognized.

'In fact, we would like to build on your obvious skills by giving you a new position. The estate at Pengaree near Digboi requires development and expansion, particularly in factory terms – and we are appointing you to the post of production manager.'

This was excellent. A new position, a new estate, new responsibilities. There was also to be a salary increase. Good news indeed!

Stuart had visited Pengaree, which was the most isolated of all the estates, so his pleasure at promotion was tempered by some reservations. But he was ambitious and welcomed the chance to move on. The next two hours were spent discussing the detail of the planned investment: in essence a whole new manufacturing facility was needed. Then there was the problem of transferring the finished product to a railhead for shipment. Digboi was the obvious destination but the track from there to the estate was in a bad condition and often impassable when the rains came. Stuart was to start his mind working on possible solutions but in the meantime his supervision of the construction of the new factory was the priority.

Stuart had one personal request: might his bearer Daniel be included in the move? The wish was regarded as of little consequence and dismissively granted. As Stuart returned to his bungalow he smiled at his subterfuge. Daniel came from the Pengaree area, and Monglee's family lived in the tiny village only a few kilometres from the Pengaree estate. They would hardly object and Stuart would be able to continue his liaison.

The move was to take place in four weeks. Movement between tea estates was not unusual, and Mackie and the others were pleased to give Stuart their congratulations and to help him with the arrangements for moving on. There was to be a new junior assistant at Budla Beta and he was scheduled to arrive as Stuart departed so there would be a degree of continuity.

What Stuart had not done was to think through the consequences of his new relationship with Monglee. The managerial visit had coincided with the busy season, and the combination of humidity, factory breakdowns and planning for his move had exhausted him to the extent that he would often crash into bed without thought of other activity.

One lunchtime, two weeks after the managerial visit, Daniel asked if he might have a word. Petrie was scheduled to be in the fields all day, supervising new planting, so Stuart simply slumped in his chair on the verandah and asked Daniel what he wanted.

'My niece has asked me to speak with you, sir. It seems that she has developed what we might call a problem.'

The sweat on Stuart's face seemed to chill as his mind analysed the possibilities. What a fool! Unless the problem was an illness, his next question appeared inevitable.

'Is it a problem or a consequence?'

'Poyser Sahib, you are quick in your thinking, clearly we understand each other'.

'What do you suggest?'

'Sahib, there are ways that Monglee would not want to take. She is happy with her condition provided her parents are happy also. Their reaction concerns her, however, and she wanted me to speak with you before she talks to them.'

'What do you think her father will say? He is well respected in his community and although we have not met, I do not wish him to be dishonoured.'

'Thank you, Poyser Sahib, that comment helps me. Tomorrow I am travelling to Pengaree to ensure that the arrangements are in order for your new accommodation. With your permission I will find time to visit the village and speak with her father.'

Stuart had an uncomfortable two days. Unusually Monglee did not appear. He had formed a huge affection for her – in his way he could almost say that he loved her; and yet he was an Englishman and she was a native woman. Others had conducted similar relationships and children had been the result – how had they dealt with the situation? What was to be done for the best? And what was going to come out in terms of the company? Mackie and his wife were no longer relevant since he was moving on but how would the estate manager at Pengaree react if the situation became known?

Daniel returned. 'Poyser Sahib, I have spoken with my cousin's parents who know of you, indeed they say that you are called "Chanchal Sahib" by Monglee so that has been the title used within the family. As you know, "chanchal" means "full of life". It seems that they have known of the association with their daughter for some time and although they do not wish to approve they do not strongly disapprove. However, the new situation means that their daughter will be looked down upon by the others in the tribe. To have a child but not have a husband is a bad thing, you understand?'

'Of course, but how can we resolve this? The company regulations do not permit me to marry, and I am powerless to change the rules.'

Stuart knew that Daniel had knowledge of the regulation against marriage for ten years from first appointment. All assistant managers were required to sign. For his part, Stuart had always very much hoped that if he should find an English wife then the regulation might be relaxed, but had not contemplated taking a native wife, however strongly he might feel about Monglee.

'My uncle says that the solution is for you to marry his daughter under Adivasi customs. That would be a ceremony in the village using our customs and traditions, following which you would be husband and wife within our culture. In that way any children would be legitimate children within our tribe.'

Stuart scratched his newly-grown moustache as he thought this through. Really he could see no alternative, and such a marriage would surely not be seen as valid under any English or other recognized law. He was not happy, but he had created the problem and if this suggestion would solve it then he must co-operate.

'Please convey my respects to Monglee's father and say that I am happy to agree.'

CHAPTER ELEVEN

The move to Pengaree tea estate went smoothly. Stuart travelled by train from Doom Dooma down to Makum Junction and then on the branch line to Digboi. From there an estate truck took him along the eighteen kilometre track through the jungle to Pengaree. The lorry lurched and crashed over the potholes and deep ruts now hardened but it seemed clear that the road would be little more than mud in the rainy season. The jungle had been cut back a few metres but it was dense and in places the canopy touched overhead. Adams had talked to Stuart about the difficulties of transporting the tea from the estate and had asked him to report back once he had seen the situation at first hand. First indications from the state of the roadway were not encouraging.

Stuart was to share a bungalow with the field manager, Tyrrell. He had met him before and enjoyed his company. More importantly, Tyrrell had heard a rumour about Stuart's association with Monglee and when they first met he had volunteered that if this was to continue he would have no objection. This was excellent news since Monglee could now be accommodated in the rear quarters of the bungalow without difficulty. Daniel had already installed himself and organized the other staff and Stuart could see that his own domestic arrangements would run smoothly.

Pengaree had seven hundred hectares of tea, smaller than Budla Beta, but the factory side was also small and the leaf was processed elsewhere. Stuart's task was to build and develop the factory, install the necessary machinery and make the estate self-sufficient.

Gregory was the estate manager, a pleasant man some ten years older than Stuart and easy to get on with. There was also Hodgkins, similar in age and rather austere but reasonable company. The junior assistant, Scott, had arrived only a month earlier. Stuart could see much of himself only two years before in the enthusiastic young man introduced to him and extending a sweating palm in greeting.

A month later Stuart found himself standing in what he could only describe as a jungle clearing. He had already seen Singpho village houses since there was a village of the Singpho tribe much closer to Budla Beta, and he had even sent home photographs of the stilted construction of their dwellings. This was very different. The huts were closer to the ground, still built on stilts but with a form of balcony in front perhaps four feet from the jungle floor rather than the nine feet or more of the Singpho construction. The stilts were formed from tree trunks, the supports of the balcony and hut tied across with creepers and ropes. Behind was a covered area with woven branches above. There were perhaps a dozen huts, each thirty feet or so from the next and forming a circle around the beaten floor of the clearing. In the centre of the clearing was a fire pit, huge leaves lying across the top of whatever was smoking underneath, and primitive long tables, a foot or so from the earth floor, were on the side furthest from the path leading to the cleared area. One house was larger than the others, and on its balcony five tribal elders were squatting, each naked save for a cloth round their waist and each with body and face painted in white and yellow stripes.

Daniel had explained to Stuart what was to happen. Stuart had taken Ross into his confidence and Ross had agreed to visit Pengaree at Stuart's invitation under the pretext of a short hunting expedition. The two of them, armed with unloaded revolvers and carrying machetes, represented the bridegroom and his armed friends who would approach the bride's house in a warlike manner. Men from Monglee's community, similarly warlike, would meet them and there would be mock combat which would resolve itself into a dance. The couple would then be led to a bower in front of the bride's house and stand on a curry stone which was laid on top of a sheaf of corn. The bride and bridegroom would be marked with red lead to symbolize bloodletting and then be drenched with water from vessels on the bower. They would retire to change their clothes and return as man and wife. The feast would then begin.

Looking back on the events later the next day, Stuart felt that he and Ross had done rather well. Shouting 'tally-ho!' was perhaps not as bloodcurdling as the response from the cavorting and rather terrifying figures on the bride's side and the Englishmen's dancing was perhaps nearer to a Scottish reel than a depiction of battle, but the beating of the drums and the chanting of the villagers added to the atmosphere and they stamped and pranced with enthusiasm. Stuart stripped to the waist and was duly adorned with red and black stripes, slightly incongruous against his moustache, but he submitted to the decoration with good grace, supported by Monglee's amusement and encouragement. Her spoken English was improving daily and she was able to interpret for her friends as the proceedings continued. It was hot, and the dousing with tepid water caused much merriment to the crowd whilst serving to cool Stuart down. He was not certain whether the changing of clothes was meant to incorporate an actual or symbolic consummation of the union, but a passionate embrace seemed to meet the needs of the audience and the shouts and acclamation that greeted the pronouncement of man and wife were clearly to the satisfaction of all present.

The feast was served on the long tables and eaten cross-legged on the ground. Monglee's father made a long and impassioned speech of which Stuart understood little, and Stuart in turn, prodded by Daniel, rose to his feet and responded in traditional English form. Daniel and Ross seemed appreciative and the rest of the congregation nodded happily and continued to consume their haria or home-brewed rice beer. The pit had yielded up roasted goat, served on leaves the size of a dinner plate and eaten with rice. Stuart reflected to himself that it was an entirely acceptable wedding breakfast and soon realized that the beer was no less potent than the champagne he might have contemplated in English climes.

The festivities went on for many hours, enriched with more tribal dancing both from the warriors and from separate swaying lines of silken sari-clad women. The heat and the rhythm and the atmosphere was arousing and when Stuart led his bride to the privacy of the bower, as encouraged by Daniel, the union was duly celebrated.

Later that year Monglee went into labour. Daniel told Stuart that she had returned to her mother in the village. After an anxious day, Stuart was proud to be told that he was now the father of a baby girl. He took a jeep and drove to the edge of the Pengaree estate from which he could easily walk the final two kilometres on foot. There he was greeted by Monglee's father and conducted to the hut where he could see mother and child. Monglee put the baby into his arms. Looking down, Stuart felt a great rush of affection for this strange small creature, and when asked by Monglee what name they should give he said simply:

'Mary'.

CHAPTER TWELVE

Fatherhood was strange. Stuart had not readied himself for the emotional change of witnessing the development of his own child. He had thought that he would be able to detach himself from the image of a full-time loving father. In the months leading up to Mary's birth he had somehow imagined that he would be able to see the product of this rather furtive union in a slightly distant but paternally friendly role. Not so. Holding Mary, watching her face, seeing the beginnings of recognition in her, witnessing her first sitting up, urging her on in her crawling progress – all triggered the pride of fatherhood. His surprised pleasure was matched only by the enormous frustration of not having anyone to whom his delight could be communicated. Certainly Monglee's parents and extended family were happily involved but on Stuart's side he could not share these small successes with parents or sister or English friends. Nor would it have been considered good form to have mentioned these things within the closed European community in which he lived and moved and had his being.

So, a strange and frustrating situation for a proud new father, but this was largely overtaken by the continued excitement of the recent promotion and move.

The downside was that the Pengaree estate was more remote than Budla Beta, transport being restricted by the state of the muddy track from Digboi. Inevitably it was a considerable journey to reach the Doom Dooma Club; but the Digboi Club was substantial and more convenient, and there was also golf at Digboi, played mainly by the oil executives some of whose houses overlooked the course which ran alongside the railway line. The other side of the coin was that it was of considerable benefit that Monglee and her family were now very close. Since Mary was born Monglee had been staying in the village for much of the time but it was now planned that she would move into the servants' quarters in the bungalow. She could move back and forth easily: the village was only a few kilometres down the jungle track, over a forded river but readily accessible.

The new bungalow at Pengaree was an improvement on that at Budla Beta, and with Tyrrell turning a blind eye Stuart was able to enjoy the opportunity to have something of a 'family' life, albeit of rather a back-door nature.

As to the factory work, Stuart had designed and was starting to supervise the building of a new tea house. The latest Crossley engine had been ordered and this would be housed in a separate building alongside the Tangye engine house. The whole of the factory process was to be streamlined. As soon as November came Stuart threw himself into the challenge. His Urdu was now coming along well and with the help of the sirdars he was able to organize and direct the workforce to erect the new structures.

Stuart's further brainchild was to contemplate a small railway track all the way to Digboi. It meant widening the existing road through the jungle and laying simple tracks, but the ability to transport the boxes of tea by this method would avoid the morass of the present track which could be impassable in severe weather conditions. To streamline the delivery of the leaf would transform the capacity of the Pengaree estate to meet its production targets. Adams and his fellow directors were enthusiastic and a small type of locomotive engine was identified. Stuart had to make many submissions to satisfy Shaws that the railroad was viable and now, to his delight, the engine had been commissioned.

All this had taken the winter of 1935 and as the estate moved into the growing season of 1936 the pressure of other work meant that the railway project had to be delayed. The next winter months would provide the opportunity to finish the task.

Stuart was relieved to be able to describe all this engineering activity in his letters home. He was acutely conscious that he could not share details of his domestic activities. He loved playing with his daughter, although he had to be careful to do so out of sight of Gregory and the others who did not officially know of the situation. In reality he recognized that the men were probably well aware of what was happening, but it seemed that the proper conduct was to ignore liaisons like his so Stuart made no attempt to explore what his colleagues knew or thought. The wives were a different matter. Stuart was well aware that the European ladies' view of associations with 'garden girls' was highly critical and he risked being ostracized at social events.

Instead he was able to regale his family with descriptions of his settling into the new estate and to send photographs of the erection of the buildings and installation of engines and, as time passed, of the new railway project.

Time came for another Assam Valley Light Horse camp. Stuart was by now quite expert in the military manoeuvres and rather admired himself in his uniform. He enjoyed the camaraderie of the corps, and particularly the way in which he was taught to develop his horse-riding skills. He had always been a good shot and enjoyed pitting his skills against others in rifle-shooting competitions.

Stuart's holiday that year was by way of a major expedition into Burma to a Burmese temple many miles up river. This had been months in the planning. Peter Carter, a friend of Stuart's from the club, made the detailed arrangements and they journeyed by elephant and then dugout canoe with a small group of bearers, marvelling at the scenery and wildlife. It was a joy to be away from the confines of tea estate life and Stuart found it extraordinary that their small party was in such complete isolation in this almost unknown and remote area of the country.

This kick-started another winter season and in his short absence elephants had been set to work clearing the jungle, moving the felled trees out of the way and finally laying the sleepers on which the narrow-gauge railway lines would be laid. Returning from his expedition Stuart moved back into organizing the labour. It was tiring work but as the winter months passed progress continued. There came the great day when the truck carrying the Crossley engine for the tea house arrived at Digboi, and had to be nursed along the track to

Pengaree. Once more, elephants and teams of coolies were needed to persuade the lorry to navigate the churned-up roadway and to unload the shining machinery and install it in the new tea house. Stuart's engineering skills were tested to their limit in the process of connecting the engine, but he was relieved to find that the manufacturers had sent two of their own engineers from Calcutta to help him.

It was an even more glorious day when the little locomotive, designed to be operated by a single driver, reached Digboi. The rail had now been laid and it was decided that the engine should make the journey to Pengaree under its own steam: this would save another tortuous journey by lorry. Stuart was anxious. Would the engine stay on the recently laid tracks? Would technical problems cause embarrassment?

A party was laid on, the train was bedecked with bunting and the wife of one of the directors was on hand to cut the ribbon and inaugurate the service. All the planters from the estates from miles around gathered to see the fruition of the project they had all heard about. The engine was fuelled, the tape was cut and Mrs Hughes, majestic in an appropriately feathered hat, declared the railway line open. Stuart was nervous but proud to watch it move away from the siding without incident, and as it set off he ran alongside in order to jump on to one of the small tenders and ride on his brainchild as it slowly chugged through the jungle to the Pengaree estate. His vision had come to pass.

CHAPTER THIRTEEN

Stuart was coming home!

To think that five endless years had passed without my hearing his laugh or seeing his face. My rites of passage, first as schoolgirl, then college student, finally gym mistress, had passed him by save in the crisp flimsiness of airmail notepaper. In turn, that same medium was my only record of his conversion from inexperienced youth to tropical-hardened factory manager.

Since September 1936 I had continued to live in Derby, enjoying and developing my role as PT and games mistress at Derby High School. I was proud to be on the earning ladder on the huge sum of sixty pounds per term. I had so much to tell my brother and I was so excited to hear in his last letter that he had been able to arrange to return home for six months' leave, arriving in the spring of 1937.

For us as a family Stuart's return was the main topic of conversation for months before the great day. Unusually my recollection of his arrival is imprecise save that I know that for some reason my parents were not able to meet him in person and so I went on my own. I well remember travelling to London by train and underground to welcome my long-lost brother from the boat-train that came in at Waterloo. I hardly recognized the mature, tanned figure, now moustachioed, in linen suit and white trilby hat. It was just wonderful to see him again.

We were both very excited and talked at the same time so that neither of us really heard what the other was saying. It was when we were in a taxi on the way to St Pancras that Stuart suddenly exclaimed, 'I've got engaged – I met a super girl on the boat!'

I was stunned and could only say, 'What is she like, what's her name?'

'Her name is Louise Rogers, she's very pretty, lovely blue eyes and dark curly hair, only her teeth stick out a bit, a bit worse than yours!'

This typically brotherly remark caused something of a quarrel as I had never considered I had teeth that were remotely protruding. Behind the pretence of anger at the insult the truth was that my stomach had knotted at the shock of Stuart's announcement. I had so looked forward to having my brother back again as a confidant, and I didn't want to think of now sharing that role with an unknown girl. I had not lived with Stuart's frustrations nor with his desperation to find a wife during the time of his leave and the breath had been knocked out of me by his casual announcement.

When the family actually met Louise some weeks later we all agreed that she was reasonably attractive apart from her teeth – Stuart was accurate in her description in that respect. We were all relieved to find that we liked her very much. She was quite shy and quiet but as my brother was outgoing and talkative we saw that as perhaps a good thing. Stuart certainly seemed happy in her company.

My father had excelled himself. He had bought a small second-hand Ford for Stuart to use during his leave. Stuart was ecstatic and this rather odd-looking yellowy-cream car with red wheels became his pride and joy. He was not discouraged by the family's naming it 'Blood and Pus', and the name stuck. The car meant that he could visit his friends and also hop down to Yelverton in Devon where Louise lived with her parents.

Once the initial rejoicing at Stuart's return had begun to subside we all went off for a family holiday in Scotland. This was the only family holiday undertaken since Stuart and I were in our teens when we had been taken to Shoreham so it was quite an event. I was twenty-one and had just finished my first year's teaching in Derby, and faithful to family traditions I recorded the whole event in an exercise book, adorned on the cover with a piece of white heather.

Suffice it to say that we took two cars, ours and Stuart's. Stuart had been told by my parsimonious father that he was to fund his own accommodation, and in consequence he spent much of the time in cheaper lodgings than the rest of us. Nonetheless we had a wonderful time; my mother was almost back to her old self, galvanized by Stuart's outgoing sense of fun and constant cheerfulness.

Louise wasn't able to come with us and on one or two occasions I thought that Stuart was rather pensive and wondered if he had begun to have second thoughts about his whirlwind romance. He was always quick to praise the virtues of his fiancée but his words seemed carefully chosen, and when friends naturally asked to see her photo which he had brought with him he tended to be apologetic, saying that it did not catch her in the best light. During the second week of the holiday we met our Scottish friends with whom I had stayed previously. Those of my brother's age included the irrepressible Isla Black, black haired and strikingly beautiful. I was watching my brother as I introduced them since I had always thought he would get on enormously well with her, but he seemed struck dumb for a moment. He passed it off but there was a brittleness about his customary exuberance and that night, for the first time in the holiday, he drank very heavily and was like a bear with a sore head in the morning.

Talking to Stuart during the holiday I realized for the first time how isolated he felt in Assam, and how dearly he wanted to find work so that he could stay in England. This was because the London tea companies had certain rules of engagement to which Stuart had signed up without much thought. One was that assistant managers were not allowed to marry for ten years. This may seem strange nowadays but there was no air travel then. Children of a marriage would have had to be sent home from an early age to be educated; the journey by boat and train would take a month and so there could be no returning home in the school holidays. During the early part of his leave Stuart travelled to London to beg the company to allow him to take Louise back to Assam and marry her but this was refused. It was a tremendous blow to him as his quest for a wife had been to enable him to build a family life over there. His engagement had achieved nothing.

In consequence, and despite his having only a few months before returning to Assam, Stuart tried very hard to find a job in England. Sadly he was offered nothing that attracted him. There is no doubt that he had led a privileged existence in terms of accommodation and service by staff in India, and it must have been difficult for him to consider the alternatives in some minor management role that would have been his likely lot here. As the weeks passed without any tangible job offers he seemed to become more resigned to his return. He spent a lot of time with Louise and she had now become his confidante more than I, which was hardly surprising since I was in Derby most of the time.

I loved our holiday together in Scotland and all the other activities which Stuart included me in when I could get away from Derby. Now that Stuart was home Arthur Mitchell visited a great deal and it was with him and his sister Christine that Stuart and I went to London for George VI's coronation.

It was a memorable experience. Everyone was in high spirits and all the procession routes were closed to traffic. We set off the morning before the event and spent the day amongst the crowds, queued endlessly to have something to eat in a Lyons Corner House, danced around Eros and then walked up Oxford Street in the middle of the road. Although it was still early evening the pavements were already beginning to fill with spectators and we continued to enjoy ourselves. Eventually, after more than a few drinks at a nearby pub, we managed to get into the second row of the crowds lining Oxford Street. This must have been at about 2 a.m. and from then on we cheered everything including the dustcart sweeping the road at 5 a.m. The whole city was crammed with people and there was a wonderful atmosphere. That was just as well since we stood there for fourteen solid hours until the procession came by at 3 p.m., and we stayed there till well after 5 p.m. I remember Stuart driving us back to Birmingham in the evening with none of us having had any sleep for thirty-eight hours!

It had been wonderful to have my brother home again, but as the days of his leave came to a close it was as if a black cloud was coming over us. Particularly my mother seemed to decline behind the surface of a fragile cheerfulness that we could all see through. We were all desperately sorry to have to say goodbye once more. Once more we would have to revert to arm's length correspondence, inevitably delayed by the days and weeks that the mail took to come by sea.

CHAPTER FOURTEEN

It was the second time in the twenty-six years of his life that Stuart had watched the chalk cliffs of Dover fade into the horizon. As the shoreline receded in the pale morning sunshine Stuart tried to analyse his feelings: eagerly looking forward to seeing his beloved Monglee and his daughter Mary but acutely conscious of his responsibilities and affection for Louise. How complicated he had made his life and what a strange life it was when set against the domesticity of home.

Had his engagement been a mistake? He had justified the suddenness of his decision to Mary by reminding her that all those in his position had only the six months of leave to find a wife before returning to the isolation of Assam. To find a girl on the boat home with whom he felt an immediate rapport had been marvellous. To discover that she was used to living abroad and so was content with the thought of a life away from England was even better. To realize that she shared his sexual frustrations and was happy to join him in releasing those particular energies was unbelievable. A joyous voyage, romanced by the calm waters of the Mediterranean slipping by the stern of the ship as they kissed, was a sure recipe for the consummation of their new relationship. Surely it was not a mistake; but then what complications seemed to have emerged before he could contemplate marriage.

During his few months' leave he had managed to put out of his mind negative memories of the isolation and boredom of life on the tea estates of Assam. Yes, he thought to himself, he had enormously enjoyed the privileges and liberation of an existence far removed from the restrictions of a Great Britain only slowly emerging from the economic depression of the decade. Set against that was the virtual bereavement represented by such a long separation from family and friends, and from the simple normality of English life where one did not have to strive to convert dialogue with the population into Hindi, Urdu or tea estate baht.

As he watched the broken churn of the wake he argued with himself, recognizing that on the one hand he had loved being cocooned in a life with servants and staff waiting on his needs. He thrived on the work, the responsibility and the use of his engineering and now well-developed managerial expertise. He knew how he revelled in the exotica of such rare sports as pig sticking and tiger hunting, and how he enjoyed the privileged atmosphere of the planters' clubs. On the other hand he now had to face up to the immediacy of his solitary return to the limitations and remoteness of a planter's existence.

Stuart had hoped that it would not be so. In the past months he had answered advertisements, attended interviews and even enlisted his parents and friends in repeated attempts to find a worthwhile job at home, but in vain. To an extent this would have been a betrayal of his position with Shaws but he had anticipated that arrangements to terminate his contract, albeit with the loss of some accrued benefits, could have been negotiated. Had he succeeded an early marriage to Louise would have followed and he could have started his new working life in familiar surroundings.

After failing to find a job at home, his contracted return to Assam had been complicated by the engagement to Louise and his overwhelming desire to set up home with her in Assam and live with her there. She was quite happy to make that move, having lived in a variety of far-off places owing to the constant mobility of her father's employment as a medical officer during her childhood, so they had both been taken aback by the refusal of his employers to 'bend' the rules to allow their marriage. In vain had he travelled to Shaws' offices in London to plead his case.

Whilst Louise had certainly spoken of 'joining him' as soon as they were allowed to marry, that could now only be after his next term of duty had finished, a distant five years away. He supposed he could try to travel back home to marry in the meantime but he would need to speak to his area director, Hughes, to find out in how many years he might be allowed time off for that purpose. The impossibility was that he had no funds to return from Assam for a wedding, but what would be the point if he could not live with her in India? And what would happen to Monglee and his daughter? Time would tell but he was conscious of his failure to meet the imperative of finding employment in England. The die for his return was cast.

Apart from the disappointment of not finding alternative employment, leave had been an enormous joy and success. He had been impressed to find that his shy young sister was now a mature and delightful companion. Her prowess at games was formidable and seeing her five years on brought home to Stuart how much he had missed being part of the day-to-day life of his family. This was emphasized by meeting up with his old school friends who had proved to be tremendous company during his leave, particularly Arthur Mitchell from Epsom College days. He had loved the trip to London for King George VI's Coronation, when he and Arthur and Mary had travelled up to watch the procession – fourteen hours in all but wonderful for Stuart to be surrounded by a crush of English people after so many years in which he would see only coolies gathered in similar numbers.

As for the girls, Grace was still unmarried, and Beth also. Of course he was now a respectable engaged man, acutely conscious of his proposal on the boat on the way home some five months before, but then Louise was at the other end of the country most of the time, and a brief renewal of his tryst with Grace somehow did not seem disloyal. Whilst in England Stuart had found that he could simply pull down the shutters on his life in Assam. Quite what his parents would have said to the revelation that they were now grandparents of a small Indian child could not easily be contemplated. Better that such matters were put out of mind, and only dwelt on in the same guilty but detached way as the romp with Grace that devalued his new loyalty to Louise, somehow neither real nor permanent.

But on the other side of the world he had both the expectation of a happy reunion and the parallel problems that his clandestine relationship would continue to cause. Scarcely a day of his leave had passed without Stuart wondering how Monglee was coping with little Mary. He could not deny that he missed them both very much and was constantly bemused by his ability to betray that relationship with his engagement. He told himself that society demanded that he take a wife with whom he could appear in public. He convinced himself that he was doing exactly what anyone else would have done in his position. Quite how to conduct himself if given immediate permission to marry Louise and return with her to Assam was a dilemma he did not need to confront at present. He was able to close his mind to that concept at this stage.

The other side of the coin was that during the time Stuart was seeking other posts he had been forced to consider how Monglee's and his daughter's lives would have progressed without him if he had stayed in England. He had always planned to send them some money through Gregory, on the understanding that this would ensure that the funds were put to good use. He could well imagine the anguished impact that Gregory's words would have caused had he been directed to announce that Stuart would not be returning. It would have been a traumatic contradiction of Stuart's impassioned promise on his departure, his expressed determination that he would definitely return to Monglee. The suggestion that the reunion had in some way been frustrated would surely have been seen as the greatest betrayal, and he would have missed them desperately.

The greatest pleasures of the leave had been his father's unexpected provision of a car and the trip to Scotland, the only family holiday since the trip to Shoreham many years before and therefore quite an event for Mary and his parents. Stuart had enjoyed driving his brightly coloured Ford, it having been decided that two cars were needed for the journey in view of the volume of luggage and also the decision to take the family Cairn terrier, Jinx, on the trip. His father had insisted upon piloting his new Austin so they had travelled in convoy.

Stuart had to laugh at his recollection of the financial arrangements for the holiday. Although Mary was now qualified her father had paid for her accommodation; but on the first night in

Yorkshire he had taken Stuart on one side and explained, in his kindly but firm manner, that he expected his son to fund himself as he was now financially independent. So there the others had been, luxuriating in the facilities of the Coach and Horses on Bowes Moor, at ten shillings a night for bed, breakfast and garage for the car, whilst Stuart had found cheaper lodgings at only four shillings and sixpence. He had so enjoyed Mary's indignation with her father when at seven the next morning he had met up with her for an early morning walk before returning to breakfast at their separate establishments.

'And I had to pay a further shilling for the privilege of bathing in a smart pink bath,' she had snorted.

Then to Bamburgh in Northumberland, where again Stuart saved himself money by finding bed and breakfast in the village whilst the others stayed at the Victoria Hotel. Finally on to a touring holiday of Scotland, during which they all met up with the Blacks, family friends whom Mary had been to stay with previously. Perhaps it was as well that he was leaving for India, Stuart thought, when he remembered his feelings at meeting Isla Black, stunningly beautiful, vivacious and precisely his own age.

So, all attempts to find suitable employment at a reasonable salary having failed, here he was returning to India. His father knew of his worries but was strong in his encouragement that Stuart should return and achieve promotion within the tea industry. Vernon had reasoned that once his son had a senior post, perhaps in sole charge of a large estate, it would be much easier for him to return to a significant position in England. Duty first, so although he was sad to have his son so far removed, the return to India seemed destined to be.

Before going down to his cabin Stuart finally let his mind open to the farewells of his last few days in London. His parents probably did not know that he had arranged for Louise to join him in a room at the Regent Palace Hotel to indulge in a final night of lovemaking before his departure, but he assumed that Mary had guessed. She and his parents had accompanied him to London by train, crowded into a taxi to the Regent Palace Hotel and sat awkwardly over a silver service tea before they returned to Edgbaston. He had expected his mother's distress as she clung to him at the end but he also sensed Mary's desolation in saying goodbye, and wondered when he would see her again.

Later he had consoled himself in the arms of his fiancée, but he was unable to put out of his mind the slender and more inventive body of Monglee and the passion with which she would welcome his return.

CHAPTER FIFTEEN

13th October 1937

My dear Daddy & Mummy

In the 'Bay' now, not been sick yet but I don't feel too steady! I am in a three berth cabin, with a R.Q.S.M and his young son on leave from Egypt. At my table there are two jockeys going to Calcutta and a naval officer's wife and a nurse going to Gib. We saw one of the new transatlantic airliners as we left Southampton, otherwise not much of interest. Dr Rogers is on board, Louise apparently did not know otherwise she would have told me, he is going to Egypt for a short holiday. I will add more to this as we go along and post it at Gib. I do hope that all goes well with you

Monday: Just eaten a hearty breakfast! ...and felt much better. I was expecting to be sick at any of the meals yesterday, about a third of the second class passengers were absent at meals but I managed to attend them all. I have not spoken to many people yet, I spent a quiet day reading and went to bed early, I expect I shall be a little more energetic today. We get to Tangier tomorrow.

Tuesday: 7.30 am. Got to post by 8.30, we stop at Tangier at 9.30. Not much else to add, I played Poker for an hour or two and danced twice yesterday evening. Will stop now, I'll post some more P'Boat envelopes at Gib. We are due at 3.30 this afternoon, Doubt if I'll go ashore.

Much love and best wishes
Stuart

14th October 1937

My dear Daddy and Mummy

I am afraid I could not post at Gib. The box is cleared one hour before reaching port and between Tangier and Gib it was not opened. Whether the post mark will be Tangier or Gib I don't know, possibly this will arrive at the same time being posted at Marseilles. I did not go ashore yesterday, although many people did at Gib. We left at dark, and heard gunfire off North Africa – probably only practice. We also saw a rebel armed trawler only about 100 yards off. At the moment we have a destroyer running parallel to us, British I think.

Life on board is beginning to liven up now we are getting into warmer weather, today is lovely, calm bright blue sea. I've met another planter going to Lower Assam and now know the history of half the ship! Now I've got Louise I can sit back and watch all the various 'affairs', I'd like to run a sweepstake on who takes who ashore! Wonderful stuff this Mediterranean air!

Thursday: Nothing else to add, we dock at Marseilles this evening and I think stay 24 hours. Passed more destroyers as we came along yesterday.

I do hope all goes well with you all.

Much love

Stuart

In reality Stuart was finding his declared fidelity to Louise sorely tested. It was early days, but he had now to contemplate whether or not he should remain in line or perhaps consider whether his seduction techniques were up to the offspring of the aristocracy:

17th October 1937

My dear Daddy and Mummy

Left Marseilles in the earlier hours of yesterday morning and get to Malta today. Many thanks for your letters and wishes, I am so glad all has gone well with you so far. I went ashore and did some shopping and also went and had a drink on the 'Rawlpinde', a sister ship to this, on its return voyage to England, but I knew no-one on board. Still, one fellow from Digboi, Hopper by name, who has been to my bungalow after a hockey match, joined us at Marseilles. The boat has more or less settled down and everybody found their respective drinking partners. I've palled up with Mac (a Doom Dooma planter) and a fellow going to Hongkong, (if I have any P'boat letters left over I will get him to post them after Bombay).

I've found a member of the peerage on board, I wonder if Mummy can rake up any family connection with this one, I had three dances last night with a Miss D'Horsay (Admiral's daughter) niece of Lord or Earl Cardigan (Balaclava)!!

The sea is very choppy and a lot of people down, nearly all who joined at Marseilles, were absent from breakfast this morning but I feel OK!

Much love
Stuart

19th October 1937

My dear Daddy and Mummy

Oh what a time we've had since I last wrote, we ran into a storm at Malta – Thunder, Lightning, Rain. Yesterday we pitched and rolled all day, the blue Mediterranean was a rain swept grey, no games or anything of course and at least half the passengers were ill, in fact at tea time hardly anyone was about, I managed to keep going and not actually sick. I just had a roll of bread and soup for lunch, I am beginning to think I am a good sailor! But I don't want any more tests!! We are in calm weather again now, sun is out again, and everyone looking happy once more. The deck games and things have started again, I shall pack my 'Blighty' clothes today. East of Suez this time tomorrow, we get into Port Said this evening or early in the morning, I shall go ashore I think and I will see what I can do about some stamps for you. I am looking forward to some more letters at Port Said, I feel quite lost not hearing, that is the worst of being on a mail boat, unless you send by air the letters don't catch up.

Well I will stop now and go and take some exercise. Send my love to everyone.

Much love
Stuart

23rd October 1937

Dear Daddy and Mummy

We get into Aden early tomorrow so I will post this today, I hope I get a letter.

Whew! It is hot, last night we had a slight sea and the portholes had to be closed, I just lay and dripped and it is none too cool now. We get to Bombay on Thursday and I gather I should reach the tea garden about ten days later.

I don't know if these stamps are much good but I got the control numbers of a few.

Send my love to Mary
Much love
Stuart

26th October 1937

Dear Daddy and Mummy

Nearly there now, only one whole day left, it is much cooler now and the sea is like glass. I went ashore in Aden and had a bath and only just got back to the ship in time.

I am out of all the deck games now except the singles of the Deck Tennis. Dog racing, dancing, etc still fill in the time. We had the children's sports and party yesterday. Fancy dress and Gala tonight.

I wonder if I shall get any letters at Bombay or Calcutta, nothing since Marseilles. I do hope all goes well with you all. I will finish off tomorrow.

Wednesday: Everyone suffering from thick heads this morning. The fancy dress was a great success! I went as a schoolgirl!

Got to do all my packing, etc today.
Love Stuart

The Grand Hotel Ltd, Calcutta
30th October 1937

My dear Daddy and Mummy

Another stage, quite a good journey over India. Bombay was very hot and I nearly went mad at the Customs. I got on the wrong side of a native Customs Officer, he tried to make out that my Air Pistol was a lethal weapon and required a licence, in the end he stung me for nearly everything, I had to pay 90 Rupees at Customs and excess baggage in Calcutta!! Swine!

We had eight hours in Bombay and had a drive round and saw the sights. We got to Calcutta yesterday morning. I leave on the Assam Mail train tomorrow night. We went to the pictures last night and are going to listen to a band concert this morning and a swim this evening.

I got another letter from Louise yesterday but still no letters from you since Marseilles.

Love Stuart

CHAPTER SIXTEEN

The train left Calcutta at 10 p.m. Stuart had a moment of déjà vu recalling his reaction only five years before to the poverty and the press of people on the streets. He had then been overwhelmed by the sights and sounds that confronted him and yet now he was indifferent. He had the company of his drinking companion from the boat, Fergie from the nearby Doom Dooma tea estate, who was travelling back to Assam and was in the same sleeping compartment for the long journey.

Fergie O'Connor was an amenable companion, happy to listen to Stuart's account of his leave. To pass the time they swapped stories about their respective backgrounds and how it was that each had come into planting. Stuart explained about his training as an engineer with Tangyes Limited and was even able, after a couple of whiskies, to recite how the company had started in 1857, and to tell the tale of their dramatic claim to fame coming with their part in the launching of Brunel's huge ship, the *Great Eastern*. He was encouraged by O'Connor who said he had read somewhere that a set of Tangye jacks had recently been used in Australia to raise the Sydney Harbour Bridge. Stuart was able to counter by describing the large number of Tangye hydraulic jacks commissioned by Brunel for the *Great Eastern* launching. They joked that only two engineers could have enjoyed such a conversation.

In Calcutta, Stuart once more reported to the Shaw & Wallace company offices and received the depressing news that he was to return not to Pengaree but to the Kharjan tea estate near Panitola. He had visited Kharjan in the past and knew it as habitually understaffed, overworked and with poor accommodation. He remonstrated but was told that after his success at Pengaree his proven skills were needed to restore normality; production at Kharjan had fallen behind and the company would be grateful if he would accept the challenge and restore order, but he was assured that he would very soon be transferred back to Pengaree. Stuart reflected, ruefully, that he was given no choice as to his acceptance of that particular challenge – only an affirmative was required since there was no alternative offered. The one consolation was that he would be very near the large Panitola planters' club so at least social life would be more readily accessible. Anyway, despite the disadvantages of the Kharjan estate perhaps a plunge back into hard work would take his mind off the black thoughts that had begun to descend as he contemplated the isolation that was to be his lot for the next few years.

Kharjan
4th November 1937

My dear Daddy & Mummy,

Well, here I am. No letter from you yet!

I can't quite realize I am back or how I feel, one thing the weather is perfect. The Factory and Bungalow are the most tumbledown rotten places in the company, but I know that and I think I shall be transferred at the beginning of the rains. Miller is manager, Giles outside assistant, Chetham who has been in the factory is off home in three weeks to get married, so I am using his furniture till he comes back and leaving mine up at Pengaree. I am going up there on Monday to get my linen, Polly, etc. Poor old Mary is dead.

I am writing this in the factory office! Already! I only got back yesterday and here we are running till 8pm. I was going to call on Hughes this evening, in fact Hill (assistant at Kanjikoa) came over for me (nice fellow Hill). Also Gregory is manager at Pengaree, he was over this afternoon for tennis with Chetham. I managed to get a few sets.

Friday night. Yet again! Not shutting down till 9.30 tonight. Miller and Chetham have gone to Dibrugah Club for the evening. So I have not yet been off duty since I got back, and it will be the same tomorrow I expect.

I haven't seen Hughes yet so I've heard nothing more about any chance of marriage but I don't think there is much hope till 1943!

I had more letters this morning including from Leicester but still nothing from you. I expect you have written and they have gone astray somewhere. Or else you have got the address wrong.

Saturday: I said so, closing down at 8.30 (in half an hour). This morning inspected the bungalows and Hospital, etc. Giles and Hill came in for tea but could not stay long as the factory was running. Tomorrow Sunday we hope to finish early and go over to Hughes in the evening. On Monday I am going up to Pengaree in a lorry to collect odd bits of furniture, etc.

My gun is much admired. Well, I think that is all. I do so hope all goes well with you. Please send my love to Mary and Leicester. I will write soon. Also to Arthur.

With love

Stuart

The Mary who died was the parrot, not his sister. During his leave Stuart would often show off photographs of his beloved parrot and tell how he had taught it to speak some chosen words. Following the receipt of this letter the news of the parrot's decease became a temporary topic of conversation of Stuart's parents. They would later tell him by letter of the time when his mother, travelling by train to London, gave the sad news to the friend who was with her. The other passengers in the compartment did not know that Mary was a parrot and assumed that a close friend or relative was being referred to.

'I'm so sorry to hear that Stuart has written to say that Mary has died, how old was she?'

'About twenty I believe, yes it was so sad and completely unexpected.'

'How did it happen?'

'We're really not sure, Stuart's letter only says that Mary was found dead at the bottom of her cage.'

The collective gasp of horror given by the other occupants of the compartment remains part of the folklore of the Poyser family.

It was not only the odd bits of furniture that Stuart collected from Pengaree; he had determined to bring Monglee and daughter Mary back with him and install them in the quarters at the back of his bungalow. The reunion with Monglee was rapturous. It was clear to him that despite his protestations when he left her four months earlier she had feared that he might not return. Their daughter Mary was now nearly four and irrepressible, chattering away using a mixture of Hindi and tea estate baht with the occasional word of English.

Stuart had still not fully reconciled himself to fatherhood, furtive as his paternity had to be in many quarters. Now he was reeling from the latest unexpected news with which he had been welcomed, it being immediately obvious when he had opened his arms to greet his lover that she was pregnant once more. 'Seven months,' she had announced proudly, smiling at her recollection of their impassioned lovemaking on his departure and the tangible evidence of his fertility. He could not imagine how his parents would have taken the news of their becoming grandparents for the second time, again reflecting that they might never even have knowledge of the first.

Stuart had delayed collecting Monglee and Mary because he wanted to gauge the reaction of Miller, who as area manager of the Shaw estates had the capacity to cause considerable difficulties if he disapproved. Chetham, who was off to England anyway, was relaxed about the arrangement; he had met Monglee at Pengaree in the past and knew the situation. In consequence Stuart had decided that he would gently sound Miller out himself, explaining that his bearer's cousin and her child were needing somewhere to stay and that he was prepared to help out. Miller had looked at him over the rim of his round steel spectacles, raised his eyebrows and uttered the words, 'No problem with me old lad, make your bed and lie on it as far as I'm concerned.'

Stuart had not sought to dignify the answer with a token denial of what was implied and allowed his silence to signify such challenge as the other might wish to read into the dialogue. So it was that he was now bumping his way back from Pengaree with a happy Monglee wedged into the cab between him and the door, cradling a sleeping little Mary pressed against the front of her sari, as the estate lorry driver heaved the swaying vehicle around the linked potholes that represented the road.

CHAPTER SEVENTEEN

We heard in 1938 that my father had been promoted to Regional Medical Officer for Leicester and so I began to help my mother and my father in their quest for a rented house in that city. Few people could afford to buy houses outright in those days and whilst some mortgages were available the financial climate was such that borrowing was not encouraged. We eventually settled on a spacious Edwardian house, number 23 Morland Avenue, which was in a cul-de-sac in the fashionable suburb of Stoneygate on the south side of the city. The move from Edgbaston was completed and my mother and father seemed very happy in their new home.

I was able to come back from Derby most weekends which also enabled me to visit 64 Highfield Street, a terraced property in a popular part of Victorian Leicester near to the railway station, where my grandparents had their home.

My grandfather had been headmaster of Wisbech Grammar School in Norfolk, and had been retired for many years. Their health was giving some cause for concern and I used to provide such support as I could in my short visits.

My mother had suffered some further bouts of her depressive illness but she loved the new house, except for the scullery – and as we had a maid I'm afraid this particular room didn't cause great concern. She seemed to take on a new lease of life, we had more money than before and she was allowed some new things for the house. She had good taste and the house looked very well; there were three big downstairs rooms in addition to the kitchen and scullery and she chose lovely chintz curtains in the drawing room, and a new sofa and armchairs. My father's stamp collection, which grew ever larger and followed us from house to house in its rather ugly custom-built bookcase, was banished to the dining room.

I had thrown myself into the organization and coaching of sport at Derby. I have explained how lucky Stuart and I were to have inherited our father's aptitude for games, and whilst in my teens in Edgbaston amongst my other sports I had played a lot of cricket – this being encouraged by our games mistress who had once played for the English ladies' team. She persuaded the captain of Warwickshire Cricket Club at Edgbaston, the renowned R. E. S. Wyatt, to coach me and I became a good bowler, a very good 'in-fielder' and a good bat. In consequence I had a head start when seeking to pass on my playing skills to the girls at school and did my best to instil my love of games into them.

I thoroughly enjoyed playing cricket. On occasions before going to Derby I had been asked to play for the Birmingham Women's Cricket Club but unfortunately Derby High School was not a cricket school, so on moving there I could only play cricket at weekends, returning to play for the Birmingham team.

There then came the great moment when I was chosen to play for the Midlands against the first ever touring team of women cricketers from Australia. This was very exciting and I opened the batting and got my photograph in the newspapers under the headline 'Out to Face the Aussies!'. Sadly I was run out for only four runs; I still wonder whether I might not have scored well had that not happened. Anyway, there was then a three-day match against Australia at Edgbaston County Cricket ground and I was invited to play in that too. I went to seek permission from my headmistress; to my distress she told me that I had taken quite enough time off already, that Derby High School needed me to stay on duty, and she refused me permission to take the three days off work. So that was really the end of my cricketing career. Perhaps otherwise I might have gone on to play for the England team – we shall never know.

Looking back it is not surprising that Stuart's regular letters in the early months after his leave reflected the increasing political concern that occupied all our minds in the late 1930s. When he was at home on leave we had talked about Germany a great deal, it was constantly in the news and there was still a lot of ill feeling following the end of the First World War a decade earlier. It was natural that people should be very worried that Germany was again becoming powerful, and it had been as recently as March 1936, only a year before Stuart's leave, that news had come of the first direct breach of the Treaty of Versailles with German troops' reoccupation of the Rhineland.

We rather glossed over seriously ponderous articles in the newspapers which expressed the view that it was our fault that the atmosphere in which Hitler had flourished had been created because we had imposed the 'humiliation' of punitive terms following the end of the First World War. Our own initial thoughts were that he seemed to be such a funny little man with his 'toothbrush' moustache, we laughed at the way he strutted around and we found it hard to take the threat seriously.

Nonetheless all Europe seemed to be unsettled and my father muttered even more darkly, in his consistently gloomy way, when the Italians under Mussolini went into Abyssinia and then signed a treaty with Berlin. The year 1936 had been such a turbulent one. July had seen the start of the Spanish Civil War, and indeed if Stuart had not been returning to India I wouldn't have been surprised if my freethinking sibling had not involved himself in some way. But it was the little-discussed news item describing the signing of a pact between Japan and Germany, promising neutrality between the two of them if either was at war with the USSR, that would prove to be the factor that would most affect my brother's hitherto peaceful existence.

Now, following the time of Stuart's return to India in October 1937, there were many in Britain who began to see war as inevitable and this feeling seemed to strengthen as we moved into 1938. Stuart's descriptions of seeing destroyers and other warships on his voyage back to India illustrate how sensitive we were all becoming. For my part, although the 'war clouds' may have been gathering I do not recall feeling particularly threatened. I suppose I was at an age when I did not much concern myself with political matters.

Certainly my father was worried and he would regularly sound off to anyone prepared to listen. He shared the views expressed by

Winston Churchill, namely that the country was 'lamentably under-prepared'. Sadly this warning seemed to have singularly failed to produce any great enthusiasm for major spending on rearmament. Perhaps this was inevitable following the severe economic depression and high unemployment that had been a feature of the first part of the decade.

I have said little about my love life over those years. There had been occasional boyfriends and I was as interested in the opposite sex as were my friends but opportunities were less easy to come by. Five years before, when he had first left for Assam, Stuart had enjoined Arthur Mitchell to 'look after' me. I was very young so this was nothing more than a sort of brotherly relationship. However, by the time Stuart came home on leave I was twenty-one and Arthur had come rather more into the centre of my life. It was with Arthur and his sister Christine that Stuart and I went to London for George VI's coronation and stood in Oxford Street from 2 a.m. to 4 p.m. to watch the procession. Then when Stuart moved back to India Arthur began to visit more and more often. Although I was in Derby most of the term he began asking me to dances and to the occasional point-to-point meeting or theatre trip. He visited my parents regularly.

I suppose that I should have seen it coming but I was totally taken by surprise when, after we had been going out together for some time, he proposed to me. I was so unsure of myself, and selfishly so enjoying my new-found independence, that I am afraid I turned him down – I was very fond of him but not yet sure that I was 'in love' so I failed him and said no. I felt sure he would ask me again and I did not know what to do. My father was not the sort of person with whom I could be comfortable discussing such an emotional issue, and so in the anguish of my dilemma I decided to write to Stuart.

Usually I had to make do with letters from Stuart being to the family as a whole, taking such comfort as I could from a brief sentence sending his love. Now there arrived an envelope addressed to me alone. I recall taking a knife to open the airmail envelope, being careful to preserve the postmarked stamps in case my father thought them of some value. Not that he had any great enthusiasm for Indian stamps, but it was a necessary ritual for him to scrutinize the postmarks through the magnifying glass that he kept in the leather box with his other philatelic equipment.

I had waited for this reply for over a month. So would it be approval or disapproval? And I still found myself questioning how my outgoing brother seemed to have managed his first five years in Assam, and the best part of another two years since his return there, without any hint of a regular girlfriend. Not that I thought there was much availability in such a remote spot, but my lusty brother had not totally satisfied me with his denials of any association when I had cross-examined him during his leave.

I opened the envelope.

14th August 1938
Kharjan Tea Estate
Upper Assam

My dear Mary

Well! Well! Well! Many thanks for your letter, good wishes, and staggering news!

Yes, I had suspicions, Arthur has always had you on a pedestal and I knew for years that he was fond of you. No, he never has actually told me, nor will I breathe a word to him, the only remark he passed recently was something like this:

'I have seen quite a lot of Mary recently, and we hope to see more of each other in the future'!! It certainly made me think, but I said to myself 'no, it can't be!'

I don't know what remarks to make, as you have not accepted him I can't very well say 'Congratulations' and I wouldn't dream of giving you my advice. But I must say this, 'Old Arthur' is a damn good bloke and has a heart of gold. I have never known him bad tempered and he has a much better character than your big brother! He always acted as a brake on me and looked on any of my escapades with amused tolerance. He is hard working and loyal and would make a damn good husband (if and when he can afford it) for someone.

But love is a funny thing, and you must love him if you accept him. That is obvious of course but a girl has other things to think of, one thing you can't pick and choose quite to the same extent as a man, you have to wait to be asked and it must come to most girls … is a life of companionship and a home of your own with a man you are very fond of, worth accepting rather than missing the bus altogether! I am sure YOU won't, Mary – you will probably get lots of proposals. But I wonder if I am right and you have ever thought that way?

It comes to us poor blokes out here, we only get four months in the time from 20 to 30 years old to meet one's mate and I think we grab at a certainty rather than a gamble. I am not trying to give you advice because I really don't know what that advice would be. Also I'm perfectly sure that advice from Daddy or Mummy is equally useless. If you find that you love him or you may grow to do so you will marry him and if you don't you won't.

I should quite like old Arthur as a brother-in-law and of course that is probably his reason for asking you! He wants me as a brother-in-law!!

The reason for my writing this, is one: you may get help from my experience, two: it is the middle of the night and I am in the Factory Office with nothing better to do! What you have to consider is:

1. Physical attraction
2. Cash (to be able to live the same life after marriage as before)
3. Same mental attitude to life (more or less)
4. Similar pleasures (games, dancing, music, etc)
5. Same attitude towards Sex (very difficult but hopeless to leave with a taboo till after the marriage, best to discuss it fully)
6. Age (in relation to 1, 3, 4 and 5) Will the position be the same in 10 years?

I have been engaged twice, you may not know that!! to two entirely opposite types, yet I am perfectly sure I loved both and still do. Neither of them would get 100% of that list though. Also I know one or two people who would probably get more marks than either Grace or Louise but they fall flat as I just don't love them. I have only met one girl that I fell for at first sight and I only met her for two hours, so I never had the chance of seeing how many marks she would get!! and I don't expect I ever shall and anyway I was engaged at the time and to break off an engagement requires at least 20 extra marks!! It may interest you and probably make you roar with laughter that the first sight one was Isla Black!!

Also you may not know that I was engaged to Grace for four years and it was only that I told her that there wasn't a hope of marriage for years that she looked at the next best thing, I told her to. She got full marks for nearly everything except 3 and 4 (games). The mere fact that she was born in different circumstances made not the slightest difference, she would have got on perfectly well out here, in fact I am quite an aristocrat as far as class goes in the B. B Tea Company.

Louise gets full marks for nearly everything except 1 and 4 (games) but as we grow older it will make less and less difference, I expect you got a bit of a shock when you saw her, people out here have seen both Grace's and Louise's photos and think I have gone mad! From this you will realize that I am a cynic and do not believe that you can get everything perfect and Arthur is a first class bloke as far as I am concerned.

Having said what I have about Louise, you might try and improve her for me, you may see her sometimes in the next five years, try and get her to pluck her moustache! Use a little more lipstick and do something about her clothes, when she is in a cotton frock, her hair blowing in the breeze on the moor she looks almost lovely, but when she puts on her Sunday-go-to-meeting hats and things she looks terrible.

Having written all this tripe, I shall probably tear it up when I read it through in daylight, my thoughts are a bit muddled at 3am! Well I will close down.

All the best and many happy returns.

Love Stuart

I will always treasure my brother's philosophical reply. It was such a change to have a letter from Assam that did not major in political comment – fraternal frustration with the world in general and Britain's political leaders in particular. I read and re-read the letter, seeking meaning between the lines and sensing that Stuart's underlining of the word 'love' was perhaps a recognition that in his engagement to Louise he had fallen into the very trap that he had described. Also, I could now make sense of his reaction to the meeting with Isla Black on our Scottish holiday. What a match that would have been!

Despite the advice I am afraid I still did not know what to do about my feelings for Arthur. I thought about him all the time but I was nervous of the future.

Arthur proposed for a second time during the time we spent together over the Christmas holiday of 1938. Instead of throwing myself into his arms I prevaricated once more. I could see how my unwillingness to commit had again caused him pain, but I think he recognised the weakening of my hitherto negative resolve. As each week passed I became more and more committed to him and less and less able to imagine life without his attentions and obvious love.

Stuart's letters continued to stimulate, but typically now reverted to the political climate. This was causing huge concern. Following Neville Chamberlain's weak attempts at appeasement, Hitler had annexed Austria in March 1938 and on 15th August, which would have been just as Stuart was penning his brotherly advice to me, the German army was mobilized. The letter to me had arrived in mid-September and it was on 30th September 1938 that Chamberlain returned from his infamous meeting with Hitler, waving a piece of paper which he described as evidence of what he called Germany's peaceful intentions towards Czechoslovakia.

My father was apoplectic. He insisted that we all gather round the radio and listen to Churchill's speech of condemnation of Chamberlain's government whilst he sat beside us, nodding grimly in emphasis.

We have sustained a total, unmitigated defeat. We are in the midst of a disaster of the first magnitude. All the countries of Middle Europe and the Danube Valley, one after another, will be drawn into the vast system of Nazi politics. And do not suppose this is the end, it is only the beginning.

As one might imagine my brother had strong opinions on all of this. He very much took after my father in his view of the world.

23rd October 1938

My dear Daddy and Mummy

Many thanks for your letter ... I was looking forward to some more personal details of your A R P experiences, did you get gas masks? Also, has Mary joined up? If not, why not?

I think that either one must be absolutely pro-Chamberlain and be prepared to trust Germany, re-distribute the colonies and adjust trade barriers, etc, Disarm all round, say and believe Chamberlain is right, nothing is worth a European war, we must try for Utopia OR Get rid of him, be prepared to vote for Labour if necessary, Utopia is an impossibility, we can't trust Germany, if we don't smash her, she will smash us sooner or later (probably sooner), unless we use a firm hand, ruthlessly firm ...

Much, much more in that vein.

CHAPTER EIGHTEEN

So there was I, far more concerned about whether or not to marry Arthur amidst all this turmoil than about Chamberlain's weakness. Whilst I remained undecided Stuart's letters to the family continued to arrive.

New Year's Eve – 31st December 1938

My dear Daddy and Mummy,

Many thanks indeed for the cheque and letters. I will put it towards the car.

I am off down to the club to see a Jack Hubbard film and see the new year in afterwards, not that 1939 gives me a great deal of pleasure in welcoming it but I shall delight in saying boo to 1938!

My evenings have been full every night, also my work has been likewise, the new engine is causing me a lot of anxiety and trouble, I keep finding fresh things wrong and now have it completely in bits all over the engine room.

I wonder what 1939 will bring, the situation in Europe seems to be back again to about the July tension 'Peace in our time'! In fact I think the general opinion out here in August was – 'War? Never!'; 'Can't afford it'; 'Hitler doesn't want war'; 'Bluff' etc etc. Now opinion is very different and people talk as if it was quite settled for the Spring!

Personally, I don't think so, I think the Autumn is a more likely time! But I am ignoring it and carrying on collecting furniture, etc. Heaven knows why, I am quite convinced it is a waste of time and money, the reason being I think, is, that if I was dead sure war was coming I would chuck Tea now and come home, but as I am not dead sure I am pretending that I don't think it will come.

I am more and more convinced that Chamberlain was wrong and that the present government is a hopeless pack of well meaning fools. You are right in saying 'you should now be in the third month of the war' Yes! But that is better or would have been better than three months before the war. A war against a much more powerful enemy and what is worse, especially in regard to prestige in India and elsewhere, we have shown that we were not prepared to fight for right against wrong or because of honour, but only because it is a question of self preservation as far as the Empire is concerned.

I am perfectly sure that Chamberlain would hand back the German colonies if he felt that it would be peace, but unless he is a b fool he must realize that all Hitler and Musso want colonies for, is tactical advantage in war time.

Apart from Europe the situation in India is going to alter a lot in 1939.
I must go now or I shall be late for the Pictures
A happy new year to you all
Love Stuart

6th February 1939
You may not get another letter for ten days as I am off to camp on Monday. I am busy or at least my bearers are, spitting and polishing and packing. It may be a good camp, I always enjoy it anyway – except for the expense – I wonder if people will take it more seriously since the last one has made some people realize that it is supposed to be a serious business. Upper Assam always do especially well DD (No 3) but I am afraid most of the Lower Assamites just join it for horse-allowance, play polo at Parade and look on camp as a 'beat up'. We have a new adjutant now and hear he is going to lick us into shape! He has got a job on!!

The news never seems to lose its interest, we seem to go from one War scare to another, at the moment anything may happen on the Franco-Spanish border, I feel that people are pessimistic about the spring. I think that things will keep on boiling without bubbling over for a long time yet …

11th February 1939
Just got back from Camp, we had the usual very enjoyable time at the same time grousing at our extreme discomfort.

The first few days were wet and everything was miserable, we could not do Pukka Parades, so did things like map reading in our tents. But after that *it cleared up and we carried on as usual, P.T., musketry, drill, etc. Two field days against the Gurkhas, one night, an awful night, in Bivouac, ten in a tent about 12 feet long and six wide!! Hardly any food and guards and false alarms, etc half the night. We were very very tired and fed up when we got back to camp the following afternoon.*

I managed to get off during guard, the only one in 20 who escaped, I am beginning to be an 'Old Soldier', our SS1 is a Bruminghamite so that may have helped! ...

20th February 1939

Work is much the same, there is still a tremendous amount of work to do before we shall be ready for manufacture, I think the leaf will be ready early this year, I expect to be manufacturing the first week in April.

I hope to send you some snaps in my next letter, ones I took at Camp. That is about all I think, Europe seems very peaceful, the lull before the storm?

On 15th February 1939, just five days before this last letter was written, Arthur proposed to me for the third time. Finally I was sure that I loved him. I accepted, to his great joy and pride, and the announcement was duly made to our respective families, including an immediate letter to my absent brother.

Predictably my father was not enthusiastic about our announced intention to marry during 1940 and I sensed that the wedding date would be a battle still to be fought but, happily and now very much in love, Arthur and I began to plan our future. Stuart let his feelings be known when the news finally reached him.

12th March 1939

Dear old Mary

Well. Well. Well!!

Congratulations! So you have made up your mind at last. I am glad. You couldn't choose anyone more sound than old Arthur.

Also I shall now only have to write to one of you instead of both!!

I am glad you are going to get married quickly, 1940, I wish I could be there to help, I have got a grouse against Arthur! He promised to be my best man so now as he has let me down you will have to provide the bridesmaids and pages, you ought to have enough to carry Louise's train by the time I get married.

I am glad, and know you will both be very happy.

You will have had my 'news' from 23 so I will cut this short and write to about-to-be-brother-Arthur. By the way I am still waiting for a reply to my last letter and remarks on Louise. Take old Arthur down to Devon and take Louise out and see what you can do about her. Now you've fixed yourself up you can both get together and help me.

I am pleased Mary,

all the best to you both and love

Hitler's final betrayal of his agreement with Chamberlain came with his occupation of Czechoslovakia on 15th March 1939. It now seems selfish looking back at the world situation but my vivid memory of that month is the skiing holiday in Val d'Isère that Arthur had arranged to celebrate our engagement.

I had not skied before and we had a magical holiday – few lifts so a lot of walking up before skiing down again, but I loved the sport and also the company of the friends we went with, including six foot five Bill Gaman and his wife Hulda from Birmingham. It was a memorable time and I was able to put the fear of war out of my mind for that short while.

Looking back I suppose I was very self-centred. I think it was perhaps therapeutic to carry on with the normal rituals of life but with the benefit of hindsight it was not an ideal time. Still, I was young and in love, that spring and summer were blessed with wonderfully hot weather, and Arthur and I were very happy. There is one lovely entry in Arthur's diary on a date in late May of that year:

Another absolutely perfect summer's day. The cathedral in the morning and an inspiring sermon by the Provost. Mary and I had the car after lunch and we sat in it in a field at Burton Overy for four and a half hours!

Good to know that we were inspired by the sermon.

CHAPTER NINETEEN

Although, to my great sadness, Arthur was not able to join us, in late August 1939 my parents and I set off for a holiday on the Isle of Skye. My mother and I were rather surprised that my father agreed to go away at all and we remained conscious that our planning for this break was overshadowed by the knowledge that the country was regarded as being on the brink of war.

Arthur could not come as he and his great friend Keith Neal had now set up a small engineering business; the plan was to both manufacture and sell door 'furniture', door and window handles and the like. They were both hard working and entrepreneurial and felt there was a niche in the market and good prospects for the future. They had rented premises, bought equipment and employed staff. Understandably Arthur was totally immersed in the new venture and I could not tempt him away. Anyway, the three of us had a lovely week on Skye and then carried on travelling around Scotland.

We were near Inverness on 1st September when it became clear that we must return home because of the political situation. In what the papers described as a 'brilliant move for Germany', Hitler had made a non-aggression pact with Russia. Then, secure in the knowledge that he was safe from the east, on 1st September 1939 his armies marched against Poland. We were told that Britain and France had sent an ultimatum demanding the withdrawal of the German invading army and warning that there would otherwise be war. I do not think any of us were confident that the threat would be a deterrent, in which case war seemed inevitable.

My father was Assistant Hospitals' Officer for the Midlands region and consequently had considerable responsibilities in the event of war breaking out. As soon as news of the ultimatum broke he instructed me to drive him to Perth railway station where he caught the train south. My mother and I then drove all the way back to Leicester from Scotland with only one stop on the way – that was quite an achievement on the roads as they then were. As soon as we got home, and almost before we had unpacked, we started putting up blackout curtains and blinds at all the windows. Everyone was running around in small circles trying to do something, expecting that if war came air raids might start immediately.

On the day of the declaration of war, 2nd September 1939, I remember that Arthur came over from Birmingham: he arrived that morning to be with us at 11 a.m., the time when we had been told the Prime Minister was going to make an announcement on the radio. We all gathered round the radio set in the drawing room at Morland Avenue and in silence heard Chamberlain's announcement that Hitler had failed to give the necessary undertaking to withdraw German troops, and that 'consequently this country is at war with Germany'.

It was such a lovely warm September morning. Mother and father were both very depressed and quiet. For four years from 1914 to 1918 father had been a surgeon in the First World War front line, operating on the thousands of casualties, and it must have been dreadful for him to know that history was in danger of being repeated. Arthur and I went out into the garden to discuss our plans and future – marriage in 1940 now looked impossible. Arthur's new business, only just set up, was in the building trade and it seemed unlikely that there would be any volume of residential building work for the duration of the hostilities. He and Keith Neal were planning to discuss the situation later that week but it seemed likely that all their hard work would be wasted.

The next few weeks and months would come to be called the 'Phoney War'. Little may have happened in Britain but the war must have seemed far from phoney in Poland where we knew the German blitzkrieg was sweeping through the country. Poland was caught in a pincer movement when on 17th September Russian troops moved to occupy the eastern provinces in accordance with the Nazi–Soviet pact. After sustained bombing Warsaw capitulated ten days later. By 6th October the last remnants of the Polish army surrendered. Hitler had overcome Poland, despite fierce resistance, in only five weeks and we read that although there had been a loss of some 13,000 Germans, more than 200,000 Polish were dead or wounded and a further 700,000 men had been taken prisoner.

We felt encouraged by the news that five British army divisions had been sent to France the day after war was declared – we knew them as the British Expeditionary Force which we understood was to be our contribution to the Anglo-French Alliance. Sadly, we were later to find that it was little more than a large defensive force with no armoured divisions, few tanks and limited air cover. Apparently even that limited air cover could not be deployed since the French persuaded us not to use the RAF to bomb the factories in the Ruhr in case it caused the Germans to retaliate by bombing French cities.

No doubt the Germans could not believe their good fortune: the Allies failed to counter-attack at the very time when Hitler was at his most vulnerable, during the Polish invasion. Instead the Allied forces dug in and reinforced their defensive line and then went on to shiver through one of the coldest winters in living memory.

Arthur was in his late twenties and wanted to be called up. He was keen to be involved in the war but as he was not already a member of the armed forces he had to wait his turn. He and Keith Neal had concluded that the business which they had worked so hard to set up in Birmingham must be closed, so he decided to go to Harborne to apply to join the Austin car company which was converting its production lines to the war effort. Austins agreed to take him on and he also applied to join the Auxiliary Fire Service in Birmingham; it was logical in those days to work during the day and then do such volunteer war work as was needed in the evenings and at weekends.

Arthur had found the closing of the business traumatic, his diary entry for the day recording:

A gloomy day during which it was decided to part with all the staff and close down.

Ten days later he started his new job and the diary records:

Up at 6am and started work at Austins at 9am. Quite a successful first day in a friendly atmosphere. Began what promises to be a hell of a cold. Got back to flat at about 7.30pm.

Arthur settled into the new regime and told me he had made new friends. He continued his fire-fighting training but would complain to me about the increasing bureaucracy, commenting in his diary in November:

on duty at 9pm to find yet more changes to the rules and regulations. Most seem unnecessary.

I have a photograph of Arthur duly kitted out in uniform as an Auxiliary Fire Service Officer. He was also issued with a small hosepipe trailer to tow behind a car so that he could become a one-man fire engine – but no bells or siren!

The extremely harsh winter of 1939 meant difficult conditions for travelling back to work after weekends in Leicester, me to Derby and Arthur to Birmingham. I well remember how the snow and ice of that terrible year dragged on, delaying warlike and domestic activities alike. Nonetheless over the winter Arthur and I continued to plan our wedding. In this we were encouraged by mother but discouraged by my father. He had nothing against Arthur but simply thought it was wrong to be planning a marriage at such a time. We had several rows about it, particularly as the war situation developed and became so worrying.

Now Arthur decided to move on from Austins in Harborne to work on a project at the SS car company at Coventry where the now famous William Lyons, of Jaguar fame, was engaged in specialist engineering work for the armed forces. Arthur left Austins at the end of January 1940 and found some digs in Coventry. It was sensible for him also to transfer to the Coventry section of the Auxiliary Fire Service so that he could keep up his voluntary efforts in that direction. I knew that he felt he ought to be fighting, and that whilst he was waiting to be called up he was determined to do all that he could to help in other directions.

At last spring came. As in the previous year the weather was superb: it seemed so strange that lovely spring weather should go hand in hand with increasingly desperate war news. Still, life had to go on.

Arthur and I met up most weekends and were often pretty energetic, illustrated by a diary entry in March 1940:

Mary and I cycled 42 miles through Leicestershire and enjoyed a good day in some splendid country, Ashby Folville, Thorpe Satchville, etc.

I must have been pretty fit in those days.

It was in early April 1940 that Chamberlain announced to the nation that we had 'done well' since war had been declared in September. He told us we had added enormously to our fighting strength and he believed that Hitler now had few reserves and had 'missed the bus' in seizing the offensive.

My father was unconvinced and his pessimism as to Chamberlain's optimistic beliefs was justified when only three days later German troops invaded Norway and Denmark. Chamberlain's credibility was gone and within a month the German blitzkrieg had swept onwards into Holland and Belgium.

CHAPTER TWENTY

The shock waves of the declaration of war had travelled round the world. Stuart and his fellows felt they were in limbo – far from the action but needing to be involved. The Indian army was in full recruitment mode and it was appropriate that British nationals working in the country would join up and so further the war effort.

Stuart had been transferred from the Kharajan estate to the larger Bokpara tea estate. This was yet further promotion as a more senior factory manager. Bokpara was much better established and he was not only managing a larger number of people but able to concentrate on improving the flow of production, rather than the constant redesigning and rebuilding work that had dominated his time at Kharjan and before that at Pengaree. As his business confidence grew so he became more relaxed in his involvement with Monglee, feeling sufficiently comfortable to have relocated her to the new estate enabling him to delight in his relationship with Mary.

Stuart had also continued his membership of the Assam Valley Light Horse. There were other similar cadres such as the Northern Bengal Mounted Rifles which mainly recruited planters from Dooars and Darjeeling. Membership of the AVLH had been almost a matter of routine for Stuart and his fellow planters in the area, but although its peacetime role was relaxed it remained an auxiliary force and effectively a unit of the Indian Defence Force. Other such units included the Calcutta Light Horse, the Sylhet Volunteer Rifle Corps and the Sylhet Mounted Rifles (to whom colours had been presented as recently as 1930 by King-Emperor George V, as he was known in India). Each unit tended to service its own geographical area so, for instance, Sylhet was part of Bengal (now Bangladesh) and the troop's area included Calchar.

Peacetime camps such as those attended by Stuart were held each year and the activities typically included Tactical Schemes, Field Operations (which included bridge building and fording rivers) and Manual and Firing Exercises. Of course in the pre-war days the main *raison d'être* of these volunteer forces seemed to be the love of polo and the enjoyment of pig sticking and other such horsey delights, but now that war had broken out the skills that had been acquired were valuable.

As the political situation became more acute Stuart thought long and hard about what he should do. On the one hand he could leave Shaws, abandon the tea estates and make his own way back to England and seek to be called up for the army from there. It would take time, particularly if he wished to train as an officer, starting from scratch. On the other hand he could join up where he was, already at officer level because of his position and qualifying training with the AVLH. If he stayed he would not need to incur the considerable cost of a passage home to England, nor would he have to abandon his job – and to do so could well jeopardize any future career once the war was over. The problem with joining up in India was that there was less certainty as to where he might be stationed: he was not keen on fighting in one theatre of war when all his family and friends were in another campaign altogether.

After thinking the situation through, Stuart opted for what he realized might be considered the easy way out. As the war expanded within Europe he, Teasdel and fellow planters Roach, Turner and Groves volunteered to become full-time soldiers and were immediately incorporated into the Indian army as part of the Allied war effort.

Stuart was at Bokpara, still waiting for the army authorities to decide the date for training to commence, when the time for the baby's birth fell due. It had already been decided that Monglee should go back to her village so that her mother and the village midwife could look after her. Stuart would have preferred her to live in the bungalow and then go to the estate hospital when the time came, but inevitably that would have meant some formal recognition of his paternity so he decided not to intervene. In the final month before the due date he travelled to Pengaree and walked the jungle path to the village as often as he could, taking great pleasure in seeing Mary running towards him as he came near.

There came the day when, as Stuart was tasting the fermentation infusions in the factory, Daniel appeared at the factory and quietly told him that Monglee had gone into labour. As soon as transport could be found Stuart drove to Pengaree. Parking in a corner of the estate he hurried down the path to the village to find to his delight that he was the father of a second daughter. Monglee was well and happy, and wanted Stuart to decide on the name. Stuart had chosen his sister's name for their first child, and he told her he thought that the name of his grandmother – Ann – would be right for the second. When he left Monglee was trying to mimic his English pronounciation of the name in her own dialect amidst much laughter from her mother and friends.

After what they saw as their dramatic commitment to join the army Stuart and his colleagues had expected to leave the area almost immediately but clearly this was not to be. In the early days there was much bureaucratic discussion but little real activity, so the new recruits continued to work on the tea estates but with greatly intensified training through more frequent camps. It would be many months before the powers that be finalized their plans as to the precise military need and took control of the volunteers' lives.

Stuart's skills and training as an engineer were such that it made sense for him to be seconded to the Royal Engineers, otherwise called sappers, and when the call came to leave the estates and start full-time training he, Teasdel and the others were all to join that discipline.

Of course the real dilemma for Stuart, and one of the factors that influenced his decision, was the situation of Monglee and his two daughters. They could not stay in one of the bungalows without his being there: any successor to Stuart's post and accommodation would naturally question such an arrangement, and a garden girl who had chosen to associate with a planter was certainly not approved of within the estate hierarchy. So where could they go? Monglee's parents lived in the village within walking distance of the Pengaree estate so it was logical that the family should stay there, but Stuart was anxious to ensure that the children had a better start in life than that of the ordinary native children of the village. Additionally, he was acutely conscious that the caste system was not sympathetic to what would be termed 'half-breed' children: Anglo-Indian children were a source of some controversy and were often treated badly once they left their father's protection. Those children whose mothers were pure Indian and whose fathers were European were less well regarded than 'true' Anglo-Indians where both parents were of Anglo-Indian descent. These Anglo-Indians had developed their own supportive communities over the years since the early days of the Raj when the interbreeding had begun.

Stuart consulted Daniel – after all it had been Daniel who had introduced and seemingly advanced his niece Monglee in the first place, and it was under Daniel's protection that Monglee and the children presently lived.

Daniel had clearly given the situation some thought. He suggested that Stuart provide funds to buy an area of land on the edge of the village and further finance to build a modest dwelling on the land. That would mean that Monglee had some status in the area, living in her own house on land which she owned, and it would also provide somewhere for her parents to stay when necessary. They would be a valuable support for the children as they grew up. Finally, he said that Stuart should try to provide some small income to ensure that Monglee could care for the children without needing to work: her status as the former partner of an absent European planter would not be helpful in finding suitable employment.

Acting on this wise advice, Stuart secured an area of land near to Pengaree village, thinking that since Monglee's parents lived in the village they would be close at hand to provide support. It was only a short distance down the track and over the river from the Pengaree tea estate, and he made arrangements for a traditional busti hut to be built so that Monglee could live there with Mary and Ann. Monglee had a sister who proposed to move in with them and help cultivate the land on which they planned to keep a cow and goats. The land was nearly ten acres in all – only the headman of the village had more – and with both the hut and the animals Monglee would have a home, income and some status.

Despite knowing that he had done his best to make provision Stuart remained concerned, although he knew that Daniel and the rest of her family would look out for them as best they could.

Stuart did not know what more he could do. Inevitably he had to contemplate a situation where he might not return, but in that event would the existence of Monglee and his children ever be known outside the confines of the village? She was illiterate, she had no particular skills or training, in the eyes of Shaw Wallace & Co. she had no official standing, and the fact that she had two children by him was more likely to be seen as a negative rather than a positive factor. The company would certainly not take her side. He could leave her with papers which should convince his father in England that the children were his: but would his father and mother want to acknowledge two half-Indian grandchildren with no knowledge of Western ways? His sister Mary might show some sympathy but he had to remember that he had taken the decision not to confide in her during his leave, and he could see that this might well cause her to be less than enthusiastic. What could she do anyway?

After a number of sleepless nights Stuart made up his mind. Although he was conscious that what he had decided was something of a weak compromise, he would leave Monglee with sufficient documentation to prove his identity and also his paternity of the children, together with some mementos that might strike a chord with his parents, but he hoped that she would not need them. He would tell her that if all else failed then she should take the documents to the company and ask them to make contact with England, but make her understand that he had no way of knowing what the reaction of his family might be. He would also explain all this to Daniel.

The time came for Stuart to say goodbye. In the days leading up to his departure Stuart had purchased for Monglee the cow that was to be kept on the land and he had carefully put together an album of photographs of his family back in England. To this he added other paperwork acknowledging that the children were his.

Mary was five and Ann had just reached three months. A tearful Monglee held them both in her arms as Stuart kissed them one by one, and then turned away from the entrance to the mud house and walked out of the village along the path into the jungle. He wondered whether he would ever see them again.

CHAPTER TWENTY-ONE

Now the events of the war dominated everything. Following the invasion of Belgium and Holland, Neville Chamberlain had at last resigned. Winston Churchill was voted in to take charge, to the enthusiastic approval of my father. As the news came of the Germans advancing along the Western Front we again gathered round the radio at Morland Avenue to hear Churchill's call to arms. It was 13th May 1940.

... We have before us many, many long months of struggle and of suffering. You ask, what is our policy? I will say: it is to wage war, by sea, land and air, with all our might and all the strength that God can give us; to wage war against a monstrous tyranny never surpassed in the dark, lamentable category of human crime. That is our policy.

You ask, what is our aim? I can answer in one word: it is victory, victory at all costs, victory in spite of all terror, victory however long and hard the road may be; for without victory there is no survival ...

Fear was in the air and Churchill's words gave us strength.

My father was based in Nottingham and was in charge of 'Emergency Regional Staff'; there were about a dozen middle-aged, experienced doctors who could be deployed to any suitably large emergency which occurred. He spent the war travelling backwards and forwards to Nottingham and sometimes staying overnight. He coped with the evacuation of hospitals and the inspection of first aid posts and convalescent homes. Because of the bombing and also the evacuation of casualties it must have been a big job. Unfortunately this meant that he was not often at home to support mother in her bouts of depression.

It was an odd time because despite all our worries our reasonably comfortable existence continued. Certainly there was rationing, there were shortages, there were endless rules and regulations from blackouts to gas masks to air raid shelters; but we were still feeding ourselves and living in the same houses and going about our business in the usual manner. But what could we do but continue to back the government and the troops in every way possible and carry on with our lives in the meantime?

We had terrible fears and the extinction of our army in France seemed certain. There was very little real news but then, suddenly, came the extraordinary announcement of the evacuation of the expeditionary force from Dunkirk. Hearing of the rescue armada of small boats crossing the Channel and listening to the stories of the survivors over the radio gave us all great encouragement.

Whilst my mother and I tried to persuade my father that this was at least partial victory out of defeat, he was sensible enough to realize but discouraging and harsh enough to remind us that the country was in a desperate state, standing alone against Germany. As he put it, France was defeated, the whole of Europe was occupied save for Spain and Portugal, the country faced imminent invasion and there was I thinking about weddings.

He was right. None of us knew what was going to happen to us. If the invasion took place our lives, if we were spared, were going to change dramatically. Arthur and I wanted to get married as soon as possible, partly to face this new terrifying world as a couple and partly to enjoy some time together while we could. So I continued, notwithstanding all the threats around us, to work on persuading my parents to permit the wedding to take place.

It was not the best time to be seeking parental approval for any sort of celebration. Nonetheless after a stormy family conference they relented. Arthur's diary note summarises:

An absolutely perfect summer's day. After the grandparents left we had a long and exhausting family conference which left us all limp but we safely cast the die. In good spirits in spite of the Germans entering Paris.

Which shows how our future and the events of the war had become inextricably bound together.

CHAPTER TWENTY-TWO

The hurricane lamp suspended from the central ridge pole of the tent gave out an incessant hiss, almost blocking out the cicada shrill of the tropical night. Wrapped in a khaki towel, Stuart sat at the low table as the tip of his tongue mirrored the movements of the fountain pen across the flimsy sheet of airmail paper. A bead of sweat had just smeared the customary opening of 'Dear All', and he moved on to the 'Here I am' hoping that the censor would see no reason to require anonymity of the location of a training camp.

'PoonAH' he wrote, hearing in his head the rarified accents of the British officers in this long-established military garrison and wondering whether being stationed for so long in the heat and humidity of central India caused some strangulation of the larynx – but immediately dismissing the irreverent thought, otherwise his eight years in the higher humidity of Assam would have altered his own accent.

Five of us from Assam and twenty-four men in all, and here for six months at least.

Stuart's scratching pen went on to relate brief detail of his two thousand mile journey from the Burmese border, including the three nights in Calcutta en route. As he wrote, his mind sought to imagine the scene at 23 Morland Avenue in Leicester, visualising his father reading the letters out loud to his mother; smelling the pipe tobacco and imagining them waiting to turn on the wireless for the nine o'clock news. At least they might now feel that he was closer to some active participation in this war: eighteen long months since the declaration, and they still seemed not to understand that all his efforts to return to Europe to join up had been frustrated. What little purpose his years of volunteer involvement in the Assam Valley Light Horse seemed now to have been. All right, it had provided a route into his present situation, but with none of the flexibility of choice or purpose that he had hoped for.

'Come on Poyser, old man; let's go and see what this camp cinema can offer. "French without Tears" according to the noticeboard. Queue up for the rear stalls and hope for some spare floosies?'

'Fat chance of that, you silly bugger.'

Stuart came out of his reverie and started to dress as his companion hauled himself out of a canvas chair, stubbing out a third cigarette since dinner in the mess. This was Teasdel from the Budla Beta tea estate in Assam who together with Roach, Turner and Groves made up the remainder of the five planters who had waved their farewells to those staying behind on the estates only a week before.

In the first lecture that morning they had been told that the target was that they should complete their training as Royal Engineers and emerge as full-blown commissioned officers in the 'Sappers' within six months, less than half the usual time. And bloody hard work it had sounded.

'Swimming, rowing, tennis, hockey, even a primitive golf course; all the facilities but are we ever going to have time to use them?' They were walking back to their tent through the moist and humid clutch of the night.

'Christ knows – bridge building, drill, and then bookkeeping tomorrow. What a combination, and half of it in Urdu.'

The colonel had talked of the crash course of all crash courses, and that if Italy came into the war they would need another hundred sappers in addition to the twenty-four now in training.

Would he end up in Italy? Would it be the Libyan desert? Why could it not have been Europe where he would have felt connected to the world, rather than on some distant planet looking down and not knowing when he would be able to join in.

Frustration was not limited to his inability to fight. It was scarcely a week since his last desolate pleasuring of Monglee's pliant body, hearing the sounds of her passion yielding to convulsions of grief in contemplation of his departure. Did she, like him, seek solitary relief from their enforced abstinence? It was two years since she had welcomed him home – he supposed he was now entitled to call Assam home – following his five months' leave in England. Remembering his return, reliving Daniel's warm but deferential greeting on the front verandah and then, behind the door, the vivid memory of Monglee joyously launching herself, almost crushing three-year-old Mary in their embrace. Only four months later the arrival of baby Ann, what was she now – eighteen months? How well little Mary had taken to her new sister and how he missed them already.

How would Monglee be coping back in the village? He had bought the plot of land and put the busti on it, sumptuous by the standards of many; but the money he had left would run out, and the money he sent to Daniel to pass on to his niece was very little.

The days marched by. Stuart was pleased to find himself second out of the whole section in the rifle course, proud of his 87 points out of a possible 100 – the game shooting in Assam had obviously stood him in good stead. He was less successful, with 26 points out of a possible 50, in the revolver course; but he found it intimidating to have targets on rails rushing forward from ten yards and having the stress of trying to fire three straight shots in five seconds. Still, he enjoyed the weaponry, wondering how strong he would be under fire and whether he would have qualms about seeking to kill another human being in response.

Less enjoyable were his daily struggles with subjects as diverse as the mechanics of field geometry and the intricacies of military law. There was so much to learn – the geography of different terrains, use of local materials to construct roads, carpentry skills to direct the building of wooden structures, mixes of concrete for foundations and pillboxes, explosives for demolition, methods of dealing with a gas attack – an endless list to equip him to become a cross between a construction engineer, a builder and a soldier. But construction included destruction, he thought, and in a war situation destruction might well be his lot.

It was all-enveloping: as a future officer he needed leadership skills, and Stuart joined the other officer cadets as they drilled and inspected the Indian troops on the one hand, but then had to be taught how to survive the intricate but irrelevant formalities of the officers' mess on the other. The sheer physicality was immense: the thousand techniques of the army engineer included joining the troops in heaving on wire ropes, swimming with mawls, using blocks and tackle, carrying heavy weights and learning to operate the massive variety of machinery. When there was spare time they went swimming in the open-air pool or played tennis. Stuart was pleased to be selected as centre half for the regimental hockey team and also for the football team, notwithstanding continued pressure from the 'rugger buggers' to give his allegiance to the oval ball.

Then there was the golf. Not the bracing winds of the links course at Bamburgh overlooking the long sands of the North Sea, where Stuart had so often played with his father. Here the greens were called 'browns', a fair description of the areas of flattened earth which so reminded Stuart of the first XI cricket pitch at Epsom College. The parched areas of coarse grass between the encroaching scrub were unhappy fairways and the few trees added little to the bleak terrain. Above all the fierce sweat-inducing glare of the Indian sun dominated each sporting experience.

Early mornings were glorious. The sun came out of a clear sky and Stuart would often walk across to the pool and swim thirty lengths before breakfast in the mess. As he swam he would think of the incongruity of his being able to carve through the cool waters under the strengthening sun, whilst his parents and sister endured the bombing, deprivations and continuing uncertainties of the war in Europe.

On that particular morning Stuart was wrestling with the news last night of the invasion of Denmark and Norway. What would the Germans do next? Would they not be repulsed before they reached France? As he hauled himself out of the water he realized that the sky had darkened, and before he could reach his tent his bare shoulders were stung with the first pellets of heavy rain. Two days previously he had made his first tentative use of explosives, blowing up a concrete bunker – surprising himself and terrifying his instructor when the flying debris had reached his chosen place of shelter behind the iron legs of the water tower which supplied the camp. They had joked of the flood of water had the tower collapsed. Now the power of the rain suggested a similar calamity. The heavy drumming had become a roar and a fine spray forced its way through the distended canvas of their shelter.

Throwing their belongings together, protecting watches and valuables, the men floundered as a river of water rose above the coconut matting and flowed across the tent.

'Provided by the colonel for early practice for the Regatta!'

Stuart's reaction started the laughter. The Poona Regatta was regarded by the senior officers as a major event in the calendar and they had insisted that the erstwhile planters be entered into a four. The planters' blistered hands bore testimony to the daily training sessions under the eye of the commanding officer whose enthusiasm was not shared by his subordinates.

Stuart and Teasdel spluttered and started to sing as they waded through the flood, gathering ruined textbooks and papers from the chaos.

'Jolly good boating weather …'

The old refrain mingled with the diminishing roar of the downpour as the freak cloudburst ran its course and the rain suddenly stopped.

A week later the Regatta was held at the man-made lagoon. A long dais with a canvas roof to protect spectators from the sun ran along the centre section of the bank and loudspeakers announced the competitors and exhorted the crowd. Full military dress was the order of the day and the few wives who were stationed in the area were incongruously resplendent in their hats and long dresses. Stuart and three other planters comprised the only novice four; despite the hated practice sessions sandwiched between their other duties they had found difficulty in mastering the timing necessary to succeed. They refused to be seen to be taking the event seriously, but when they approached the starting line, sideways at first to the amusement of those watching, they found they were nervous rather than nonchalant. Their opponents were an experienced crew from another regiment, suitably disdainful of their amateur opposition.

At the starting gun the novice crew went off sharply. They heard the loudspeakers saying 'Sappers four nicely together and holding well' and 'Well done the novice team!' and their pride and fitness began to carry them through. It was exhausting work, having to maintain the speed of strike set by Teasdel who was stroke. Pouring with sweat under the glare of the sun and constantly cursing they stuck at the pace and were finally rewarded to hear the crackling declaration, 'Novice sappers first – very well done chaps!'

A fatal loss of coherence and failure of confidence prevented success in the semi-finals. 'Lost by a canvas' was the final verdict. But Stuart felt that honour, and the colonel, had been satisfied.

That night there was a fancy dress dance at the Ordnance Depot, decorated as a Paris underworld club. Stuart braved the damp heat of a woollen balaclava, quickly cast aside, and noted that imagination was not the strongest suit of the men. Cloth caps, scarves half covering the face, tweed jackets with the collar turned up – more the flavour of a football terrace than of a seedy nightclub.

Across the concrete of the arena Stuart spotted the wondrous sight of rouged faces and slashed skirts. In an instant he was weaving his way through the crowd towards a trio of girls standing uncertainly by the entrance.

'Ladies! Allow me to find you a seat and a drink! My name is Stuart …'

'Otherwise Poyser – one of the new trainees, and far too insignificant for you to be talking to,' said Major Connor, the corps adjutant, as he cut Stuart out of the conversation, taking the elbow of the tallest of the girls and encouraging the others to follow him to a roped-off section of the hall where the officers were gathered. Two junior officers fell behind him, blocking pursuit.

'The answer to your unspoken question is that they are nurses from the military hospital,' said Hamilton, one of the training instructors, as he steered Stuart back to the trestle table of the bar and put a bottle of Kingfisher beer into his hands.

'Seems the nice girls love a sapper as much as a sailor – and rumour has it that, like sappers, they're pretty good at finding ways of demolishing erections. Trouble is, your progress over the next six months is dependent on Connor, so seducing his bit of stuff may not be wise.'

'Proper quarters' were promised. Others of their number had been moved into the brick-built barracks which offered bathrooms in each corridor and ceiling fans to stir the burning air. The six Assam cadets were left until last.

The intensity of the training was relieved by occasional nights out in Poona, barely five miles away and a truck was usually available for transportation. Stuart was well used to the ordered chaos of an Indian town, and Poona matched his expectations with a heaving mass of people amidst an uncontrolled and uncontrollable mix of bicycles, carts, rickshaws, animals and traffic. There were a number of eating places catering for the visiting military. A mixed grill was the common target of those off duty – not that the meat was always identifiable or ever had much flesh on it, but when washed down with a few bottles of local beer it was palatable.

The constant discussion menu was the progress of the war. Whilst Stuart had joined up six months after war was declared in September 1939 it had been many months before their training had commenced. Thereafter they had all followed the traumatic news of Hitler's progress through Europe and Chamberlain's attempt to stem the tide. Then came the invasion of Norway and Denmark closely followed by that of Holland and Belgium. Stuart in particular had rejoiced to hear in May 1940 that Churchill had come to power but then further days had passed, the German advance had continued and they had listened to the devastating announcements of defeat in France and the evacuation from Dunkirk. Now they had the news of Italy coming into the war.

Every evening in the mess, after the meal and the formal toasts, the duty officer would put on the wireless and there would be total silence whilst the measured delivery of the newsreader filled every corner of the room. As he finished there was an instant cacophony of fierce argument. Most were determined to express an opinion though a minority were withdrawn and pensive, perhaps thinking of what was happening to the families from whom they had been parted for so long.

'Maybe the defeat at Dunkirk will prove to be a good thing?'

'Why, oh why can't we be sent to Europe to help?'

'We also serve – old chap.'

'Fat lot of use our service is going to be unless Japan comes into the war!'

'Italy may be in – but we're safe as a rock, sitting on the biggest arsenal in the East.'

'Shall we all end up posted to the Libyan Desert?'

Stuart was desperate to fight. With hindsight he felt he should have resisted the natural progress from the tea estate to the training camp. Should he have obtained a passage back to England and joined up there? He decided to put in an application to see whether, even now, he could force the issue.

'So, you want to just abandon this training and go home?' Major Steele was sitting behind a huge mahogany desk as Stuart stood to attention in front of him.

'I accept there would be a cost involved – I'm prepared to pay for the passage out of a suitable replacement if that would be acceptable?'

'No, it bloody well would not be acceptable. You are being trained at great cost to be an officer in the King George Vth's Own Bengal Sappers and Miners – "God's Own" as we're generally known – and you, Cadet Officer Stuart Vernon Poyser, have taken upon yourself to decide that you rather fancy swanning off to fight the war in Europe. You are bloody well going to stay here – and pass out – and be posted where you are chosen to be posted – and you are bloody well going to look happy about it! Dismiss.'

The next morning, immediately after morning assembly on the parade ground, Major Steele made an announcement:

'For the avoidance of any doubt whatsoever, you are all members of the Indian army. You cannot leave the Indian army. Some of you may be posted to the Balkans, some may go to Libya, some may go to Malaya. Wherever you go you will remain in the Indian army. If you are injured, then you will be returned as a casualty to India. There is not, repeat not, an opportunity for you to choose where you wish to fight this war. DisMISS.'

Stuart, Teasdel and Bekhtawar Singh, the latter also training as a full officer rather than as the usual Viceroy Commissioned Officer, were sitting together in the lecture hall later that day.

'It's all very well for you, Beggar, you were born in ruddy India, being shipped back here as a casualty is fine – but not for the rest of us.'

'Poyser Sahib, if we remain in Asia and if Japan doesn't fight there will be no opportunity for you to be injured, and if you are not injured you will not be a casualty and if you are not a casualty you will not be shipped back, always assuming you are sent anywhere in the first place.'

Stuart saw little point in answering his Sikh friend's usual stolid logic and turned his concentration back to the droning lecture on the evils of gas warfare.

'The odour of gas may be unnoticeable due to the smell of corpses ... if your eyes are affected, scrubbing your eyeballs with a nailbrush may bring relief ...'

Stuart wrote home at the end of June 1940:

It seems there is no holding Germany – it will be a long and bitter war. I cannot believe that France has packed up, now it is Britain against the world. Still no news from you all at home. The news over here of air raids simply talks of coastal towns and 'the Midlands'. No names of towns or cities are given. I fear for your safety but have no means of knowing but to wait for your letters. I am not able to say anything in my letters to you, I can only tell you that I played hockey against a famous 'British Regiment' last week. Also that I am the Sappers ping-pong champion! There is a huge amount of work – explosives and demolition, continuously blowing things up. But how I wish I was home to join the fight.

I am not the same person that I was four months ago.

CHAPTER TWENTY-THREE

The wedding was duly arranged for 2nd August 1940. My trousseau was collected together, my wedding dress made by a local dressmaker, veil and shoes purchased and the invitations sent out. I broke up from school just two days beforehand and as Arthur was working every day including Saturday mornings we planned that he would take just Friday and Saturday off, marry on Friday, honeymoon on Saturday and Sunday and have him back at work on Monday morning.

Arthur believed he was now close to being called up and he completed the formal registration process in Coventry, but he heard that the specialist work on which he was engaged might block his recruitment. His fire officer work escalated with the expectation that air raids would now commence in earnest. On 17th June he wrote in his diary:

France ceases hostilities, a fact which causes some thought and rather upsets the day's work. I wonder if the raids will start tonight?

History books tell us that Hitler had thought that Britain might sue for peace but by early July 1940 realized this would not happen and so had issued instructions for Operation Sea Lion, the invasion of England, to move forward. The invading force was assembled in France but it was first essential that the Luftwaffe destroy the RAF to gain control of the Channel. This was to be the beginning of what would later be termed the Battle of Britain. It seems there were to be four phases of the Luftwaffe's battle plan: from mid-July to mid-August they were to win superiority over the Channel and southern England; from mid-August to early September they were to destroy the RAF and its airbases as a fighting force; during the rest of September they were to attack London to force any remnants of the

RAF into the air in defence, where they could be destroyed; and in the final October phase they were to concentrate on night bombing of London and other major cities.

Not that we were aware of any of this – we just continued with our preparations for the wedding. But as we moved into July there were constant reports of the air battles taking place over the south of England and we all kept in touch with what was happening through newspapers and radio. Inevitably the news given out in those desperate times was more optimistic than the reality but in consequence we saw no reason why our wedding plans should not move into top gear.

On 1st August Arthur left work at 5.30 p.m. to catch a bus to Leicester and after an evening at Morland Avenue he retired to the Bell Hotel in the city centre for his last night as a bachelor. The actual wedding day dawned and was beautiful. The weather was magnificent, my mother had organized everything marvellously and many friends came from far and near. The one great disappointment was that Stuart was not able to be present. Instead of Stuart being best man, as would have been certain had he been there, Arthur's great friend and short-time business partner Keith Neal stood in.

The *Leicester Mercury* newspaper must have been rather short on news that day judging by the detail of the wedding that was recorded:

The bride is the granddaughter of Mr A W Poyser of Leicester, who is the only surviving member of the staff of the opening of the Wyggeston Boys School. He was later headmaster of Wisbech Grammar School. Mr and Mrs Poyser celebrated their diamond wedding in December 1938. The bride was given away by her father Dr A V Poyser and wore a gown of cream slipper satin trimmed with heirloom Limerick lace. Her tulle veil was secured with orange blossoms, and she carried roses and stephanotis.

Of course there were no wedding bells at the church. By now we all knew that in the event of an invasion church bells would be sounded right across the country – in every parish bell-ringers were ready to give the alarm in this way – so bells at our wedding might have alarmed the entire nation!

After a short reception we set off on our brief honeymoon, staying at a hotel called the Cotswold Gateway in Burford in the

Cotswolds. The weather was good and we put the world out of our minds and enjoyed each other. It was not unusual for both bride and bridegroom to be virgins, and despite the 'heavy petting' of our courtship Arthur and I were no exception. I am happy to report that all went well on the night: we were both very much in love.

All too soon came Monday morning with Arthur back at work in Coventry and me on my way to my first class of the day in Derby.

Stuart had written expressing his concerns about our air raids but the few bombing attacks that had taken place were to prove minor in comparison with what was to come in the latter months of 1940. As I started life as a 'married woman' the so-called 'Battle of Britain' in the air was just beginning and our lives were to be dominated by its progress from the beginning of July to the end of October 1940.

As a family we seemed to be glued to the radio set, my father by turns elated and depressed – usually the latter. His forebodings were fortified by news that by mid-August over three hundred RAF fighters had been destroyed. Still, as the continuous hot weather of that summer advanced into autumn it seemed that this crucial phase of the war in Europe was coming to an end and a new phase – the Blitz – was about to begin.

We found later that before the war began there had been a survey of the country to establish those areas that would be at high risk of attack from the air. Whether or not Birmingham was a vulnerable target was open to some discussion because on the one hand it was at the farthest range of German bombers, whilst on the other hand the wide variety of engineering production made it an obvious place to attack. In the event it proved to have been earmarked for attention when the first raid on Birmingham occurred on 9th August. There was then another larger raid on 13th August when Castle Bromwich aircraft factory was hit. Right across the country further bombing raids, still mainly on airfields and radar installations, intensified during the days after our wedding. On 12th August Portsmouth docks and town were heavily bombed. Another major attack took place along the south coast on 13th August and then on 15th August there were massive raids along nearly six hundred miles of the British coast from

Newcastle in the north-east to Weymouth in the south.

Obviously I was desperately worried about Arthur. Now that we knew that Birmingham was capable of being reached by the bombers, nearby Coventry was clearly at risk. I was acutely conscious that when raids happened he was bound to be in the thick of the action, and vulnerable to further bombs whilst others sheltered as best they could. The small consolation was that as far as we could tell these raids were all on military and some factory installations – we did not know that they would be regarded as modest compared with what was to come.

The procedure in those days was carefully laid down. There were Air Raid Warden's posts in most streets and wardens had received appropriate training. If a bomb fell or a fire started the nearest warden reported it by telephone, on foot or by messenger to the control centre, usually based in the local town hall. Fires were reported to the Fire Control or local fire brigade and decisions were then made on how to deal with the incident. The fire service had the most dangerous task. With hoses and water as their main weapons they often had to force their way through crater-torn and rubble-filled streets amid collapsing buildings in order to give precedence to fires in factories with inflammable stock. During all this, incendiaries and high-explosive bombs rained around them.

There were specialist rescue teams, first aid parties, and ambulance and police services, and in addition voluntary organizations, in particular the Women's Voluntary Service (WVS). The WVS was good at helping victims on the spot by way of organizing rest centres, street kitchens and canteens, some of them mobile. They helped and comforted people who had been made homeless and were suffering from shock.

So there in all this was my new and much-beloved husband, right in the front line – no wonder I listened with such fear and trepidation to news of air raids, desperately trying to work out which areas were affected, and I so treasured the telephone calls or messages from Arthur telling me he was all right. We still had weekends together but they were very often disrupted or even cancelled by circumstances beyond our control.

Ironically, the first major incident to involve us directly was in

Leicester itself. At 10 a.m. on Wednesday 21st August a single Dornier bomber broke through the morning cloud and released eight high-explosive bombs over the gasworks on Aylestone Road. Six people were killed and twenty-four injured. Although my parents' house was a couple of miles from the site of the bombing and Arthur was in Coventry, whilst I was in Derby, we both felt almost violated in that Leicester seemed suddenly to have been singled out. In reality a number of raids had occurred in the Midlands that day employing only one or two aircraft and it seems that Leicester was not seen as a primary target. It was not until November that Leicester was to witness the impact of a more major raid. However, that August incident still shook us up.

CHAPTER TWENTY-FOUR

On 29th July 1940 Stuart passed out as a Second Lieutenant. He had come fourth out of eighteeen cadets and four VCOs. Great were the celebrations with a riotous night in the mess and then a day off with a trip to Bombay. Much was the beer consumed and it was with pounding heads and uncertain stomachs that the new officers headed north the following morning. Fortunately the length of the journey necessitated a break in Delhi, with an opportunity for sightseeing. Stuart found the Red Fort the most fascinating of the extraordinary mix of buildings in the ancient part of a city now strangely juxtaposed with the modern architecture of the new Lutyens designs, completed only ten years earlier after seventeen years of controversial work.

Stuart somehow felt his stature had been increased by the sense of order and tradition surrounding him. Whilst proud of his qualification, up to that point he could not avoid believing that engineers in the army were both undervalued and underrated. Not that the situation was much different from the tea estates where engineers were seen as inferior to planters, he thought wryly. His frustration stemmed from the realization that the skills needed demanded a higher level of intelligence than he had witnessed in many other areas of the armed forces.

In that vein Stuart wrote proudly to his father:

I am now 2nd Lieutenant S V Poyser R.E!

I passed out 4th out of 18 Cadets and 4 VCO's (Indians). They are I.E's and we are R.E's. Sixteen of us are to be commissioned in the British Army from 1st September.

It is recognized that of those of us of intelligence in the Army: the Best

Brains are – Sappers; the next Best Brains are – Gunners; and the rest – go into Signals! I am off to Roorkee (15 miles east of Simla) soon and my address will be the King George's Own Bengal Sappers and Miners (God's Own!). For short: KGVO. B Sapper and Miners, Roorkee.

Stuart was instantly impressed by his new spiritual home, the headquarters of the Bengal Sappers and Miners in Roorkee. The gleaming white-pillared façade of the colonial-style mess building with its single-storey wings stretching out on each side was flanked by the Ganges canal and an accompanying gridlock of ordered roadways leading to accommodation blocks and other buildings. It spoke of power and tradition, with its turbaned and richly uniformed staff ensuring unobtrusive service. Stuart and his colleagues were to be there for a week before travelling on to the Sappers' northern base at Nowshara on the North-West Frontier for further manoeuvres.

In Roorkee the new officers were at last to hear their fate. Rumours as to the likely posting had been rife for weeks but if the officers at Poona knew the intended destination they were not revealing any information. Odd, thought Stuart, as he sat with his colleagues in the impressive marbled lecture hall, that you volunteer to fight a war, and after three months of waiting and six months of back-breaking training you have no hand in your own destiny.

Lieutenant Colonel Lee's piercing gaze swept around the hall. He was flanked on the dais by his intended successor, Colonel Obbard. To one side sat the Corps Adjutant Captain Percival and the splendidly moustachioed Subedar Major Jia Nand.

'I cannot sufficiently stress the secrecy of what you are now to be told. The destination will soon be apparent to all, and the country of destination may be revealed to your families at home. However, the specifics of the place where you are going, the terrain, the nature of the tasks that you are to undertake and all other aspects of your work are of the greatest confidentiality. The particular work that you sappers carry out is of the utmost value to the enemy. Fifth column spies abound, not so much here in India but in the place where you are to be stationed, and the release, however inadvertent, of any information will be a disciplinary matter which may even amount to treason. Is that clearly and completely understood?'

'Please let me be posted to a war zone so that I can fight,' Stuart thought to himself.

'Malaya is your destination.'

A collective expelling of breath, more groan than gasp. Stuart's fears were realized – destined for a country not yet in conflict and one which the war might never reach. Bitter disappointment stirred in the pit of his stomach and frustrated anger that his lust to fight might never be satisfied.

'You will be part of the 11th Indian Division and you, I should say we, will be the 3rd Field Company. We are under Northern Command. The Wana Brigade, of which we are part, includes two Scinde Horse Squadrons, the $2/2^{nd}$ Punjab Regiment, the $3/8^{th}$ Punjab Regiment, the $1/18^{th}$ Garhwal Rifles, the $2/3^{rd}$ Gurkha Rifles, the $2/8^{th}$ Gurkha Rifles, the 19th Field Company, Bombay Sappers and Miners and ourselves, the 3rd Field Company, Bengal Sappers and Miners.

'For those of you of an inquisitive nature I can tell you that at the beginning of the war there was only one Field Company in Malaya, but there will be eight including ourselves by the time Japan makes up its inscrutable oriental mind whether or not it is going to join this war.

'There are those of you who will feel that Malaya is a backwater. I am here to assure you that it is not. The risk of the Japanese coming into the war is seen by our political masters as high and if that happens Malaya will be their prime target in order to achieve dominance of the Far East. As I speak, the French Vichy Government has announced that it has allowed Japan to occupy the northern portion of French Indo-China.'

Another grunted reaction from the men. Most of those present were acutely aware of the geography of the Far East, all could visualize the closeness of the Burmese peninsula and the land surrounding the Mekong Delta to Malaya. Only the Gulf of Siam would now stand between any build-up of Japanese forces and Malaya itself.

'Whether or not the Japanese have either the appetite or the resources for war remains to be seen. There are those, particularly in America, who believe it has not. However, the stark fact remains that if Japan chooses to create a force in Indo-China it now has the capability to strike swiftly, whereas the long sea journey from Japan that would previously have been necessary would have given ample warning of any such intention. I am now going to hand over to Captain Percival to give you a first overview of what we see as your role.'

As Percival came to the lectern, Major Nand assisting him in the uncovering of a huge map of the Malayan peninsula, there was a swell of muttered comment: dismay, but little surprise, that the government of the invaded French nation should act in such a manner; speculation as to possible collusion with the Japanese; scorn in some quarters as to the Japanese capability. Stuart felt a quickening of interest: if the Japanese were to invade Malaya his thirst for action would be satisfied.

'You all know that at the foot of the peninsula lies the island base of Singapore. You will all have read of the works that have been carried out there by way of massive fortification. I need not tell you that it is not only a major port but the vital base which is essential to our presence in the East. As you will see from the map, Singapore is a very small land mass compared with the Malayan peninsula above it. Singapore Island is approximately six hundred miles south of the northern border of Malaya with neutral Siam, otherwise known as Thailand.

'Above the border the peninsula is thin, before broadening out again as it goes north into Thailand and then into the mainland and the capital city Bangkok. As to that strategically key Malayan-Thai border itself, it will be seen that this is not straight and would be difficult to defend from attack from the north. If the border were in a straight line across from its northern point it would be at a narrower part of the land mass and much easier to fortify. At this stage I can only tell you that there are proposals as to how this situation may best be dealt with.

'So above the border there is southern Thailand where it is possible that a Japanese force may invade, then there is the border area in which invasion may be the more likely, then there is the southern part of Malaya with the gulf of Johore and its causeway to Singapore Island at the bottom.

'The main problem is the long eastern coast. The bad news is that sandy beaches extend practically the whole length of the eastern Malayan seaboard and conditions of gradient, going and surf are favourable to amphibious landings almost anywhere for most of the year. Also, the immediate hinterland to the east coast is normally low lying, featureless and contains no great obstruction to an invading force. The better news is that there are numerous rivers and streams running across the area which drain the extensive high central watershed and furthermore the road is little more than a fine-weather coastal track running down the east coast where going is made difficult by long stretches being routed along beaches where no roadworks have been executed.'

Captain Percival's immaculate tones and precise engineering-type descriptions marked him down as a true Royal Engineer, interested in the practicalities of the terrain and easily conveying to his qualified listeners the kinds of works that might be necessary to provide adequate defences.

'Further good news is that the middle of the peninsula is not flat: an extensive mountain range runs practically the entire length from north to south, making overland communication between east and west coasts extremely difficult. The main north and south road from Singapore to the Thailand border, as I have said a distance of about six hundred miles, lies west of the mountains and is flanked by a metre-gauge railway. This railway crosses the mountain range in the southern part of the country, here at Kelantan, so constituting the only communication between north-east Malaya and the remainder of the country. So, in summary, as the main route southwards is to the west of the mountain range, it is more likely than not that any invasion will be in the area of the northern border so that the invading army can then travel down the west of the country. That main road to the west has an average width of approximately twenty feet, a good tarmacadam surface, and is characterized by numerous bridges over water gaps, mainly of reinforced concrete construction.'

The lecture wore on through the afternoon and yet none of the listening sappers wilted in the dry heat of the northern Indian plain. The descriptions given conjured up clear pictures in their freshly trained minds, and enabled the theory of all they had learned over the past six months to mesh with the practicality of a real war situation in an unknown tropical country with six hundred miles of eastern seaboard to defend. They could well see the near impossibility of preventing even a limited invasion, which led them on to the realities of how then to seek to defeat and ultimately repel the invading force.

'Will we be given the resources to do the work?' was the burning question asked of Stuart as they made their way to their quarters to change for dinner in the mess.

'Your guess is as good as mine – but the task is huge and it rather depends on how many of us there are, and how much army or local labour is available. We look like being in for an interesting time!'

Stuart wrote home:

Our photo was taken and we were issued with more equipment. Flea bags, folding baths, basins, beds, etc. Had to pay 90 Rupees for a greatcoat! Met Forrester of Doom Dooma Tea Estate in the Gunners.

A lot of the new officers have only been in India for a few months, we can speak the language far better than any of them. We are frantic from dawn until after dark, terrific amount of work, we often miss meals altogether. We work on Sundays and never stop.

I am not allowed to tell you more about my work. Your letters that have arrived are ancient history – so Mary and Arthur are now married! Will write to them separately. I am not allowed to say where I am going but it will soon be in earnest. For God's sake look after yourselves.

CHAPTER TWENTY-FIVE

I returned to Derby with the status of a married woman but hardly what might be termed an ordinary married life. Arthur and I would meet only at weekends at Morland Avenue. It was a strange existence but so many people were separated in the war years that it was pointless to complain. I enjoyed my teaching, the weather was lovely and at least I was able to enjoy my new husband at weekends.

So we came to the September of that hot English summer. It was on 7th September that the Blitz was to begin in earnest. There had been intermittent raids before 'Black Saturday', as that day in September came to be called, but little significant damage had been caused.

Few people will now remember the awful fact that, from the first major raid on 7th September 1940, London was bombed almost every day and every night until 13th November. We know that on 25th August the RAF carried out a bombing attack on Berlin. Anecdotal evidence is that this enraged Hitler who saw it as a violation of his capital city and that he boasted that he would raze our cities to the ground. There is little doubt that the bombing of England had already been planned but it is probable that Hitler's perceived petulance intensified the Luftwaffe's efforts to include civilian targets in the bombing campaign. Some commentators have argued that the German plan to bomb civilian targets, with a view to breaking morale and forcing the British government to surrender, actually had a beneficial effect on the course of the war. They would say that Fighter Command's aircraft and airfields were no longer regarded as prime targets. If so, that was of little consolation to the people of London and the other cities about to be devastated.

That particular Saturday, 7th September, dawned a clear cloudless day in Leicester and across the rest of the country. It was four in the afternoon when the blue sky over London suddenly darkened with the shapes of a huge number of German bombers.

In the first attack 300 bombers destroyed the East End, centring on the Royal Victoria Docks and the Surrey Docks. Woolwich Arsenal and the Beckton gasworks, the largest in Europe, were hit and all the huge warehouses on the riverside were set on fire. The warehouse frontage eastwards from Tower Bridge burned for a distance of nearly a mile and the force of the fires was such that it was said the flames could be seen from the South Downs sixty miles away.

At the sounding of the first All Clear the survivors emerged from their shelters to find major destruction and, what was worse, raging fires which were themselves to serve as a target for a further 250 bombers which came back at 8 p.m. with even greater bomb power. These were intent on destroying the whole of London's harbour installations, supplies and power sources.

There were no firemen left to be deployed: all were out fighting the flames, but their hoses were not up to the challenge of burning warehouses and the message was that it was 'Fire Out of Hand'. By the early morning forty-two major fires were raging and one of the fire officers, requesting reinforcements from the south of England, is reported to have said, 'Send all the bloody pumps you've got – the whole world's on fire.'

It was perhaps surprising that in that first raid only 430 people were killed and 1,600 injured, bearing in mind that the areas of Stepney, Whitechapel, Poplar, Bow and Shoreditch were largely destroyed and that gas, electricity, water supplies and telephone services were gone. In the next three weeks alone the London firemen would have to fight 10,000 fires – little wonder that I became fearful for Arthur in his part-time role if the bombing should come to Coventry.

We were all appalled to hear the news, we could not imagine how the country could survive such warfare and we now knew that civilians were among the targets. Each day we heard that the bombers had returned the previous night and by the end of the month the newspapers said that 5,730 people had been killed and nearly 10,000 seriously injured.

The people of London soon became skilled at identifying the different types of bomb falling: these varied in size from 110 lb to 2.200 lb, the latter nicknamed Hermann after the portly figure of Göring as head of the Luftwaffe. There were a few even larger bombs called 'Satan' and 'the Max' which weighed in at 4,000 lb and 5,500 lb, producing craters that could comfortably accommodate four or five double-decker buses. There were land mines with parachutes and there were the dreaded incendiaries. These were tiny: nine inches long and two inches in diameter, made of magnesium alloy so that when ignited they would burn for ten minutes at a frighteningly high temperature throwing particles of burning metal up to fifty feet. They were deadly in starting fires unless they were quickly located and extinguished. Later on some of these were fitted with a delayed action fuse which exploded an attached bomb some minutes later, hugely increasing the risk to the firefighters.

So the air raids went on, and on, and on. Other cities were attacked but London continued to bear the brunt. The casualties for October, the second month of the Blitz in London, were over 6,000 killed and nearly 9,000 seriously injured. It seemed it would never end. There were sporadic raids over Coventry, fairly minor by comparison with London, but they gave Arthur the opportunity to regale me with vivid descriptions of how he and his fellows had dealt with the fires.

Arthur told me that on one occasion he had seen an incendiary fall through the roof of a terraced house and had raced upstairs to try to deal with it. He found the small device lodged in the ceiling, burning intensely, but there was no water to supply the stirrup pump with which he needed to douse the fire and save the house. In a moment of inspiration he seized a china chamber pot from under the bed and used a jemmy as a lever to persuade the incendiary to fall into it. He then managed to carry the chamber pot with its burning contents down the stairs and into the street to safety.

Whether or not Arthur thought these tales of derring-do would calm my fears for his continued safety I was not certain. For our part, we all had to have an air raid shelter to go to, and also to make arrangements for shelter within our own houses. My grandparents had a cellar under their Highfield Street house, so that became their shelter. Morland Avenue had no shelter but there was a small room behind the kitchen door which was in the centre of the house and without windows. My father stacked folding deckchairs in there so that when the alarm sounded those then living in the house could solemnly squeeze into this small pantry and sit it out.

There were also gas masks issued to everyone including children, although I cannot remember ever needing to wear mine in real life. We still had to practise putting the wretched things on and off.

It was an extraordinary time. We tried to carry on our everyday existence but constant shortages and other hardships dominated our lives. Clothes rationing began on 1st June 1941 when there was a major shortage of cloth reaching Britain and much of that was needed for uniforms, tents and parachutes. The Ministry of Information issued guidance on 'Make Do and Mend' – how to repair and update existing items in your wardrobe. There were clothing and shoe exchanges organized by local schools.

Then there were two other ministries: the Ministry of War Transport and the Ministry of Labour and National Service. These encouraged people to travel shorter distances by foot rather than use public transport. They argued that this would create space for those travelling longer distances and also free up the overstretched transport system. I already walked or cycled most of the time so felt I was doing my bit in that particular respect.

I was less assiduous in my attention to the Fuel Saving Scheme as part of which households were encouraged to paint a line round their bathtub to ensure that not more than five inches of water was used, thereby helping to save water for the war effort. Line there might be, but when alone in the bathroom how meticulous were we all? Certainly my father would not have infringed, but then he took a cold bath every morning, lying in the water and washing, which was a habit I could never come to terms with. The thinking behind the Fuel Saving Scheme was to encourage families such as ours to reduce fuel consumption by setting a 'fuel target' based on the size of the house. This target was then the maximum amount of fuel that we were allowed to use and we all had to read our own gas and electricity meters and display the results to ensure this wasn't exceeded.

We also had the Ministry of Supply. As a forerunner of today's 'Green' recycling efforts it was as early as 1940 that the ministry established a scheme encouraging us all to sort and separate our wastepaper, rags and glass and deposit them in the salvage bins provided in most streets.

Perhaps the most famous of these wartime initiatives was the campaign launched by the Ministry of Agriculture to help combat food shortages in Britain by promoting the planting of allotments in gardens and on public land. 'Dig for Victory' was very successful, taking the number of allotments to nearly one-and-a-half million by 1943. Vast areas of public land including some royal parks were converted into allotment land and nearly a million tons of vegetables were grown in the peak years of production.

I suppose it was the rigours of our daily lives that provided the background against which I would later write to Stuart, castigating him for 'living in the land of milk and honey'.

CHAPTER TWENTY-SIX

North-West Frontier: a name evocative of its wild and desolate nature. Stuart was stationed in Noshwara, very different in size but not dissimilar to Roorkee in style and tradition. Regimental traditions as now anticipated, but there were only five in the Sappers' Mess: a major, three regimental captains and one second lieutenant, Stuart. The station was dominated by a battalion of infantry from the 3/4th Punjabs. Stuart knew some of them from Poona: old and new faces in a familiar setting. But the scenery! Stuart was used to huge vistas – in Assam the Himalaya range was ever present in the distant background and sight lines to the far horizon were measured in hundreds of miles, so different from his home territory of the English Midlands where a dozen miles of vision would be rare. Here the immediacy of the mountains imposed their massive presence. The word towering seemed inadequate for such neck-stretching elevation to the white-tipped peaks. It was a harsh landscape, jagged broken lines of vertical rocks cut through with passes which seemed to negate that description.

Amongst this drama was set the headquarters building, less imposing than Rorkee but nonetheless grand, well staffed and well equipped. Here the training continued for two more weeks with a concentration on the art of bridges: building bridges to span the torrents of water, working out techniques for access roads and infrastructure, and then the reverse – demolition.

Stuart found that he had a love of structure, of how things stood up, construction in all its aspects. He hated the concept of demolition, pulling down or blowing up those same beloved structures and wasting the skills of the original builders. Notwithstanding that hatred, his very affection for the bridges and buildings fuelled his knowledge of their weakest points and made him the star pupil in the positioning of destructive devices. His instructors and superiors singled him out for praise and quietly watched his continued development.

It was enormously hard work. Training was intense and continuous. Save for one game of hockey all sports and other leisure activities were abandoned. In addition to the building and demolition work they practised night-time attacking and defence techniques. They worked on Sundays and ate when the opportunity arose. It was exhausting.

Towards the end of their few weeks in Noshwara Stuart and his team had to demonstrate the demolition of a building in front of an audience of GOC staff. It was a nerve-racking experience and Stuart retained visions of his overenthusiastic demolition of the water tower in Poona. He lay awake at night before the demonstration with wild imaginings of the debris from the anticipated demolition slaughtering the watching officers. In the event all was well, the explosion was of a size appropriate to the task and the visiting superiors declared themselves pleased.

That night, in the mess after dinner, Captain Percival invited Stuart to join him in a peg of whisky. Comforted that such tea estate expressions were being used, Stuart was pleased to accept. Percival led the way to a couple of basket-weave armchairs in a quiet corner of the bar under one of the big overhead fans.

'You've done extremely well. It has been noticed. Your techniques as an engineer are excellent, you are also developing well as a soldier – but how do you feel you will react in a battle situation?'

'Do any of us know until we've been under fire? I'm desperate to do my bit, and can only hope I shall be as brave as the next man – if that's what you mean?'

'Let me put it another way, and in total confidence. In two weeks we'll be in Malaya – assuming we're not torpedoed on the way – and I've been asked to seek out a number of volunteers for special duties. I believe you possess the qualities that are needed. However, there is a downside and I need to tell you about that before you decide whether or not you wish to have your name put forward.'

Stuart was sitting forward in his chair, willing the other man to go on. The words 'special duties' were music to his ears. Was this the chance he had been hoping for?

'Malaya is largely jungle. Warfare in the jungle is very different from conventional warfare. Skills have been developed, and continue to be developed and it is believed that small highly mobile units may be needed alongside the more traditional formations. Some of those units may be involved in pre-invasion preparations, under cover, in Thailand. Some may need to operate behind enemy lines once an invasion occurs. At least one demolitions expert will be attached to each unit – those that have experience of the tropics and also language skills are favoured. However, those chosen must have not only a high level of fitness but also the ability to fight.'

'Sir, this sounds just up my street, assuming you think I have the skills.'
Stuart's enthusiasm was obvious, but when Percival held up a hand he fell silent.

'I mentioned a downside. You are a second lieutenant, the lowest commissioned rank. You and Beattie and Teasdel might be regarded as competing for promotion. I am confident that, in time, that promotion would be yours enabling you to move up the leadership ladder. The problem is that those nominated for special duties are going to be involved in a great deal of training, and in exercises and operations away from the main body of the 3rd Field Company. Present indications are that in the short term you would be likely to be passed over for promotion in favour of those who will be constantly available as future leaders. That's not to say that swift promotion may not follow after the special units have proved themselves, nor indeed that the opportunity for being decorated may not be greater …'

Percival raised his eyebrows and laughed as he tailed of, implying that of course he was in no way suggesting that Stuart might regard a decoration as in any way desirable.

'The other thing to say is that the need for even greater secrecy will be fundamental. You will not be allowed to tell your family anything of your selection. If the war goes badly they may never even find out. You will have to be coy with your friends outside the units, and not be tempted to tell them of the situation even if I am right in my prediction that you will be passed over for short-term promotion. In short, the present stringent conditions of secrecy will seem delightfully relaxed by comparison with the new need for total confidentiality if you accept.'

'Please put my name forward.'

The words came involuntarily. Stuart desperately wanted to be involved. His one sadness was that his family would not know. He knew of his father's unhappiness, constantly expecting to hear that his only son was going to be in the centre of the war effort. He knew the views of his sister Mary, hinting in correspondence that Stuart was enjoying a holiday whilst the rest of the world was fighting. He realized how frustrated he would become in being prevented from giving an explanation, but deep down he knew that his father would approve and one day, hopefully, be proud of him.

CHAPTER TWENTY-SEVEN

Depressed as we all were by the news and evidence of the Blitz, life had to go on as best it could. On 14th November I was in Derby, busy organizing things for the school prize giving; I had been sleeping on a camp bed in the staff room during each weekday of that term, and travelling home at weekends, so I was alone in the school most evenings. I was teaching by day but also doing first aid work at the Rolls Royce factory on evening shifts, so it was usually quite late when I got back to the empty school.

It seems that in the late afternoon the rest of the staff had heard on the radio that a terrible air raid had been launched on Coventry and they had decided to say nothing to me. That evening I remember so well going down to the big empty hall in the dark. The hall had been filled with parents and children together with the staff all afternoon and was now eerily deserted. I switched on the only radio which was attached to the radiogram we had been using for playing records. I was terror struck when I heard commentators talking of the 'near destruction' of Coventry.

Standing silently by the radio in the darkened hall I heard that an estimated 10,000 incendiaries had been dropped by an advance force of light bombers and that waves of heavy bombers had then followed and were continuing to come hour after hour – Coventry was alight from end to end. The newsreader, in measured tones, said simply that a city 'firestorm' had been created, explaining this as a wave of uncontrollable fire sweeping through the streets.

I was not to know that only a few days earlier Hitler had been due to speak at a major rally in Munich, celebrating the anniversary of his attempt to seize power in Bavaria, when British bombers had attacked the city and the event was disrupted. In his rage Hitler had summoned Göring and agreed with him that they would exact a newsworthy revenge, selecting Coventry for a massive retaliatory attack.

Coventry was a compact and effective target being a city of 220,000 people with aircraft factories and many engineering works all within a limited area. Notwithstanding its industry it was a city containing many beautiful medieval buildings, quite apart from being the city in which my new husband was a fireman.

I could not believe that Arthur was still alive. I stayed, sleepless, by the radio in the darkened hall. I was at the station at dawn the next day and caught the first train to Leicester. When I reached my parents' house the news announcements were saying it was now believed that between 400 and 500 heavy bombers had followed the first pathfinders. There were estimates of the huge tonnage of high-explosive bombs dropped, it was said that fires were still raging out of control and that more than one hundred acres of the city centre had been destroyed. The 600-year-old cathedral of St Michael's was burning.

My father was ashen faced. Although Coventry was thirty miles from Leicester they had not only heard the sounds of continued bombing but had watched the glare in the night sky until dawn broke.

I was convinced that Arthur must be dead. It was not until mid-morning that we heard on the radio that the bombing had stopped. There was little more on the radio save for constantly repeated reports that the air raid had been catastrophic and that the city was in ruins and still burning.

Most of our friends knew that Arthur was in Coventry and there were several well-meaning telephone calls seeking news. My parents had already spoken to Arthur's parents in Stratford; they lived near enough to Coventry to have watched the constant waves of bombers and to have heard the continuous impact of bombs and were desperately worried. I could only sit numbly and leave my parents to deal with the calls.

It was early afternoon when I heard the telephone ring again. My father picked it up, listened for a moment and suddenly said: 'Arthur!'

I tore the phone from my father's hand. Somehow Arthur had found a working telephone. As if in a dream I heard him telling me that he had survived but was desperately tired and needed sleep. He said there was no transport and that he would start walking to us in Leicester, some thirty miles distant.

It seemed like a miracle. I told Arthur I would borrow my father's car and drive to Coventry. I was stopped at Walsgrave – the police would allow no one to go further because of the terrible damage and all I could see was the burning city in the distance and a long column of refugees coming past the checkpoint. Eventually my exhausted and fire-blackened husband trudged into view and I ran towards him.

This was the night that a new word was added to the dictionary: 'Koventrieren' in German or 'to Coventrate' in English – to lay waste by aerial bombardment. This was the night that others would later call 'our Guernica'. This was the night the German bombers pioneered the 'pathfinder' technique of sending specially equipped advance aircraft to drop parachute flares with incendiary bombs to mark targets for the main force of bombers following behind.

Perhaps surprisingly in view of the enormous devastation only 568 people were killed, but of those some 400 were so badly burned that they could not be identified. For the first time in the war mass graves were created so that the bodies could be buried whether or not identification was complete. There were over 1,200 seriously injured, and in the immediate aftermath between 50,000 and 100,000 people fled from Coventry fearing a repeat attack the next night.

Only five days after the destruction of Coventry, and in a much lesser way, the Blitz came to Leicester itself. The first incendiaries fell across the city from the gasworks in Aylestone Road to the Great Central Railway station in Belgrave Road. High explosive bombs then dropped on various factories including that of Freeman, Hardy & Willis in Rutland Street. Residential properties were blasted over a wide area including parts of Highfield Street where Granny and Grandpa Poyser lived.

My grandfather's memory had started to fail with the passing years and by the time the war began he was senile and apt to repeat himself. There were two elderly companions living with my grandparents and they had all been advised by my father that when the raids started they must move into the cellar which they had equipped with deckchairs.

When Highfield Street and nearby Saxby Street were bombed all hell broke loose in my grandparents' house with the windows blown in and incendiaries all around. Down to the cellar they all went and as each crash and crump was heard overhead my grandfather would ask:

'Why are we sitting in the cellar, Annie?'

To which my grandmother would reply:

'There is an air raid, Arthur, we're being bombed by the Germans.'

This confused my grandfather who still recalled the Germans from the First World War but remembered little of recent events, and he would say:

'The Germans – how did they get here?'

'We are at war with the Germans, Arthur.'

But then another crash would be heard and my father would say:

'Why are we sitting here, Annie?'

'There is an air raid, Arthur, we're being bombed by the Germans.'

And the whole cycle would begin again.

This went on all night. It must have been very frightening for four old people in a cold cellar, but at 5 a.m. the wardens started to evacuate the entire area. My grandmother thought the banging on the door upstairs was the sound of yet more bombing and refused to allow her companions to leave the cellar.

At about 8 a.m. my father arrived to find the whole area cordoned off. Fearing the worst and having been told that everyone alive had been evacuated to the rest centres he started to search each centre but to no avail. It was not until 9.30 a.m. that my grandmother at last allowed one of the companions to emerge and a warden spotted her, went down to the cellar and duly evacuated them all to one of the centres which my father had already visited. In the meantime my father had managed to obtain permission to go inside the cordoned-off area to search the house, but by the time he got there it was empty. It was not until mid-afternoon that my father finally found the four old people and took them to Morland Avenue where they all sheltered in the hall against the next night's bombing.

It was extraordinary to see how well people's morale held up in the bombed cities and towns. The propaganda and newsreels gave a rather artificial 'we can take it' flavour to the reality of life in those times but we survived. There was real fear and dreadful uncertainty and it would not have surprised me if morale had not collapsed but somehow it remained high. Winston Churchill's landmark speeches helped, and the 'stiff upper lip' tradition of those days meant that there was less introspection than there might have been today.

It is often forgotten what huge destruction and loss of life was caused by the Blitz. Between September 1940 and May 1941 no less than two million houses were demolished. The figures for those who died in air attacks show that nearly 30,000 were killed in London itself and 31,000 elsewhere in Britain; there were 86,000 admitted to hospital and 150,000 injured.

Of course we fought back, and Bomber Command subsequently carried out heavy raids in Germany with the destruction of Dresden being one of the most awful acts of retaliation. Ultimately the German civilian losses through air raids were equally heavy, but comparisons of that nature do not in any way reduce the sense of personal tragedy and loss involved in each death wherever it occurred.

From our own personal point of view we were just thankful that we had all survived, but I can imagine Stuart's agonies of frustration. I feel guilty that in my letters to him I hinted at his enjoying 'the good life' whilst we were suffering, which must have been very hard for him to bear. It was not as if he could do anything about it, and the fear that he might never be involved in the fighting must have been unbearable for such an enthusiast as my brother.

CHAPTER TWENTY-EIGHT

Dear All,

I am somewhere in the Indian Ocean! Courtesy of the British India Line. I am baggage officer for several hundred men. It is a crowded troop ship, down below it is like the Black Hole of Calcutta. Not a lot of the men are sick but one doesn't like going near the latrines. I am in a cabin with Richards. It was odd when we left as there were no farewells, but then there was nobody to say goodbye to. I fear it is going to be dull and boring – but we may be in a tough spot if the axis means anything when things get going. It is not what I had hoped for. I feel so homesick leaning over the rail. I wish I could be with you all.

4.11.40

Dear All,

Malaya. That is all I am allowed to say. We have missed the war unless the Japs come in. We came over in convoy, no particular thrills. Are we here for keeps? It is a glorious country, beautiful scenery, clean and happy faces, first class buildings and roads. Vegetation not unlike Assam, but more like the South Seas. If we were not being involved in a war it would be paradise. I am in a hotel and a courtesy member of various clubs. There are cinemas, dance halls, cabarets and a night club. I am off with a small party on a special job next week. It is a lovely and interesting country, truly a land of milk and honey.

But a land of enormously hard work – two weeks of immense activity from Stuart's point of view. First there was the sorting of the men and all their equipment – embarkation, disembarking, entraining, detraining, and all the logistical tasks associated with moving hundreds of men from one country to another, and then from the south of Malaya to where they were now stationed, close to Penang. Second came the leadership meetings to plan the tasks that were programmed for delivery. Thirdly, local volunteers had to be selected who were to form the bulk of the team effort required to produce so much in so short a time. They had now set up groups organized under non-commissioned and VCO control and those units had started the construction work: shutters for the defence sites; temporary boarded huts to house the Malayan labour that had been recruited; transoms ready for bridge construction; the list was endless, and they had not yet travelled to the actual places where the defence and construction systems were to be deployed.

Stuart moved from unit to unit, checking the design drawings, ensuring that the work was in accordance with those designs, arranging for the materials to be in place, bullying those in charge of each unit to maintain a high speed of construction. There were endless briefing meetings at all levels, and the most fascinating were those where Stuart learned of the defence plans for the country as a whole.

Stuart's notes set out brief detail of the four principal anti-invasion defence projects to which the different Field Companies were committed. Reading through his jottings for the tenth time, before destroying them in accordance with standing instructions, he checked the list of the four main areas upon which the various Field Companies of sappers would be working:

1. Probable landing beaches on the eastern side at Khota Baru
2. Beaches near Mersing in the south in Johore State, seen as the back door to Singapore
4. Beaches on Singapore itself
5. The Jitra defence line, an intended 'stop' position in North Kedah, 10 miles inland from the Thailand border.

The first project would involve the 3rd Field Company in some degree, but it was the last task, the Jitra defence line, which would be of his particular concern. Would there be the time and resources to set up a sufficiently mined and pre-prepared position when other offensive issues had also to be considered?

'Operation Matador is the key to our defeating a Japanese invasion!'

The words came from Lieutenant Colonel Steedman, to give him his full title. Stuart and his fellow officers, and all the other officers of the units making up the 11th Indian Division, were gathered together in a specially commandeered hotel in Penang. Both the hotel and the conference room were guarded and had been checked for infiltrators. Refreshments were set out on side tables but no waiters or other staff were allowed to be present; even the hotel manager was excluded and had been allocated to the external guard to ensure compliance.

'Matador is a plan whereby we, the 11th Division, will make a sudden advance into Thailand, with the objective of forestalling a Japanese assault in the Singora-Patani area. As will be seen from the map, this advance to the northern coast will create a new and narrower defensive line across the peninsula, and also secure the vital railway junction near Singora where the only railway line from Thailand divides and creates separate lines down the west and east coasts. The advance will be by road and rail simultaneously: the major force will depart from the north-west, with a smaller advance from the inland area of Kroh. Together we intend to force a route and occupy what is known as 'the Ledge' which you will see marked here – forty miles inside Thailand and astride the Kroh-Patani road.'

The colonel had the undivided attention of the assembled company. The huge wall map showed the tactical advantage to be gained. The thought of being an attacking force, rather than simply a defensive one, fired their imaginations.

'You mentioned a sudden advance – how soon is that likely to be before a landing force arrives?' Stuart had raised his hand to put the question.

'Thank you, Poyser. I can only say that I am told there will be two triggering factors, the first being a request for military assistance by the government of Thailand. I fear we should not hold our breath for that. The second is, and I quote: 'provided a Japanese invasion of

146

Thailand is imminent'. I do not know how or when that decision will be made. At worst, one must assume that it will not be until an invasion force has been spotted, which is likely to give us very little time to prepare. That issue of preparation conveniently brings me on to the necessary preliminary work.

'I will also tell you that necessary reconnaissance will be carried out in southern Thailand. That is a country that regards itself as neutral, thus our making preparations for war over the Thai border is likely to be regarded by the Thai government, and others, as an act of provocation. Some of you may be involved in these incursions, but in conditions of great secrecy. Of particular importance will be the role of those of you who are Sappers, not only in preparing the way for Matador but also in the preliminary work for demolition of river crossings and roads in the event of a retreat becoming necessary.'

Stuart's pulse quickened. He had already been notified that he would be needed for a 'course' for two weeks, starting in four days' time – was this to be the beginning of his special training?

CHAPTER TWENTY-NINE

13.11.40

I am a long way from where I last wrote. Have left the good life. I might as well be back in tea again with the climate more like Assam. Living in a coolie hut on hard tack. 24 hours on duty continuously. Have radio contact and heard last night that Coventry was wiped out in an air attack. Last letter I read was written in August so no idea how you all are. Hope Arthur is all right in Coventry. Should tell you that before I left India I volunteered to return home and join the home guard, offered to pay a substitute to come out – given short shrift! Heard from tea estate – Swansell and Cummings gone (gunners and signals). Not seen a female of any colour for over a month.

Everything seems to have changed so much.

Yes, at last he had heard from the tea estate. He had sent letters to Daniel each month in the hope that they would be read to Monglee but replies had been rare even when he had been training in India itself. He had often tried to imagine how they were managing in the village with work on the estates being so reduced. Stuart had steeled himself to a total lack of news of his children, and he was delighted to have the crumpled airmail sheets on which he recognized Daniel's careful handwriting. He visualized Monglee dictating to him. He read that baby Ann had flourished and was now walking well, and that her sister Mary was doing well in her early classes at the primitive little school adjacent to the Pengaree tea estate. The estate was functioning, but at a low level of productivity in view of the limited number of staff. Monglee had been able to help with the picking. She sent her love.

Stuart closed his eyes. '… sent her love' – he had always tried to avoid that word. Love seemed such a formal expression. The commitment of love would be natural with an English wife in an open world; was it right to use the word in his clandestine circumstances? Louise was his fiancée, that was where his future love must lie, but how complex he had made his love life and how would it end?

'I love my children.' He found himself speaking out loud, lying on his bunk in his solitary tent. There, he had acknowledged his feelings for Mary and Ann; but even that natural paternal love seemed somehow diluted by the knowledge that he would one day have to decide whether or not to acknowledge them in public. He had seen McTavish and Andrews, both men of integrity, ignore their children and walk past them and their mothers on occasions when their wives were visiting from home. Would he do likewise, or would he be proud of his own offspring and declare them to the world?

And what about Monglee, his child bride; he had taken her innocence and was in no doubt that she loved him passionately. He remembered some phrases from a new poem he had read by Auden:

'my noon, my midnight − my talk, my song'

− but how had it finished?

'I thought that love would last forever, I was wrong.'

Was this how Monglee would feel? And how should he fit Louise into this emotional equation − could he love two people at the same time, and what was love anyway?

Stuart thought he was going to die. He had thought himself tough. He had thought himself fit. Tough or not, the seeming sadism of the Special Operations Executive commander Spencer-Chapman defied belief. Now hunkered down in a shallow hollow of ground, pressing his body into the earth, Stuart winced as small fire laced the air above him. In the last hour he had run two miles in full kit, additionally burdened with the destructive weight of a Bren gun and ammunition; he had waded three rivers, crawled through a swamp and thrown himself into a ditch to avoid detection. It was dark, he was sodden with the heat and humidity, painted ochre with mud, and he still had to cover another mile of jungle-clad hillside to attempt to capture the hut that had been designated as the enemy position. Sight lines, camouflage technique, dead ground, diversions: the instructions of the last ten days streamed through his consciousness as he planned his final route. As he began to move he winced as his back, bruised in the unarmed combat session the previous day, made its silent protest.

16.12.40

News of war in Africa. Got four of your letters written but in August. Time lag frightfully difficult, feel we are drifting apart. Japs seem to have climbed down a bit – their usual tactic? Working from 7am until dark, can't say what I am doing.

But I long to tell you exactly what I have been doing, thought Stuart. After the complete secrecy of the SOE course, which he was required to conceal from the rest of his section, there had been further short specialist training sessions of the same nature. The advanced combat techniques were at once the best and the worst of this new secret world. The learning of skills in stabbing, strangling and garotting – to name but three – concentrated his mind on the face-to-face involvement of infantry war. It was so different from the remote laying of demolition charges. And yet, he reflected, would he feel more fulfilled by the personal touch of an enemy hand as the piano wire cut into the throat than by detached obliteration in the impersonality of timed explosion?

Overriding the driven exhaustion of the training were Stuart's suppressed fears of failing to stand firm under fire. What must it really be like to experience the deliberate aiming of bullets and shells? How would the more numerous sepoys, upon whom any defence or attack would depend, face up to that same fundamental?

Three months later in Malaya letters from home continued to make their spasmodic appearance. Stuart maintained his regular flow of restricted news:

13.1.1941

Had a whole bunch of your letters. A raspberry from Arthur (and one from Mary a few weeks ago). My work is of military importance, being a Royal

Engineer makes it more so than any other branch. I have never felt so far away and separated before.

12.1.1941

Got letters re: bomb damage. You were lucky to escape. It hurts like hell to have letters 'hope you are enjoying your good life' – 'hoped you were in Africa chasing the Wops'. I was only four days in the land of milk and honey. If the Japs come in I will feel I am pulling my weight – and how! Nine years in the tropics and only five months in a temperate climate. Going to be an awful flop if nothing happens. We are warned to say nothing, especially the sappers.

14.4.1941

News of Blitz and again Coventry. Japan sits on the fence and snarls. Been in this place nearly two months, cut off – no roads – only rail. Malay people are mainly Chinese (best of the lot). The Malays, Thais and Javanese are like the Assamese: they just live on the land and work only to live, mainly rice and fishing. Thick jungle and a lot of swamp, hot, sweltering and harsh climate; and no particular seasons. If I had done ninety-nine years rather than nine I would still not understand the Easterner. Crowned heads of Malaysia visited this week. Major Wright and CRE coming to look round in next few days.

24.5.41

Tried sending letters via America, hope you receive them. Been in hospital with fever, instead of the tea estate cure of quinine and a good sweat, and back in a couple of days – I have been kept in bed for seventeen days with strange dope. Still, good rest. And still we wait for Japan. Troop movements in South Thailand, wish I could tell you more about things but I can't. Not discuss military matters but plenty of hard work after return from hospital. Been with rest of company and not returned to the 'old place' but off again tomorrow to a 'different spot'. Crete now in the headlines and Hess landed in Scotland – strange life!

CHAPTER THIRTY

1941 was a most depressing year save for one thing: I was still in my first year of marriage. It was a strange start to married life with constantly depressing war news, the Blitz and rationing. Arthur and I had no marital home as such – he was in Coventry and, during the last part of 1940 and in the early months of 1941, I was in Derby. As I have said before, we only met at weekends at Morland Avenue. We had our own room but little privacy otherwise. Indeed I remember that when we moved our first double bed into the room in Morland Avenue in which our Cairn terrier, Jinx, had been accustomed to have his basket, Jinx refused to let Arthur into the bed. Not an auspicious start to our life together!

The Christmas of 1940 was ghastly. We were all exhausted from the trauma of the Blitz and both spoken and unspoken fears as to the progression of the war. My mother's depression meant that there were good days and bad days, and the bad days were very bad. My father's diary entries for each day would show an upward arrow for a good day, a sideways arrow for a neutral day, and one or more downward arrows depending on the severity of the bad ones.

Since the bombing of Leicester, and the destruction of the Highfield Street property, Granny and Grandpa Poyser had been living with us all at Morland Avenue. Grandpa was senile and occasionally incontinent, and Granny was far from easy to live with at the best of times – and these were not the best of times. There was a maid living in the property which was good in terms of help, but not so good in that she added further pressure to bedroom and bathroom accommodation. My father was commuting to Nottingham to work, fire watching on regular evenings, and trying to cope with both his parents and my mother when he reached home at night.

It became apparent that my father could not cope on his own and the maid could not manage to look after my grandparents and my mother on those days when my mother was at her worst. As my mother went into another bout of melancholic depression it was clear that I would have to care for her. There seemed to be no alternative to my giving up my job in Derby. This was a huge blow to me. I felt I would become isolated without contact with the teaching which I enjoyed.

It was with a heavy heart that I abandoned my career. I saw my teaching as good for the war effort and believed that I was performing a valuable service. Simply reverting to domestic duties was a great wrench and seemed worthless in war terms but I could not see what else I could do.

Eventually my father managed to move my grandparents to a nursing home in Mountsorrel, to the north of Leicester. This was not too bad for him to visit on the way back from Nottingham but it was a difficult journey from Morland Avenue on the south side of Leicester city. Even then, the added burden of visiting Mountsorrel added to the pressures on him. I was still needed to look after my mother whose condition became such that she could not really be left.

News of the war continued to depress. From March to May 1941 no less than 412 British, Allied and neutral ships were lost at sea, mainly to German U-boats. Churchill even ordered that shipping losses should no longer be reported in the press, using the argument that the information gave too much information to the enemy. I suspect the true reason was that the news would further lower our morale.

In May 1941 the Houses of Parliament were bombed and the Great Hall of the Palace of Westminster all but destroyed. Nonetheless the early force of the Blitz had diminished and although air raids still happened they were on a lesser scale than those of the terrible few months from September 1940 onwards. Then we heard that the battleship *Hood* had been sunk, although there was then better news when it was announced that its attacker, the *Bismarck*, had in turn been destroyed by the Royal Navy.

In June came the extraordinary development of Hitler launching what was called Operation Barbarossa, attacking Russia and advancing on Leningrad.

My father was in what might be called an apoplectic dilemma. For years he had seen Russia as a deadly enemy and now Churchill was calling upon us to regard our former Russian opponents as allies – it would take some time for him to come to terms with the change. However, even my father could see that for Hitler to launch an attack to the east would be likely to dilute his efforts elsewhere, so after due reflection he was able to regard the news as positive, a good thing as there were not many positives around.

Arthur was still in Coventry during the week and a number of our communications tended to be by letter. I was never sure how he found time to write to me during the times of the air raids but I treasured those letters that I received. One such letter after a further major raid on Coventry in April 1941 read:

My darling

This may be another letter in instalments, as I probably won't finish it tonight. I sent you a postcard this afternoon though, so you won't be without news of me.

Well, last night was hell let loose in Coventry. It was the longest and worst raid since November and it really was pretty horrific. The ATS had a real night out and were fully, and more than fully, occupied. I stayed in bed until 11 o'clock (in spite of a bit of gunfire) and then went up to the depot as things started dropping. From then until 7 o'clock this morning I was busy fighting fires and you can imagine that I'm just a little bit weary tonight in spite of a few hours sleep this morning.

I left work at 5.30 this evening, gave up my Home Guard lecture, and am now sitting by the fire, ready changed except for the outer layers, and waiting for the sirens, which should sound within the next half hour.

Last night's experiences were indescribable, because when things happen so quickly one loses count of time and one's 'balance': as a result all that remains afterwards is a blurred impression of what went on.

The crew I was with worked chiefly in one of the working class districts of the town and we seemed to have the brunt of the bombing in our part of the world. This time Foleshill district escaped the full force of the attack. At one very big fire, there were dozens of pumps at work, including crews from Birmingham, Nuneaton and other surrounding towns.

If we get many consecutive nights of this sort of thing, I shall evacuate myself to Leicester for a night and out of the firing line, in order to get some sleep; because otherwise I shall be 'spark out' in a few days. Today I couldn't get down to any real work and everyone really felt the effect of nearly twelve hours in shelters. I'll drop a postcard to your mother to warn her that I may turn up at a few hours notice for a night in bed, but I don't suppose it will be necessary.

Sirens! 7.40 Off we go!

Here is the timetable of events for last few hours:

7.40   Sirens

7.42   I am on my way to the depot – walking

7.45   Down come dozens and dozens of incendiaries, all so it seems on wretched Foleshill. I pick out the nearest one, on the pavement nearby, and smother it with sand with the help of some civilians.

7.47   On the street to a small shop, burning very nicely with the incendiary under a sofa in the back room. I procure a stirrup pump from somewhere and with the help of two willing ladies from nearby houses, and after kicking in the doors, put out the fire.

7.55   Just round the corner, in the Foleshill Road, fires are everywhere. I tackle the nearest one in a haberdashery shop. Neither fire extinguishers from the cinema next door nor a stirrup pump have any effect on the blaze and after five minutes I have to leave it for the attention of a better equipped crew.

8.05   Report at the depot

8.07   Away with a crew to attend a timber yard nearby. This is blazing furiously and occupies all our efforts for the next few hours. Four other crews come to help us and eventually we are able to leave it – pretty well blacked out but still smouldering. Meanwhile we have put out another fire in an empty house 50 yards away. During all this time we have provided a grand target for Jerry and he knows it.

12.00   midnight. All clear (thank God!)

12.15   *Return to the station*

12.17   *Turn out to investigate a fire reported at a bakery which has received a direct hit from high explosive. It turns out to be the smoke from the baking ovens and we make it safe before leaving.*

12.30   *Back to the station*

12.31   *Off to a house with an attic bedroom burning (incendiary as usual)*

1.00   *Off to a call to a 'military objective' – which was Jerry's biggest bag the previous night and where a fire had broken out again. Found the situation well in hand and after waiting about for some time, came back. I was driving on this occasion – in thick fog.*

3.50   *Back to the station. The 'white' now being through, I toddle off home to get out of my clothes which have been saturated since 8 o'clock*

4.30   *After knocking up Mrs Rush for a hot water bottle and hot whiskey, I have a rub down and get to bed*

4.31   *Asleep*

10.00   *Wake up*

10.45   *Having breakfasted and written to my wife, I must hurry up and get dressed for a late arrival at the works*

So that's that, my dear. We have a warning in progress now, and Jerry is somewhere overhead, but it is still foggy and who's afraid of the Big Bad Wolf anyway. A good night's sleep I am now fit as a fiddle again and ready for what the night may bring. I really must finish …

Now that I was back in Leicester and as we moved further into 1941 Arthur decided that he could safely commute to Coventry rather than working there all day and being on fire service every night. He obtained a transfer to the local Leicester fire service for evening duties. We discussed the arrangements at Morland Avenue and both agreed that we could not go on as we were. We determined to find a small rented house where we would at least have some sort of married life on those occasions we were together.

We were fortunate to have the offer of a small property in Uppingham Road. I would have to cycle the three miles from our rented house to Morland Avenue every day to look after my mother, but that was a small price to pay for our new independence. We bought some furniture, a bed and a table and chairs, we had some crockery and glasses as wedding presents and my aunt Kitty gave us some items. Thus we were able to equip ourselves in a modest but adequate way. The journey to Morland Avenue meant crossing most of Leicester and I would cycle along Green Lane Road (which was anything but a green lane) and across the city in that way.

I loved having a home together with Arthur. It was so sad that there was a war on, but we enjoyed our lives as much as we could. We were only there at Uppingham Road for about four to five months before the Horsfall family from whom our house had been rented decided that they were moving back to Leicester. It seems that they deemed the major risk from bombing was now over, so we were put on notice to move out.

Initially it looked as if we were going to be homeless or have to move back into Morland Avenue. However, after many enquiries and a number of disappointments we managed to rent a top-floor flat in Springfield Road which was within walking distance of my parents' house. We rented this from a retired solicitor and his wife, Mr and Mrs Plummer. The flat was reached via two long flights of back stairs, steep and difficult to negotiate.

As Arthur was working long hours I worked hard on the move, carrying loads up and down stairs. On the day we got possession I did a huge amount of fetching and carrying but that night I felt very ill and fainted, which was unusual as I had thought myself pretty fit with all the sport and cycling I had been doing.

I went to the doctor the next day. He told me I was pregnant and that the baby was due in May.

CHAPTER THIRTY-ONE

The six coolies in soiled white cotton shalwar trousering and torn shirts shielded their faces under the wide brims of their straw hats. Throwing their picks and shovels into the open back of the tuc-tuc the three tallest crammed themselves into the cabin as the others struggled to find space to sit amongst the equipment in the rear. The overloaded machine coughed its way along the jungle road towards another coastal clearing near Singora.

Crushed between Bechtar Singh and the big Malayan guide, Stuart made further markings in the folder of maps and plans that contained the fruits of their journey of the last three days. Striking north across the Thai border from Khota Bharu they assessed every bridge and river crossing for both structural strength and destructive weakness. Each beach and seascape clearing was surveyed for landing potential, the six men apparently relaxing and cooling off by splashing in the shallows but in reality constantly checking for gradients and footings, lines of fire and areas suitable for storage. Others had been before and others would come after, but each assessment added to the picture and identified the places where supplies would be cached ready for the advancing forces of Operation Matador to make use of them.

Further inland, both the east and west jungle roads down which an enemy force would have to advance were similarly surveyed. Here the river crossings were more substantial: some were rusting girder bridges, some heavy timber structures, some with rope suspensions, others simply chained and fixed logs over narrower gullies. Then there were the rail bridges, punctuation points as the narrow-gauge railway line and its cuttings tore a passage through the tropical forest and rubber plantations. At each crossing the nature and stability of each structure was noted.

The group's target was the Ledge, a strip of the Kroh-Patani road crossing a raised north-facing area of scrubland breaking free from the thick jungle canopy. Here the line of sight extended fully two miles to the north. The steep incline rising to the plateau of the flattened ridge made vulnerable any advance to or from the south. To the east of this natural platform the north-south railway line could be seen. In the centre the Ledge straddled the road so that any attacking force would be forced into the open if it sought to advance.

Caution was vital. Stuart's party had passed groups which he suspected had similar missions to their own; no acknowledgement passed between them but the height and bone structure of some of the working parties denied their native origin. The native Thai people seemed relaxed by their presence, friendly faces suggesting an open acceptance of their attempts at subterfuge, but were there informers behind the veneer of acceptance? Rumours that the Japanese had their own teams of observers in this ostensibly neutral land were unsubstantiated. Secretly Stuart hoped that the stories were true as this would make more certain the intention to invade, and bring to pass the action that he both craved and feared.

South of the border, defence routes to Jitra were now in an advanced stage of construction. Matador would take the Allied forces north of the border, but if the Japanese broke through there would be a fall back to the Jitra line. Cutting the roads, thereby slowing or even turning the feared Japanese advance, was a strategic necessity. Demolition chambers were at the approaches to bridges, in high embankments and in deep cuttings. The chambers consisted of twelve-inch-diameter pipes: only a limited number were available and Stuart and his local volunteers improvised others. These hollow tubes were laid under the roadways ready for the insertion of cylindrical sheet-metal canisters containing the explosive charge. After loading the canisters were to be sealed and left ready for detonation by the retreating force. After Matador – on the pessimistic but realistic assumption that it would probably be turned and ultimately fail to defeat the Japanese force – the charges would be inserted and primed ready to destroy and delay elements of the invading army.

'All very well in theory,' said Teasdel when they had returned to their base and rejoined the mess, 'but it rather depends on the Japs sticking to the roads and not breaking out into the jungle. It also depends on us poor sapper buggers setting off the charges. Could be a bit wearing on the old nerves with a ruddy great tank bearing down as we light the blue touch paper!'

Stuart and his group had a brief respite before they returned to their duties in the north. They all caught up on their letters.

1.6.41

Dear All

News on Crete and the Hood, not good, thank heavens we got Bismarck. Heard the Roosevelt speech 'let me hold your coat'. Better if they got off their backsides and came into the war. Can only say we are enjoying ourselves, sort of holiday camp and work till 3.30. Lovely spot, burnt black. Glorious view but can't describe it. Made whoopee with two other subs in local town – hotel – cigars –cinema –cabaret – 2am.

Drawings and accounts to do now, hardly training for a fighting man. Never get out of Malaya unless the Japs come in, which I doubt more and more.

Lt Bhajat whom I knew in Poona (tennis) and saw off from station is first Indian VC of the war. The brother of Bhajat was with me in the mess when the news came through on the wireless. Back to old spot at end of week. Hear we are about to enter Damascus – troops on German/Russian border – still Japan does nothing, we wait and wait and prepare for trouble.

Back to the rubber plantations and surrounding jungle, back to the defence lines and the surveying of roads and bridges. Back also to constant exercises to develop and refine the fighting skills of the troops. Making the disciplined but inexperienced Indian sepoys and their VCOs work as a team with the laid-back Australians who were now a significant presence in the area was proving difficult. There were two- and three-day exercises, fought in the humidity of the jungle where every tree could hide an enemy and where tree cover meant that circling aircraft could not detect movement under the canopy of trees. For the sappers these fighting exercises were a diversion from their construction duties, but they grumbled amongst themselves at the unfair division of labour since they alone, as engineers, still had to work on after the infantry had finished their war games.

There was also the need to maintain contact with each man's distant family, individual exhaustion at the workload always overlaid by the constant fear that news of some personal loss or disaster would be concealed in the spasmodic and out-of-date correspondence.

23.6.41

Two months since I last heard from you. Now Germany has attacked Russia, we don't know whether to laugh or cry. If we and Russia and the States can't beat up Europe I would like to know the reason why. Japan have to make up their mind one way or other. Manoeuvres all week. Three day blitz, 22 miles in 24 hours once, RAF dive bombing, bombs and crackers. At one time I was tip of spearhead in bren carrier. Captured and recaptured by famous British Regiment! Boots not off for three days.

Miss the sea – at present we are as isolated as in Pengaree. Off on a trip for two or three days tomorrow. If only one did not have to talk in riddles! Shall hang head when I land in England – one of the few who missed the war!

Time ceased to have meaning. Each dragging hour dissolved into the next, weeks melted into months, and still Stuart waited. Frustration became a pain, a constant sickness of the heart. That sickness of being was fuelled by news of the war spreading across Europe, sinking deep into Russia, dominating North Africa and stretching long tendrils into Italy. Letters from home, intermittent and vastly delayed, painted images of hardship and deprivation. These elements expanded in the minds of the waiting forces, exaggerating their fears but sharpening their fighting appetite.

Stuart dreaded the nightly news bulletins; no longer did he open the rare letters from home with eagerness. Yes, he feared for the safety of his family, but he hated the immediacy of their involvement, juxtaposed with his own inaction.

Yet inaction was hardly an appropriate word. The pressure of work increased: there was growing intensity in the building, construction and preparation of yet more defences and fortifications. The constant advancement of the state of readiness gave some comfort and partly eased the hunger for battle. But would that battle ever come?

28.7.41

Had letters re Blitz on Notts and fire spotting. Sick and furious that I'm doing nothing. I rushed off to Assam, 13 months afterwards war was declared, I got overseas – and to do what? I swap a tea estate for a rubber estate. Another flap on, Indo-China and the USA, so freeze the Jap credits, may lead to something.

21.8.41

Lull in Far Eastern crisis before the storm? Roosevelt and Churchill meeting – talk of 'Common Peace'. Russia slowly pushed back, Japs not made up their mind. BBC talking of 'finest British units' in Malaya. Fair enough – but three years of war and I haven't seen a shot fired, perhaps I never shall? Have to give a long lecture in Urdu tomorrow, I am one of the few people who have spent so long in this climate, ten years. Still have to say nothing about work, especially us Sappers.

20.9.41

Nearly a year since we sailed for 'war' – and the Japs even less noisy than before. We get dark about 5, bad as Assam, rain three times a day and when it stops just – drip, drip, drip. We listen to mosquitoes as our war effort. Hear from your letters that Mary had to make an address to Wyggeston Girls School, more than 80 people – so Mary wins – but I have to do it in a foreign language. There are now nine of us planters in the section, work up to our eyebrows but I hope to get on a 'course' soon.

15.10.41

Been on a course for twelve days. Very secret, interesting and thrilling and worked frightfully hard. Travelled for two days and afterwards cinemas/cabarets/dances/night/shopping. A complete change of surroundings and real live Wrens and Waafs.

The course had been a final top up of the Special Operations Executive training at the Training School on Singapore Island. The main aim from Stuart's point of view was to better enable him to operate as one of the 'stay behind' parties equipped and trained to operate out of jungle hideouts for several months at a time. The locations had already been researched and provisioned in the past six months of clandestine exploration. The plan was that when an area was overrun, the groups would emerge to ambush road and rail traffic, or any other 'soft' target they could find. Major Spencer-Chapman, appointed by Colonel Killery, was the head of the Training School. Stuart already knew his methods and techniques.

Twelve days of huge activity: attack techniques and every other sort of operational training in daylight hours, lectures all evening and often further attack exercises at night. Stuart had thought he was already fit but as the days passed he found himself surpassing his previous aerobic levels. He revelled in the new-found strength and greater powers of endurance he had acquired. Then there was the advancing of previous skills: new explosives, refined detonator methodology and advanced structural detailing for collapsing large bridges – all had their place and their own expert lecturer.

'Another drink? What about a Screwdriver?'

Stuart had found the cocktail name to be a usefully suggestive line in the past. Combine it with a flutter of the manly eyelids and the seduction was started. Reference to a Between the Sheets was more delicate territory and he judged that Betty, the slim Wren he had singled out in the restaurant bar, was perhaps not yet ready for such an advance. She had been eating alone, and there had been only a token moment of reluctance before she had allowed herself to be diverted to sit up at the bar and accept a drink.

She questioned him: 'Tell me again what brings you to Singapore?'

Stuart tapped the side of his nose. 'Walls have ears and all that, old thing. Let's just say there is a specialist establishment on the island and I was sent on a refresher course there. Refresher in the sense that I'd already been trained in the wondrous specialist skills that I'm not allowed to tell you about, but now you see an Adonis of a man whose body and attributes are honed to perfection. Which leads me to observe that your body, from what I can see of it, appears also to have achieved perfection in every way.'

Betty laughed. 'And I thought you just told me you'd spent ten years deprived of female company in the backwaters of darkest Assam? I could add by suggesting that your perception of bodily perfection is clouded by your lack of experience – which is a silly remark, because I can guess that it was about to lead you to launch into the inevitable and predictable suggestion that you would be very happy to make up for that lack of experience in your hotel room. Do I look such an easy conquest?'

'Conquest suggests an element of pursuit – I was rather looking at it as a mutual exploration of interests with neither victor nor vanquished – but since you mention it, I've been billeted in rather a smart hotel which I would be happy to show you if you were so inclined.'

Betty's needs had been similar to his own. Boyfriend a submariner, apart for over a year, she reluctant to be seen out with officers stationed in Singapore in case others heard of it. Fears and frustrations of war, uncertainty for the future and distance from home inflamed the passions of their lonely ships passing in the tropical night.

19.10.41

Japanese government resigned. Moscow in a tight corner. Expect Japs will go for Russia? Japs still huffing and puffing and talking with the States but no nearer action. I long to do something active. So fed up, will jump for joy if Japs come in. More work and rain. Sappers get the most extraordinary sort of work to do. In Malaya over a year now – where shall we all be in another four years?

There had been some light relief. Back in Alor Star, combining supervision of the continuing preparations for Operation Matador with clandestine work on 'stay behind' projects, Stuart was able to relax in the mess. Tuesday evening was the usual cinema night, newsreels of the war in Europe followed by a feature film if available.

On this particular evening a good deal of beer and spirits had been consumed and both officers and men were on good form as they joined the other ranks in the corrugated iron-roofed cinema building. The film was not well acted and attention wandered until the moment when the tearful wife embraced the returning soldier hero.

'For six long and weary months I have waited for this moment, darling!'

'Only six sodding months – I've been waiting for six fucking years!'

came the shout from the back of the audience. Above the roar of laughter the unsuspecting actor swept on:

'Buried in jungle swamps, suffering malaria, surrounded by snakes, but always dreaming of you!'

The hall erupted in pandemonium.

CHAPTER THIRTY-TWO

'So what the fuck are we doing here?'

The drawled Australian question drew a laugh from Stuart. Jim Holden came from Brisbane and shared Stuart's philosophy of challenging authority. Stuart was visiting Khota Bharu to view the beach defences and to talk to fellow sappers about the progress of the Matador preparations.

'We, my wallaby-stuffing friend, are a deterrent,' said Stuart. 'By sitting up here in Malaya we frighten the Japanese sufficiently to stop them invading this snake-infested shoreline. Our masters tell us that Singapore is impregnable, that we are the deterrent and that if those yellow bastards really do want to go to war, Thailand is the nearest they are going to get to us.'

Jim reached for another beer, sprawling back in the canvas chair as they watched a group of turbaned Sikhs drilling in the shimmering heat of the cracked parade ground.

'Heard on the news yesterday that the Japs are refusing to quit Saigon, the Yanks are determined to cut off their oil supplies – what they call stopping "trade relations", and that bloody great conference in Singapore has decided there won't be an attack because their German pals are now fighting Russia and, anyway, the winter monsoon would prevent any invasion.'

'Hope you're right. Saigon's only two hundred miles behind that Indian officer's arse, and the Japanese navy has about a million more ships down here than we have. Come on, time for food.'

So saying, Stuart led the way to the mess hall. It was good to have Jim around, visiting from the 28th Australian Infantry, relieving some of the boredom of the usual colleagues from the 11th Indian Division including his own fellow sappers. He stopped and introduced a fellow tea planter, Tom Braithwaite from the Bokpara tea estate, who promptly invited Jim to join him in a whisky back in Assam once the war was over.

The memory of Assam made Stuart wonder how Monglee, Mary and Ann were doing: no news had come through for the past three months. It was still extraordinary to think that here he was, only a few months after celebrating his thirtieth birthday, a father of two illegitimate daughters of which his family in England had no knowledge. A smile came to his lips as he once more imagined the reaction of his stern-faced father as he told him that he had two half-breed granddaughters.

A sudden klaxon blast, repeated three times. The hubbub quickly died down as the loudspeakers crackled.

'All personnel to the mess hall immediately!'

A shifting of chairs as the sergeant major took over: food on plates bolted, crockery stacked, furniture moved, seats arranged to face the staging, men filing in and being seated in platoons and sections, an air of expectation and excitement.

Marching feet, and into the hall came the available officers, straightening ties as they filed in, followed by the adjutant and then an imposing figure.

'Who is that?' Jim had manoeuvred his way to Stuart's side.

'That is the great and glorious commander of the 6th Indian Infantry Brigade, Brigadier W. O. Lay, Distinguished Service Order, to you. Didn't know he was in the area.'

'Men. Whilst I am visiting the area I asked your Colonel if I might have a moment to address you. First, your work on the defences in this area is superb and I congratulate you. Second, I am able to give you some good news. I know that sometimes you feel you are isolated and forgotten. Whilst this may be understandable, I am pleased to tell you that it is not true. As an illustration of that I can now announce that there are at this moment two battleships positioning themselves in Singapore harbour, namely *Prince of Wales* and *Repulse*. For there to be two such warships in our theatre of war is excellent news, and sends the message that our role is important.

'Whilst I am not privy to the precise role these two ships will fulfil, I confidently expect that they will patrol the eastern seaboard from Singapore up to and beyond our positions close to the Thai border, and then onwards to the eastern and southern coasts of Thailand itself. The impact upon an invasion fleet, if such is launched as we have anticipated, can be imagined. The combination of seaborne guns firing on a fleet of landing vessels from the sea, taken together with the splendid defences you are building on the shore, should be fatal to any Japanese effort.

'Some of you may know that *Repulse* is perhaps regarded as getting on in years, but it is still hugely powerful. More importantly, *Prince of Wales* is more modern and has all the up-to-date sophistications that one might expect.

'Of course, battleships can be vulnerable to air attack. However, rest assured that our RAF analysts confidently predict that the range, fighting capability and manoeuvrability of our Hurricane and Buffalo aircraft is superior to anything that the Japanese can offer. In consequence, it is expected that any attempt to attack these ships will be "Repulsed".'

The officer paused, the anticipated laughter enabling him to take a sip of water before continuing.

'As to the expectation of whether or not the Japanese are actually intending to invade, there are two schools of thought ...'

'Damn, damn, damn, damn,' Stuart swore to himself, silently but savagely. All the recent pointers had been towards an invasion. All his hopes of finally being in a pitched battle with an enemy force were built upon the increasing certainty of a Japanese attack. In these new circumstances, surely the Japanese would not attempt to force a landing? Would they not now identify the risk that their invasion fleet would be decimated by the mighty firepower of the two battleships? What chance of worthwhile action now?

Before leaving Khota Bharu and returning to his unit, Stuart was given a tour of the defences at the mouth of the Kelantan River. This estuary broke up into a delta area of tributaries, lagoons, creeks and low islands. One of those tributaries, the Pengkalan Chopa, was seen as the most likely landing spot for an attacking force: two spits of land either side of the mouth had become the focus of the engineers' attention.

Stuart shielded his eyes from the fierce sun which reflected from the endlessly crossing lines of advancing and retreating surf. He could make out the concrete pillboxes in which the defenders' Bren guns would be positioned. Slit eyed, their impassive gaze took in the barrier of wire which straddled the entire width of the beach. Stuart was professionally impressed to hear that some three hundred miles of barbed wire had been deployed: first a double apron in triangular form which presented an enemy with a six-foot-high slope of wire to the front and an identical slope facing the other way; then a triple Dannert barrier – concertina rolls of razor wire; behind these seemingly impassable obstructions, over four thousand anti-personnel mines.

'Formidable!' But his words of praise belied his inner thoughts, ignoble as they were, that an attack might well be completely repulsed, and if the enemy failed to gain a foothold, would he yet have the opportunity to fight? And would not *Repulse* and *Prince of Wales* wreak havoc amongst an invasion fleet before it even reached the fortified if desecrated beaches?

CHAPTER THIRTY-THREE

Arthur was enormously pleased to hear that he was going to be a father. The news of my pregnancy seemed to revitalize my mother and Arthur's parents in Stratford said how pleased they were. I know that my own father was actually rather glad that he was going to be a grandfather, though he wasn't quite able to express this without some gloomy comments about what sort of a world the child was going to inherit. But that was just his manner and unsurprising in view of the war situation.

Being at the Springfield Road flat at least meant that my journey to Morland Avenue each day was short – I could either cycle or walk. Although the flat was on the third floor and the stairs were steep, I was happy in my pregnancy, and well cared for by Arthur when he was able to return home at night, which was now most of the time.

Arthur would boil a kettle to shave each morning at 6 a.m. and then either drive to Coventry in our newly acquired Austin 7, of which he was inordinately proud, or take the train. He was now working on a special engineering project which he would not tell me much about. He would usually come home, pretty tired, about 7 p.m. and I would give him a meal, but then most evenings he had to go out again to the fire station for lectures and drills.

I have mentioned that my father was travelling to Nottingham carrying out his Ministry of Health duties and that he would often be on fire-watching duty at the end of the day so could be very late home. As the Blitz progressed fire watching had been seen as of vital importance. Fire brigades could not cope with the blanket of incendiary bombs without help from each local community. There needed to be a watcher on the roof of buildings and if this could not be achieved voluntarily then compulsion was needed. Eventually it was directed that all able-bodied men under sixty should train for fire-watching duties and put in at least forty-eight hours per month on the roof tops of the cities and towns. My recollection is that father did much more than that. So, like most of the population, we were all immersed in the war effort.

Rationing was a constant feature and burden of our lives. Each individual, adult or child, was issued with a ration book, those of the children having a different-coloured cover. You had to register with a particular shopkeeper, although it was permitted to register with different shopkeepers for different products – for example, you might choose one shop for fish and another shop for meat. Coupons were stamped by the shopkeeper.

Allowances fluctuated as the war entered each different phase and supplies became more or less plentiful. I seem to recall that each month an individual was allowed four ounces of butter, twelve ounces of sugar, four ounces of bacon or ham and a tin of dried egg (the equivalent of six eggs). Meat was rationed by cost which enabled you to decide whether to have a small amount of an expensive cut or a larger amount of cheaper meat. Cheese was rationed from May 1941 as were, for instance, syrup and treacle.

Queuing was a way of life. Those foods that were not rationed were in short supply and we would all join a queue as a matter of routine, before enquiring from the person in front what commodity was believed to be on offer.

There was a small cluster of shops on Holbrook Road, on the other side of the London Road from Morland Avenue. Round the corner was the Co-operative store and separate Co-op fishmonger. Hicklings was the grocer's shop and Wickens the hardware shop. There was a butcher's a few yards away and a post office also. I did most of the family shopping here rather than in the centre of Leicester – it saved bus fares and our ration books were registered here. Sometimes Mr Hickling would come to the house and take an order from my mother, dutifully stamping the ration books when the produce was delivered. On some occasions I would take a cluster of ration books – Granny and Grandpa's, my father and mother's, mine and Arthur's, even that of Jessie the help if she was going to be with us at the relevant time. It was quite a mental exercise to work out which coupons to use from which book – and to contemplate what meal might be conjured up from the lean pickings available.

For those who had money to dine out the world was more flexible. Restaurants were permitted to serve a similar number of meals to the number served prior to the war and the details were of course registered and had to be kept to; but those with influence and funds were able to eat well on occasions. The rest of us had to make do: it was a time of 'digging for Britain' so gardens, parks and open spaces were dug up for growing vegetables and any other available food. Those who kept poultry were greatly in demand – perhaps the occasional egg might wander in the direction of a friend, or the passing chicken be diverted. Unrationed food, mainly offal but also rabbits and the like, was much sought after.

The government pumped out endless advice on healthy eating and 'making do' but the memory one has of those years is that eating was dull and rarely filling. Boiling was almost inevitable: frying was difficult because lard was rationed and olive oil was only available on doctor's prescription. Liquid paraffin could be used for frying if you felt your family was of a strong enough constitution!

As my pregnancy advanced and I grew larger, the war widened its area of conflict. The German army in Russia had advanced on Moscow; Finland, Hungary and Romania came into the war; our aircraft carrier *Ark Royal* was sunk off Gibraltar.

Of course we scrutinized the newspapers for information relevant to Malaya, conscious of fears of the build-up of Japanese forces in Indo-China. However, most of the news related to trade negotiations between the Allies and the Japanese. With so much happening on the war front, discussion on political manoeuvring rather passed me by. Anyway, surely the Japanese would not threaten to invade when we had such strength in Singapore? There was an article in *The Times* which summarized the situation:

Singapore today is the core of British strength in the Far East. The history of the last eighteen months in Malaya has been one of unremitting effort to build up armed strength.

We felt rather proud of Stuart's hard work when we read this. The article went on to say:

Whilst the dense jungle of the northern Malay states makes it unlikely that an enemy will ever try to reach Singapore by marching down the 400 mile peninsula, landings off the coast might well be attempted. Singapore's significance can perhaps best be appreciated if the hypothetical question is asked: What would happen if it fell to the enemy? The answer is obvious. Neither the British nor American navies could operate in the western Pacific since they would have no base from which to operate. ... Australia, New Zealand, to say nothing of Malaya and the Indies, would lie wide open to the invader. With Singapore stand and fall the destinies, not of countries only, but of whole continents.

Our relative complacency disappeared when on 8th December we saw the headline:

JAPANESE WARSHIPS SPOTTED – Activity in the South

The Times said that Catalina flying boats of the RAF had sighted ships 'presumed to be Japanese' cruising in the Gulf of Siam towards Bangkok. The article said that it was impossible to say if this was a demonstration or an indication of 'more serious developments' but that there was still 'a tendency to counsel moderation in interpreting events and pessimism is discouraged'. Further, 'it is considered that some estimates of the number of Japanese troops in Indo-China are exaggerated'.

No sooner had we read the papers than the radio was talking of Japanese attacks.

Suddenly came the dramatic news of the Japanese dive-bombing the American fleet at Pearl Harbor. Then a broadcast talking of Japanese planes making a bombing raid on Singapore. Glued to the radio, it was only a few hours before we heard the bulletin we had feared – that the Japanese had landed in Thailand and their invasion fleet was trying to gain a foothold in Malaya.

At last Stuart had the wish that he had expressed in so many letters – he was in the front line of the fighting.

We were at war with Japan.

CHAPTER THIRTY-FOUR

The ripple of an offshore breeze gently rattled the long green blades of the palm tree overhead. Stuart took another draw of his iced gin and tonic and returned to his letter writing. Another beautiful day beckoned. Already he felt the unaccustomed relaxation of the muscles in his shoulders, the tensions of the past months beginning to fade. He took a moment to gaze again at the backcloth of green hills above the pale blue of the bay with its fringe of white sand. He fought to avoid fevered visions of the bombed cities of his home country, flames mingling with grey rain, and the contrast with his present situation.

24.11.41

Had letter (only one) but with Christmas cheque. Happy Christmas! Can't say anything, fear of number of multi-nationals that make up the Malyasian population. Anyway, now on leave – first pukka leave since joined up. Gorgeous spot, top of small hill, little hotel. Separate bungalows, sitting room as well as bedroom. Swimming pool and tennis courts. Palm trees and mountains. Golden sands. Black rocks. Japs headline news. Washington talks over?

The same day – cut to total chaos – could it be the centre of Calcutta? Of course it wasn't; but the similarity was in Stuart's mind as he threw himself, suitcase in hand, out of the slowly moving train from Penang into a mêlée of domestic and thundering military traffic mixed with running people and frightened animals, all in a state of high alert. Was it only four hours since he had sat, gin in hand, at the edge of paradise? Then there had come the hurrying feet of the usually imperturbable hotel manager, waving the flimsy telegram, breaking his reverie:

'Sir! Sir! Sir! Leave cancelled, return soonest!'

He supposed that he should have taken issue with such a confidential telegram being read by the manager but the whole country was on tenterhooks, fearing invasion, and the impact of his recall was hardly going to be capable of concealment.

The train from Penang had been held for him. Ejected from the hotel shooting brake to which he had been so gracefully welcomed seven short days before; propelled by willing hands, thrust past the ticket office; launched on to the waiting train; then the grinding impatience of the slow wheezing progression through the peaceful foothills and silent rubber plantations to the assembly point for the Matador force.

Stuart's section was a vital part of the North-West strike force. Centred on the railway line the sappers' first function was to check the line for explosives and debris: not that High Command's expectation that fifth columnists would sabotage the rails in advance was widely accepted. This precautionary slow-moving first troop train would then be followed by others, whilst alongside the railway the supporting infantry and mechanized forces would thrust forward.

The sheer volume of men, of transport and armed vehicles, of artillery pieces and equipment, assaulted the eyes. All were drenched by the continuous tropical rain. The ears were attacked by a mixed cacophony of fired-up steam locomotives, the high-revving engines of armoured carriers, the lower sound register of waiting lorries, and shouted commands and tramping feet, all overlaid by the clattering roar of Buffalo and Hurricane aircraft passing overhead.

'Enemy fleet sighted in the Gulf – enemy aircraft flying south – waiting for go on Matador – ready to roll any time now ...'

It had taken Stuart but four hours from beach to bridgehead. He was struggling into his full battledress as Teasdel breathlessly brought him up to date.

Now, four more hours passed as the columns waited for the signal to advance. In the command building alongside the assembly yard senior officers willed the telegraph to chatter out the signal to move. Frustration spilled over into anger, field telephones were cranked, communication cables checked – and still they waited.

'Seems that Brooke-Popham believes the ships may be a feint to cause us to move into Thailand and create a major incident. Unbelievable! What was the point of all this preparation if there was no one prepared to throw the switch?'

The engines had been turned off. The head of steam in the locomotives had been diminished. Sodden in the tropical rainstorm the waiting troops had taken off their helmets and webbing. Two field kitchens had been broken out and were serving a belated meal to chosen shifts of men. Anger and foreboding in equal measure hung in the steaming humidity of the monsoon in the late afternoon.

The hours crawled by. At last Stuart and his fellow officers were summoned to a meeting at battle headquarters, a mile behind the most forward troop positions. They threw themselves into the back of a lorry for the short journey. Taking what he guessed would be the last opportunity to put pen to paper, realising that the letter might never be delivered but still feeling the compulsion to communicate, Stuart wrote:

1.12.41

All leave cancelled. Lying in bathing costume when summonsed. Back in four frantic hours. Bit of a flap, was away for a week only. Writing this in back of truck. This looks like the real thing. May be the last letter for some time. Don't worry about me, action at last! Love to you all.

The briefing was short and savage. Spitting out his understanding of the situation, Major-General Murray-Lyon's staccato delivery did nothing to conceal his rage.

High Command had delayed the decision on Matador: it seemed that political factors had intervened. It was now too late for it to be launched.

The invasion was not a feint. The stark reality was that the Japanese fleet was attacking Khota Bharu and other points further north.

As yet unconfirmed news was coming in of a Japanese dive-bomb attack on the American fleet at Pearl Harbor. A Japanese force was also attacking Hong Kong.

Japanese aircraft had attacked Singapore itself.

Frozen in their seats, silent, but with their minds and stomachs churning, the assembled officers listened in fascination.

'We can only hope to God that the Jap invasion force is poorly equipped and that their soldiers are badly trained. If not, and they succeed in landing, you may think our troops are as lambs to the slaughter. What we shall do is to fight them to the utmost of our ability. However, we know that the defences at Kota Bharu are good – that is our best opportunity to repulse the enemy fleet. Because the highlands are between us and the east coast, and because the railways are ours at present, this seems to me to be our best chance.

'I am in command and I intend to start by making an incursion into Thailand to establish whether or not the planned bridgehead on the Ledge is still an achievable objective. At the worst we will be able to activate some of the demolition work to hinder the enemy. I know that with Matador cancelled this may be too late, but the invasion force will take time to group itself for advance and if conditions are right we are going to do our damnedest to cause them difficulties towards the east.

'We also need to delay them before they reach Jitra on the western side. In the meantime, maximum effort will be put into the defence line at Jitra but I want two detachments to advance northwards to delay the Japanese advance and give us more time. The detachment at Kampong Imam will make an expedition by rail, with a demolitions train and supporting forces. Your section commanders will now deal with the detail. May God go with us all.'

Stuart's 3rd Field Company moved north-west with the 1/8th Punjab, the 7th Mountain battery and the 373rd Anti-tank battery. They understood the need to use their mobile detachments to delay the advance but time was against them: breaking news was that following the successful Japanese landings at Singora and Patani the invaders were rushing south in two columns.

The jeep carrying Teasdel and Stuart roared through to the railway line where they flung themselves off and hurriedly pushed through the troops to the leading steam engine to the front of which a flatbed wagon had been connected. On its wooden base a cordon of sandbags, two deep and three in height but open at the front, left space for a man to lie facing forward over the track. Stuart waited to take up his position, chosen to watch for planted explosives and other hazards and to signal the driver as the convoy moved forward.

Stuart lay on the flatbed truck ahead of the engine. On either side of the track were the deep shadows of the jungle and neither Stuart, as he lay prone with his head overhanging the rails, nor the soldiers manning the machine guns between each troop coach could escape the torrential rain. Progress was slow, but the risk of sabotage at this stage seemed small so Stuart soon asked for an increase in speed, which request was quickly granted. He well knew that if he failed to spot the signs of buried explosives he would be the first to die, but in his mind was the need to move quickly if the expedition was to have any prospect of success. They had covered some thirty miles, minor river crossings had been made and they now approached the main bridge at Choorak. He had studied this in earlier reconnaissance, and as the solid ground under the track gave way to the open slats over the brown river beneath he saw the steel girders to which charges would need to be fixed for demolition,

A huge explosion down river to the left. For some hours Stuart had been aware of the constant aircraft overhead and the detonations far ahead of the train, but now he realized that the Buffalo aircraft were lower and to the west. Machine-gun fire, more explosions in the jungle perhaps a mile away. The train lurched to a halt. Teasdel ran alongside the bridge to the front of the engine as shouted commands brought the troops tumbling out of the carriages on either side of the rails.

'The Japs are parallel to us in the east! Christ knows how the buggers have managed to move so fast! We will be cut off if the RAF can't hold them back. Orders are to blow the bridge and then get the hell out!'

CHAPTER THIRTY-FIVE

The news of the invasion of Malaya had shocked us all, and each day after the war with Japan started we scoured newspapers for any information as to the progress of the campaign. The headlines announcing the declaration of war against Japan announced:

INVADERS BEING HOTLY ENGAGED IN MALAYA
SEA, LAND AND AIR FIGHTING

and seemed to give some encouraging news:

by 8am all remaining enemy ships off Kota Bharu appeared to be retiring northward, leaving some landing craft and troops ashore, who were being mopped up by our land forces.

Only two days later our confidence was further bolstered by *The Times*:

HARD FIGHTING IN MALAYA
MORE JAPANESE LANDINGS
Enemy striving to gain local air superiority
The strategy of making a drive towards the peninsula has long been foreseen and for several months there has been a strong force from the Empire armies in Malaya guarding the northern frontier. The Japanese will certainly come up against formidable opposition if and when they clash with those defenders.

Our optimism did not last in the face of enemy news agency claims that northern Malaya had been occupied and

unconfirmed reports circulated by the German News Agency state that Japanese formations have crossed Thailand's northern frontier and are pushing towards the Burma Road.

In the midst of this uncertainty the most unbelievable news came through. I was at the shops when I overheard someone say we had lost two battleships.

It was 11ᵗʰ December, only days after the invasion, and I rushed home to put on the radio. My mother and I were horrified to hear that the Japanese had sunk both of our great battleships *Repulse* and *Prince of Wales* off the Malayan coast.

The headlines of the sinking shocked the whole nation. It was devastating to have such bad tidings in those early days of the campaign when we were still reeling from the simultaneous Japanese invasion and the bombing at Pearl Harbor. Inevitably within our household we were to become particularly fearful for Stuart's well-being.

It was about a week after the invasion that we had Stuart's letter of 1ˢᵗ December – somehow that had got through.

Naturally we thought of Stuart all the time. My father sent frequent letters to him as a matter of course, but we knew that communications had been intermittent prior to the Japanese invasion and in the days thereafter we heard nothing more so we did not know whether or not our letters were actually reaching their destination. We did not know of Operation Matador since Stuart had not been allowed to give us any such code names. If we had read that Matador had been delayed and then cancelled I doubt it would have registered with us, but in any case that was not the sort of information appearing in the newspapers.

The trouble with the newspaper coverage was that so much more was happening on other war fronts and Malaya was often pushed into the background. I remember on one particular day, 13ᵗʰ December, reading separate headlines with accompanying articles on

ACTIVE RUSSIAN GUERILLAS
NO RUSSIAN PEACE WITH HITLER
PRESSING ON IN LIBYA
HONGKONG UNDER ASSAULT
THE OUTRAGE OF HAWAII
ITALIAN CRUISERS TORPEDOED
before finally reading briefly of
VIOLENT FIGHTING IN NORTH MALAYA

As the days went by the papers began to talk of rearguard action in Malaya so we were acutely aware that our army was retreating but detail was frustratingly elusive. We tried to draw some encouragement from a number of bullish newspaper articles talking of our strengths. One example, which was subsequently proved to be quite wrong, said smugly:

In the air our fighters have shown themselves to be faster and more manoeuvrable than any aircraft possessed by the enemy, but the latter has continued to enjoy numerical supremacy.

On another day we learned:

The enemy activity has died down in Malaya, owing to the exhaustion of his forces and heavy casualties inflicted by the defenders. British troops arriving at Kuala Lumpur from the front praise the fighting qualities of the Indian troops: 'Once we were up against it those Punjabis were tremendous ...'

These brief moments of positive reporting were rare and in the main the news continued to be depressing. As December advanced we read:

After severe fighting involving heavy losses on both sides, the enemy has gained ground in the north western province of Kedah. The situation is considered to have many dangerous possibilities, and some commentaries from London and elsewhere sometimes appear to observers to take an over-optimistic view of the situation.

This cautionary view proved to be right as we moved towards Christmas and heard on 22nd December:

The news is grave tonight. Our forces have been obliged to retreat in Malaya. This retreat exposes Penang to attack and as we have not sufficient troops to garrison it, it has been necessary to evacuate the majority of the civilian population.

Next we heard that Penang had fallen with 'savage bombing' of civilians. Only two days later the papers expressed surprise that our troops had retreated 'further south than anticipated' and stressed the necessity of forming a front upon which resistance to the Japanese advances could be made. For our part as passive listeners in Morland Avenue we were fast losing confidence in this happening.

There was one moment of great excitement in those anxious weeks after the early December Japanese landing and that was when on Christmas Eve a telegram arrived. Stuart had somehow managed to send us a Christmas message simply saying that he was 'alive and well', but without giving us any detail. It was wonderful to have even that brief word since it was clear from the news that the fighting was fierce and continuous.

At least he was still alive.

Each evening my father would settle down with my mother to listen to the nine o'clock news, but there was rarely anything that we had not heard on the news bulletins during the day.

Christmas came and went, with that one telegram to console us. The news continued to depress, on 27th December:

Our army in the North, after initial disorganization caused by the sudden and unexpectedly heavy Japanese onslaught, has pulled itself together. Even though we are still withdrawing southward, fighting is at least orderly and controlled. The country favours the invaders, as it is impossible to establish a continuous line while the enemy has sufficient men for constant flanking movements through the rubber plantations on each side of the roads, down the rivers and along the jungle tracks. It is the middle of the rainy season and every day there are heavy tropical downpours which soak the troops to the skin. The Japanese use bicycles on many roads and in certain places they have taken to the jungle streams in collapsible rubber boats. The initial fighting was severe, men who had lost contact with the main body of the British forces near the frontier returned to their units after lone journeys of up to 200 miles.

Now the New Year was upon us and we moved into a cold and wintry January. Despite the freezing weather at home our thoughts were still overseas. It seemed clear that the Japanese ruled the skies over Malaya and that dogged rearguard actions were being fought. There was talk of commando action behind enemy lines but as the month advanced we read of withdrawal to positions south of Slim River which I could see from my schoolgirl atlas would put Kuala Lumpur at risk.

On 11th January 1942 my father wrote:

My dear Stuart

You are constantly in the thoughts of us all and we can only hope and pray for your safety. The Japs are now in and around Kuala Lumpur. We continue to hope for a change of news. What a blessing it is that Russia maintains her drive. It does make the future more certain and one imagines that the Boche is feeling somewhat uneasy. ...

Now Kuala Lumpur fell. Was Stuart still alive? We had no idea. By 14th January *The Times* was reporting:

The British forces in Malaya have fallen back from their positions twenty miles to the south of Kuala Lumpur to a new line well to the south of that city. All last Saturday and all through the night and through a large part of Sunday hundreds of vehicles rolled south on the main road from Kuala Lumpur.

And the next day:

Reports indicate that British resistance up to the borders of Johore was virtually crushed. Large areas evacuated by British forces.

17 January

Our troops have been fighting with little or no rest because Japanese landings on the West coast have forced the employment of reserve troops which would otherwise have been resting. The work of Sappers and Miners has been particularly impressive in blowing up bridges, railways and roads, often only just before the arrival of the enemy. Some Indian units have been amongst those engaged in this demolition work.

This passage helped fuel my imagination that Stuart was at the forefront of this activity. If only we could be told that he was still alive.

And so the stories of retreats and rearguard actions continued. We guessed that the newspapers were probably restricted from telling us the whole truth. On 24th January my father wrote again:

My dear Stuart

No news from you since the arrival of the Christmas cable and letter news up to mid November. It may be weeks before we hear from you. Malaya is indeed an anxiety for us both from the general and personal point of view. Tonight only sixty-five miles from Singapore! How much further? Can we reply effectively? We continue to hope and personally I remain hopeful because the impossible cannot happen. And tonight another retreat in Libya! It is a good thing Russia keeps on so wonderfully. She is absolutely marvellous ...

Poor mother, listening to the news hour by hour, depressively downhearted but with an overlay of nervous energy keeping her going until the next transmission. One of her letters started:

Darling Tootoo

The days drag on and no word from you and we don't want word of as that might be bad news. We try, but it is impossible to picture what you are going through ...

Despairing, we read of the advance of the Japanese army down the peninsula, finally as far as Johore. We were now aware that the enemy forces had reached the straits overlooking Singapore Island itself. My father wrote:

7th February 1942

My dear Stuart

We have been extremely anxious for two months and now if possible the anxiety is increasing owing to the lapse of time and no news. Our main comfort is that we feel that it is probable that the exigencies of the situation prevent your sending a cable. It is now the siege of Singapore and the dice are hardly loaded in your favour. But we hope that you are back there and that you will be protected.

The whole of Britain was holding its breath. The nation had been taught that Singapore was impregnable, my father not alone in saying that 'the impossible cannot happen'. Having said that we had been knocked sideways by the news of the loss of the *Repulse* and *Prince of Wales* which had been a massive body blow to national morale. Daily news of constant retreats only added to the collective anxiety.

There was huge excitement at Morland Avenue when a letter in Stuart's distinctive handwriting finally arrived. As my mother and I identified the airmail envelope on the mat behind the letterbox we fell on it and tore it open.

25th December 1941.

What a Christmas! Last two or three days not so bad but for bombing. Got last letter in lull before storm. Went on train to Thailand, blown a large bridge day after storm broke and not many sensations have not been through in last fortnight. Not under shell fire (save mortars) but pretty well everything else. In the line as infantry – very unpleasant. Writing on knee in lorry. Lost count of bridges blown up – nearly broken my heart, smashing of engines. Have had wind up sky high at times. Fear of unknown, not as frightened under rifle and machine gun fire as expected. Lost lot of friends. Bill Williamson, etc. Hope will rebuild bridges and hope Jap success is flash in pan and we'll push them back to the sea. Lot of things to settle, lost most of kit, all mufti, photos, etc. As soon as the Yanks get going, can't lose now if we tried! Damnation to the Japs!

Once we had devoured the contents we telephoned my father in Nottingham to tell him that a letter had come through. He came home early and must have read the letter through three times before he was able to speak. It was obvious that he was so very pleased, as were we all, that we had such news of Stuart's exploits.

Depressingly, my sensible father soon poured cold water on our initial enthusiasm by reminding us that the date of the letter coincided with the Christmas telegram. In other words, it told us nothing about Stuart's survival that we did not know already. A desperate month of the campaign had passed in the meantime.

When Arthur came home to our flat that night he and I went through every word that had been written. Whilst we had at least some news to pass on to friends and family we were all aware that the absence of anything more up to date did not bode well.

The very next day the newspapers carried the headline
CAUSEWAY BLOWN; BATTLE OF SINGAPORE BEGINS
followed by a quotation from 'Lieutenant-General A E Percival G O C Malaya':

The battle of Malaya has come to an end and the battle of Singapore has started. For nearly two months our troops have fought an enemy who has had the advantage of great air superiority and considerable freedom of movement by sea. Our task has been both to impose losses on the enemy and to gain time to enable the forces of the Allies to be concentrated for this struggle in the Far East. Today we stand beleaguered in our island fortress. Our task is to hold this fortress until help can come, as assuredly it will.

Britain was in the grip of one of the worst winters in memory. Snow continued to fall and villages were cut off. In Cheshire there was continuous snowfall for twelve solid hours. My father was finding it very difficult to commute to Nottingham and even trips to the local shops were hazardous. It seemed unreal to be reading of the heat and humidity of fighting conditions in Malaya whilst we were battling with snowdrifts and huddling round our gas fire to keep warm.

On 6th February we were told that even soap was to be rationed, to only four ounces per person per week: such were the minor, if real, hardships at home as we struggled to come to terms with potential defeat in the Far East. Life was full of extraordinary contrasts.

We hoped and prayed that the news of reinforcements approaching Singapore would turn the situation round but then, often on the same day, we heard of oil tanks being ablaze and continuous bombing raids by the Japanese air force. What were we to believe?

Two more weeks of desperate anxiety, the whole country speculating about what was happening. Despite his iron external control I could see my father's dread of the outcome. Finally, on 15th February 1942, there came the announcement over the radio.

Our army in Singapore had surrendered.

CHAPTER THIRTY-SIX

The nation was horrified. We had thought that Singapore was impregnable – how could this have happened? From our personal point of view we did not know what to think, we had had no direct information, and now we began to hear of huge numbers of prisoners of war. Had Stuart survived? Was he wounded and would we hear of him from hospital? Would details of prisoners not come through soon?

Once more we gathered round the wireless set to hear Winston Churchill's words:

A heavy and far-reaching military defeat – one of those moments when the British nation could draw from the heart of misfortune the vital impulse of victory. We must not underrate the power and malice of our latest foe. But neither must we undervalue the gigantic overwhelming forces which now stand in the line with us in this world struggle for freedom.

We appreciated the sheer scale of the tragedy with tens of thousands of troops involved, we read and read again the details of the casualties as they were published, but there was so little precise information available.

Japanese claim to have taken prisoner 60,000 imperial troops at Singapore, figures are not disputed in London where, however, it is pointed out that no exact figure can be given until the casualties are known. Tokyo states that this force consisted of 15,000 British, 13,000 Australian and 32,000 Indian soldiers.

Was Stuart one of these? One could only sit and hope whilst life went on and my pregnancy advanced.

Then particular fears emerged as news came in of Japanese atrocities towards troops in Hong Kong. Our government confirmed the worrying news that

> there have been no reports of treatment of prisoners and the Government could not regard the situation as satisfactory until Japan allowed the International Red Cross to function.

As we continued to shiver and the newspapers reported that February 1942 had been colder over England and Wales than any February since 1895, we read that the Red Cross had protested over 'Japanese barbarity' in Hong Kong

> which would come as an especial shock to all the relatives of the many thousands of British subjects who have fallen into Japanese hands.

There were also fears that Australia was at risk of invasion. Darwin had been bombed by the Japanese and the Australian nation was mobilized. The fate of individual soldiers on Singapore Island seemed almost to have been forgotten.

It was on 31st March, over six weeks after the surrender, that an envelope came from the War Office addressed to my father. By chance he was at home that day and we gathered round as he opened it. I could see him fighting for control as he saw the reference at the top of the page:

0.8.2187.P (Casualties)

He read the letter carefully but not out loud, simply said 'missing' and passed the letter to my mother who then gave it to me when her tears prevented her from reading further. I remember the key passage:

> I am directed to inform you that according to the latest information available in this office your son, 2nd Lieutenant S V Poyser, Royal Engineers, was serving in Malaya during the hostilities which terminated in the capitulation of Singapore on the 15th February 1942. Every endeavour is being made through diplomatic and other channels to obtain information concerning him. It is hoped that he is safe and, although he may be a prisoner of war, it is necessary to post him as 'missing' pending receipt of some definite information.

We were at the same time enormously depressed and slightly relieved. Depressed because we all knew that a 'missing' letter was usually the prelude to the worst news coming; marginally relieved because there was no actual confirmation that he had been killed. We knew that the number of prisoners of war was huge and we felt sure that very many of them must be unaccounted for in the particular circumstances of the surrender.

That evening Arthur tried to reassure me by stressing the words 'it is hoped that he is safe'. He felt that at least there was some hope.

I occupied myself by copying out Stuart's Christmas letter and the War Office letter by hand and sending them on to relatives and friends. We of course spoke to Louise on the telephone and I sent the letters to Stuart's old girlfriends, to the Blacks in Scotland and to Epsom College.

Then, ironically but dramatically, another letter reached us apparently written on 15th January, four weeks before the fall of Singapore.

15th January 1942
No.3 Field Company S/M Malaya

I am still whole and fit, how or why I don't quite know, but I am. I've been very lucky. We are 'out of it' now for a bit, back behind the line to refit and reform.

I think I last wrote about Christmas, it seems years ago. I haven't had a letter or anything from anyone since the war started. I haven't seen a newspaper more than once or twice, and only heard the wireless about three times, we get odd pamphlets about the outside world sometimes.

I am now 2nd in command. Teasdel and I are the only one's left of the original officers of 3rd Company who sailed overseas. Beattie went three or four days ago, he may be still alive, no-one actually saw him killed, but he will be even luckier than I was if he gets back. I've lost everything I possess three times!!! That is I've collected, begged, borrowed or stolen another set including three cars and lost each one, the only original things I possess are my boots, revolver and identity discs!

I almost had a direct hit on one car by a large bomb, I have now got Beattie's clothes on and managed to collect another car. I was cut off three times in eight hours, four days ago, and lay in a ditch for the five longest minutes of my life with a Jap tank on the road within six feet of me and hell going on all around, our own guns and bullets bursting all around me. I shall perhaps be able to tell you all the details one day.

I've wandered about alone in a swamp and jungle like a hunted animal but by the grace of God I've got back. I did one walk of 20 miles non-stop, I daren't stop as I'd never have started again!

I've had adventures and thrills and frights to last a hundred lifetimes. Almost the longest retreat in history and being Sappers just about the last back all along, I can't wait to tell you the bridges I've blown up and the scorched earth I've created. I've lived through the last month's hell and now for the first time I've done everything – eaten, washed, shaved, rested and stand a good chance of being alive this time next week!!

What a life! What a war! But we'll be OK soon now that aeroplanes and help are arriving. What a lot of bridges we shall have to build. We shall become as expert as we have become at destroying them, there are not many people who have blown up as many bridges as I have, we Sappers in Malaya must be the demolition experts of the world!!

I'll try and send a cable to let you know I'm OK. We may be able to get some mail now, and there is some chance of the mail going if it reaches you (I wonder if my other two letters did?) Let Louise know, she is probably worried, poor girl.

Quite a lot of planters have got through, the devil looks after its own! Roach of Digboi, Bill Merton and Bill Williamson are the only one's who haven't as far as I know. Poor old Roach was killed quite near me. Rusty Howell is OK.

Well, touch wood I may be able to write again soon, heaven only knows but it looks as if we are out of it for a day or two.

Take care of yourselves, keep smiling and DON'T WORRY

Love to you all

Stuart

It was an amazing description of events and when my father read it I could see his enormous pride in what Stuart had been through, contrasting with his desperation that his son was missing and probably dead.

I read the letter so many times that I could have recited it word for word. '… wandered alone in the jungle like a hunted animal' – the phrases went round and round in my brain. Again I copied out the letter and circulated it to Louise and others.

But was my brother still alive?

CHAPTER THIRTY-SEVEN

The baby, nicknamed 'Boady' (being short for Boadicea), was due on 23rd April 1942 but was late. It was not the best of times. Everyone was very tense, Arthur was very tired and overworked, my father was depressed with the lack of news of Stuart and my mother was not only clinically depressed but also had very little help. Food was rationed and scarce.

On 2nd May I was admitted to Fielding Johnson Hospital and after thirty-six hours of long and difficult labour our son Christopher Stuart Martin Mitchell was born. In the circumstances it was appropriate that Arthur and I should choose Stuart as the second name.

Sadly, I was badly nursed – indeed the sister in charge resigned afterwards, apparently by way of admission of what had gone wrong. I was in great discomfort with lots of stitches and could not sleep; in my exhaustion I got out of bed when I was not meant to and went downhill as a result. I was ordered to have full-time nursing and it was three long weeks before I was discharged. I had difficulty feeding Christopher and felt wretched; I ran a temperature and deep breast abscesses were diagnosed. I was operated on at the house and the abscesses were filled with yards of dressing and gauze; my temperature peaked at 104 degrees and another operation was needed. It was ten weeks before Arthur and I were to be together again in our small Springfield Road flat.

Arthur was a very proud father and helped with the baby in every way he could. In his spare time he retired to our small bathroom where he had started to build 'the Red Engine', a three-foot-long wooden model of a railway engine with big wooden wheels ready for the toddler that Christopher was soon to become. The sounds of sawing and sanding lasted well into each carpentry night and I had to become immune to the sawdust that stood on each bathroom surface and permeated our small flat.

At weekends we would sometimes go to Stratford to show Christopher off to his paternal grandparents or perhaps to Birmingham to catch up with old friends. Bill Gaman, Stuart and Arthur's great friend from Birmingham with whom we had been skiing on that memorable holiday in Val d'Isère, and his wife Huldah had also become parents for the first time. Bill, all six foot six of him, became one of Christopher's godfathers. An example of the light-hearted exchanges they had is found in the note that Bill wrote from Birmingham in May 1942 enclosing a poem headed 'Father's Lament' which included the verses:

Christopher Stuart has boisterous poise
(and John C Gaman's noise annoys)
In later years they'll wax their skis
And soar uphill into the breeze
They'll be boys with quelque poise ...
Now Mary has a little lamb
And Huldah Mary too
Before so long the erstwhile pram
Will be somewhat 'de trop'
When Christopher Stuart is six feet two
And father ninety-six
There'll be some fun, that's mighty true
When Stuart's up to his tricks.

Not to be outdone, Arthur responded with his own poem, 'Reply to a Father's Lament':

Why should you grieve so, laddy
It really isn't right
The fact that you're a daddy

Should make the world seem bright!
I think myself quite clever
To do what I have done
In my cap's a feather
And I think it's fun
So dry your tears, you silly goofs
And let your feelings loose
For I am simply cock-a-hoop
Come, Gaman, shall we schusse?

Despite the excitement of Christopher's arrival, and the attention that he attracted from family and friends, our fears as to Stuart's fate hung over us. It was the wait that was the worst, month after month and no news. Somehow an important part of each of our lives was in limbo.

North Africa, Italy and Greece were new battlegrounds. In the East, Burma had fallen with massive casualties. The news that General Orde Wingate's Chindits were making incursions as a prelude to an Allied reinvasion of Burma failed to raise our spirits.

Inevitably we were no longer optimistic that Stuart might somehow have survived as a prisoner.

Then, nearly four months after Singapore had fallen, a letter arrived from Lieutenant Colonel Steedman from Bangalore:

6 June 1942

Dear Dr. Poyser

I was your son's CRE and was evacuated from Singapore 24 hours before the capitulation. I wish to give you the latest information I have about him. I much regret that his section went missing from the morning of the 12th February and from enquiries I have made of others who came away later than I, there was no news of him up to the time of the capitulation.

His company was being used as infantry in the somewhat confused fighting of that day and a large part seems to have been cut off. I can only hope that he is a prisoner.

I am sincere when I say that I had no officer who excelled your son in gallantry, energy and efficiency. He was always in the thick of things and where they were stickiest. His fund of humour and amusing light hearted descriptions of his adventures were a tonic to us all. I wish I were able to give you better more definite news.

Life had to go on despite the lack of news. My mother was not coping well: shortages sometimes meant that she had to queue at the town hall for such meat as might be available, mainly offal and spam, and she then had my father to cook for when he returned from Nottingham each evening. The knowledge that Stuart was still missing and the fact that the war was going so badly caused her depression to worsen.

Arthur and I were at least able to enjoy our brief family life at the flat and for many months we were a proper married couple. It was tremendously tiring to have to carry Christopher and all his paraphernalia up and down three flights of stairs but I kept saying to myself, at least I have a husband who is coming home at night.

It seems mundane, but 'doing' the washing was a constant worry as we had only one tiny washbasin with a cold tap in the bathroom and a hot-water geyser over the bath. There was nowhere to hang out our washing because our landlady, Mrs Plummer, would not permit anything to be hung either in her garden or in the back yard. All I could do was boil the nappies in a big aluminium basin on the gas stove, hand wring them, and then either drape them with our other washing round the gas fire in the kitchen or put them into the pram and take them to Morland Avenue to hang outside in the yard there. Very primitive, but at least it meant that Christopher could enjoy sitting in his pram as we walked to my mother's, and she was always delighted to see us.

My father wrote letters in his quest for further information. He addressed them both to Colonel Steedman and to the War Office. He even copied Stuart's last letter to the casualties section in the hope that this might provide them with some clue. I still have the short response:

16th April 1942

Sir

With reference to your letter dated the 31st March, 1942, I am directed to thank you for forwarding to this office a copy of the interesting letter that you have received from your son, 2nd Lieutenant S V Poyser, Royal Engineers, the contents of which have been noted. It is regretted that no further information is yet available concerning your son. Arrangements are being made to obtain from Japanese Government information of the British military personnel who were in Singapore at the time of the capitulation but it is feared that some time will elapse before official information is received.

Many more months of silence – the rest of the year passed, and still no news. The uncertainty was like a constant ache.

My father always kept a diary and it was his custom to summarize each year in one or two sentences. His entry for the end of 1942 read simply:

SVP 'missing' at Singapore, two or three days before capitulation, on 15th February 1942 – still awaiting news.

It was terrible to be left in the dark for so long.

CHAPTER THIRTY-EIGHT

Now Arthur decided to seek to be 'de-reserved' and join the army. I could understand his thinking: he was frustrated at work, he wanted to 'do his bit' and most of his friends were fighting. Also the air raids had ended so there was little activity in the evenings with the Auxiliary Fire Service save on a precautionary and training basis. I suppose that the decisive factor from his point of view was that his best friend, Stuart, was missing. Arthur felt that he was in some way letting the side down by not being directly involved. He realized that joining up meant that he was going to miss out on much of Christopher's early development and was clearly torn, but he felt that his decision was right.

I was devastated at the thought of Arthur leaving home. We all knew that the Second Front was looming, the Allies had to invade Europe to win the war, there were few 'spare' men left and thus those who were 'older' were increasingly in demand. On the other hand I was acutely aware that there were still many able-bodied men in manufacturing and other industries, the authorities having been persuaded that their importance to the production effort meant that they should maintain their reserved status. Few of them had volunteered for the AFS, few of them had been in the thick of the Blitz, few of them had fought at first hand against the fire and destructive power of the German bombers. Many of them were living reasonably comfortable surburban lives and whilst some were keen to be de-reserved many others seemed to feel no obligation to fight.

I could have argued with Arthur that he had 'done his bit' but it would have been in vain. It all seemed so unfair. I could see no point in trying to stand in his way but I feared for his safety and also knew that life was going to be very difficult financially. On joining up Arthur would receive only ten shillings a week; my family allowance was only two pounds, and my father had to support not only his own household but also that of my paternal grandparents who were in their care home in Mountsorrel, just outside Leicester. I didn't know how we were going to manage, but Arthur and I discussed what further economies we could make and how it would help if we laid up the car in a garage in Avenue Road, only a street away from the flat.

In the event Arthur had little difficulty in persuading the authorities to de-reserve him from his specialist and 'secret' function in the aircraft industry. The official War Office papers calling him away followed all too soon.

I well remember the crisp January morning when Arthur left. The previous night my proud husband presented his son with the completed Red Engine, shining in its red and black paint. Christopher was able to pull himself up on it and push it along and I watched them at play with tears in my eyes.

Christopher was only nine months old so I did not go to the station to say goodbye. It was very early in the morning and I lifted Christopher out of the cot and sat him on my lap, Arthur kissed him and then I kissed Arthur and he went off to catch his train. We both knew that in the first three months there would be little or no leave and the occasions upon which we would meet thereafter would be out of our hands.

When he had gone I sat with Christopher and cried.

CHAPTER THIRTY-NINE

Saying goodbye to Arthur had been a terrible wrench. His first letter home must be typical in demonstrating the heartache caused by such separations in the war years.

Worcester. 4.2.43

My darling

It is now close on 9.30 and 'lights out' will be in a few minutes, but I am ready for bed and so have a few minutes to spare for telling you a bit about my first day as a soldier.

When I reached the platform in Birmingham it was obvious that most of the passengers were prospective soldiers like myself, a number in Home Guard uniform, lots with gas masks and paper parcels. When we got to Worcester about 12 o'clock there were 100 of us and we lined up outside the station to await transport. After a long time some army lorries turned up and took us away in small batches. Norton barracks is well outside the town and you can see the cathedral tower down below and the Malvern Hills standing up in the distance behind.

On being decanted from the lorry, we went to a building across the parade ground and after another long wait, were received by a tall red-faced major and a short fat red-faced major (both jovial) who gave each of us a large sheaf of papers. Another wait and we gave a number of particulars to Army clerks sitting at tables, losing some of our papers in the process. Then a cup of cocoa (cold) and fruit pie in another room, where we watched other squads going through it on the parade ground and at PT. About 30 of us then formed up and marched (?) to the company office where we signed our names for the third time.

Off to the medical inspection hut where we stripped and passed before a number of doctors in a rather chilly room. My grade is A1 I'm happy to say. The camp is a sea of mud everywhere. So far I haven't met anyone to go about with as a regular thing, although we do keep together pretty well and are all on friendly terms. The chaps all seem to be good sorts and range in age from 18's to about 35. I found two more SS Jaguar chaps in my platoon this morning, making 5 out of 30 which is rather extraordinary.

Our company commander is a tall and exceedingly handsome captain and we also have a lieutenant, a company sergeant-major and, in our platoon, a sergeant, corporal and lance-corporal.

As far as leave goes, I believe we have seven days after three months, but I don't know if there is a leave when we are posted on after leaving here. We shan't be let out of the barracks until next weekend, but I am still a bit vague about such things.

So much for myself.

I have been thinking a lot about you and how you are getting on. There were lots of things I wanted to say before I said goodbye, but they just wouldn't come out. I think though, that you know how much I hated leaving you and Christopher and how much I shall miss you both. So spare a few moments to think of me when you are in bed each night, and I shall do the same wherever I am. Because I love you very much, my darling, and am longing for the day when I can come back to you and to my beautiful son.

Don't worry about me – I'm all right – but take care of yourself for me.

With all my love

Arthur

We wrote to each other all the time, the letters were our lifeline. Christopher seemed to take up all my time but I would spend part of most days at Morland Avenue looking after my mother, sometimes staying overnight when my father was on night-time fire-watching duty in Nottingham. My grandparents continued to be a great anxiety. What with Arthur's departure, rationing, food shortages and the sheer worry of the war, everything seemed to be getting worse and worse.

Arthur always kept a diary, and looking back at his entry for Monday 15th February, eleven days after his departure, I read:

ENGAGEMENT ANNIVERSARY *Very cold morning – mostly*

spent on top of a hill in biting wind. A normal routine of activity during the day with an evening of letter writing. An odd way of celebrating 15.2.39.

And so the first month of Arthur's army career passed with little of great moment until Ash Wednesday, 10th March, thirty-five days after he had joined up. Great excitement!

Posted to Warwick and wangled a weekend pass! A very good day's work! More cheerful than at any time since I became a soldier.

Arthur sent a telegram to announce his leave. I was so happy and raced Christopher in his pram round to Morland Avenue to tell my mother the good news.

I found my mother in tears, holding a letter addressed to my father from the War Office. She would not open the letter in his absence but was desperate to know what it said. Would it give us the news we hoped for that Stuart was a prisoner of war? She said she had telephoned my father in Nottingham and he had agreed to come home immediately. It was unheard of for my father to leave his office in this way.

It was over a year since Stuart had been posted as missing and the balance of our lives lay in the sealed envelope still clutched in my mother's hand.

I stayed with my mother, neither of us able to settle, drinking endless cups of tea, looking at the sealed letter which I had persuaded her to put on the kitchen table, waiting for my father to arrive. When he came through the front door he took the letter and sat down at the table and started to read it out loud.

Sir,

With reference to the letter addressed to you on the 16th April 1942, concerning your son, 2nd Lieutenant S V Poyser, Royal Engineers, I am directed to inform you, with deep regret, that a report has been received through the Japanese Military authorities that your son was killed in action on Singapore Island. I am to convey to you an expression of sympathy in the distress this letter must necessarily cause you …

He was unable to read on.

It was not until a year later, in 1944, a full two years after Stuart's death, that we would receive a brief description of what had happened. This came in a letter from Colonel, now Brigadier, Steedman dated 25th January 1944.

25.1.44

An Indian (Sikh) Lieutenant of your son's company made a get away early last year from being a prisoner of war in Japanese hands. I heard from him last month but he is not educated sufficiently to write much English in a letter and I have not seen him. His news is confirmed from what I know myself:

On the 11th February 1942 the company was detailed to hold the South West sector of the airfield on the west of the road between Neesoon and the Naval Base. Bekhtawar Singh, the Indian Lieutenant, says:

'It was about 0900 hours on the 12th when a few Japanese turned up on our left, where Poyser's section was. All of a sudden they opened fire and unfortunately Poyser got a burst of LMG fire and was killed on the spot.'

I fear that is a bald and hard statement but I can get no more unless I run across Bekhtawar Singh, which I hope I may. I have recently seen in the papers that Maj Beattie, who commanded the company and was thought lost at Slim River, is now reported a prisoner of war. Teasdel the 2nd i/c is also a prisoner.

You know what a high opinion I had of your son, I hope if I am ever near Leicester that I may meet his parents. I like many, am anxiously waiting the time when I can take an active part in taking revenge on the Japanese.'

I believe that the 'Sikh Lieutenant' must have been the very same Bekhtawar Singh with whom Stuart had trained from the beginning.

I managed to leave a telephone message at Arthur's barracks and later that day he telephoned Morland Avenue where I was waiting for his call. I told him the news of Stuart and he was devastated: from the high of obtaining leave, to the anxiety of knowing that I had telephoned, he was taken to the low of the loss of his best friend and my brother. His brief diary entry for the day reads:

Thursday 11th March. Heard of SVP's official death and felt the shock all day. Wrote several letters on account of the news.

Arthur's first leave was both happy and sad. It was too early after the news of Stuart's death for us to be completely relaxed but we had so much to talk about and Arthur had so much catching up to do with Christopher. All too soon he had to return and my life of child-filled isolation resumed. I knew that Arthur had been summoned to London for an interview for the Intelligence Service but I then heard from him that he had been unsuccessful, and so he settled back into his new routine having been transferred to Warwick. The next leave was to come in mid-April and Arthur's diary entries speak for themselves.

Friday 16th April – After a hard morning and the Company parade set off for Leicester with a glad heart and got there quickly and comfortably. A lovely evening with my own family in my own home; bath and a proper bed.

Saturday 17th April – Up at 8.30 after the luxury of breakfast in bed. Walked and shopped with the family before lunch. Tea and the afternoon at no. 23. Another lovely spring day.

Sunday 18th April – The end of a perfect weekend's leave. Up between 9.30 and 10.30; pottered; went to Queens Road to the Clarendon with the lads before lunch; 23 during the afternoon; tea at home and then comfortably back to Warwick.

Expressions of sympathy for Stuart's death came in including one from Assam:

Budla Beta Tea Co. Ltd, Kanjikoah T E, Assam.
3rd September 1943

Dear Dr Poyser

I received from our secretaries a copy of the letter which you wrote to Dr Byatt on the 24th March last.

The loss of your son has been a severe shock to us all out here. He was most popular in the Company with everybody, both Indian and European and I think I can safely say he was the youngster we missed most of all. We shall miss him in every way, not only for his cheerful and live personality but also for his work as he was quite the best Assistant we had. You say in your letter that you believe he more than proved himself in Malaya, and knowing him as we do we are quite certain that this was the case as he was always keen, enthusiastic and to the front in everything that was afoot. All his friends out here join me in expressing deepest sympathy to you all.

With kindest regards

F S Gregory.

CHAPTER FORTY

Arthur was now working towards Warrant Officer status but that would take time. Leave was hard to come by and the frustration of knowing that he was stationed at Warwick, only forty miles away, was huge. Inevitably Christopher was growing up with only the most occasional contact with his father. He was a lovely little boy – curly hair, very forward for his age, very early walking and talking, and really very easy and happy. He was popular all round. This even stretched to our landlords, Mr and Mrs Plummer, who lived on the ground floor and had been reluctant to allow the tenancy to continue when I became pregnant. They now thought Christopher was lovely and I overheard Amy Plummer boasting about him. Arthur was enormously proud of his small son, but owing to his short and infrequent leaves it always took time for Christopher to get used to his 'Daddy' on those brief visits.

By May Arthur had passed his board interview and various other tests and announced he was 'all set for Hereford'. Later in the year he was transferred to Kent which meant that travelling home on leave was much more difficult, illustrated by one diary entry:

Sunday 3rd October – Had a good day at home until 6.30pm when I started back. Had a shattering journey which lasted till 6.45 am when I got into the billet after a sleepless and uncomfortable night.

Arthur finally passed out as a Second Lieutenant at the end of November and was posted to Shorncliffe. It was a time of turmoil in Leicester because that very month both Granny and Grandpa Poyser died within ten days of each other. In some ways this was a blessing: my grandfather had lost his memory and my grandmother was not well and it was perhaps a mercy that they should pass away within such a short space of time.

My father was not a man who could easily express his emotions – his time as a surgeon behind the trenches combined with the reticence into which men were encouraged in those days saw to that – but his desolation at losing both parents was obvious. The stable building blocks of his life, mother and father, had been taken from him at a time when the fortunes of war could alter our lives for ever.

Almost immediately my mother went into St Francis Hospital for an operation. I went to live at Morland Avenue during this time in order to look after my father but also went to visit my mother in hospital each day.

When Arthur's commission came through he was given a precious week's leave to celebrate. This was the first week of December so I returned to the flat. It was wonderful to have a whole week of my husband – there had been so few nights that we had spent together since we were married.

It was during that leave that Arthur told me he was determined to join the 'Second Front'. He pointed out that volunteers were wanted and he had decided to transfer to the infantry, resolute that he should be in the thick of such action as there might be. In consequence he said that he would be going up to Dunbar for twelve weeks, joining the Royal Warwickshire Regiment.

I understood the implications of what Arthur was telling me but it was clear I had no choice but to accept his decision. I realized that he was likely to be in great danger: before his transfer he was in a fairly 'safe' position but now he was aiming to be in the front line. He had a great spirit of adventure, and although he could appear very laid back he had great determination, he knew what he believed was 'right' and he would not be diverted when he had made his mind up.

Fate now intervened. Perhaps the situation is best read from Arthur's reply to my important letter to him.

10ᵗʰ January 1944

My dearest darling

Two letters from you today (including the one with the socks) and I was extremely glad to get both of them, as your news is of such absorbing interest!

You know more about such things than I do, but I have just been counting up the weeks since December 3rd in my diary and it does certainly look as though we are in for an increase in family! Unless of course the curse has arrived since you wrote on Saturday. I find it all hard to believe, because as I said before, I had no idea that anything went wrong with the works when I was on leave. All I can say is that rubber goods must be of a very inferior quality nowadays!

My thoughts have been full of you and this unexpected happening all through the weekend and even during highly technical lectures on dynamics and starter motors, I have found myself ruminating on an entirely different subject. My feelings are very mixed but, at the bottom, I am thrilled and not so alarmed as I ought perhaps to be. I do very much want a daughter (or another son, if you can't manage it the other way) and I do think, as we have decided in talks long ago, that it is a mistake to leave too long a gap between children if the family is to be as happy and united as possible. But of course, the present is as difficult a time as any to cope with an infant, on the other hand I don't expect conditions to improve tremendously within the next two years and that is too long to wait.

It is all very complicated isn't it?

I wish I was able to be with you and hold you.

All my love is with you my darling

Arthur

So there I was, pregnant again and unintentionally. I was very worried, not only because Arthur was away and there was no likelihood of his being anywhere in my vicinity when the baby was expected in early September, but also because I had had such a terrible time with Christopher. Additionally, life in general was rather grim. Still, I soon became acclimatized as Arthur was so thrilled that we were going to be a 'family'. He kept saying that he had always wanted four children! My mother was pleased beyond measure as she adored Christopher, and having been discharged from hospital she was coming back to her old self again despite the trauma of Stuart's death. She and I were very close, and of course we saw a lot of each other and naturally had a lot in common. She was a wonderful companion when she was well.

My father was rather 'doom and gloom' but he was very proud of his grandson. I cannot remember discussing the new arrival with him in terms that he would actually volunteer that he was pleased about the 'happy event', but that wasn't his way and I know that he was pleased for me.

In April 1944 Arthur finished in Dunbar and announced that he was to be given a final two-and-a-half weeks' leave before joining what we now knew was going to be the invasion force. The whole country was aware that a second front was planned and it was obvious that this was going to start sometime during the early summer. The leave was clearly intended to be our last opportunity to see Arthur before he embarked for Europe, although we did not know precisely to where or when. American forces were massing at various locations right across the country, road convoys with heavy equipment and men were commonplace, but it was also a very tense time since German rocket-propelled V bombs were now falling on London and the south of England.

We had decided to let the flat and after discussion it was agreed that I would move to Morland Avenue whilst Arthur was abroad. It was a traumatic two weeks. On the positive side the leave was a marvellous opportunity for Arthur to catch up with Christopher and for the two of them to get used to each other, and also for Arthur and me to have quality time together. On the negative side I was five months pregnant and still suffering occasional sickness, we had a huge amount to do in the way of sorting out our possessions and getting ready for me to move out, and I was about to lose my husband for an indefinite period.

On 8th April, which was Easter weekend, Arthur and I had our last little holiday together. We left Christopher with his grandparents at Morland Avenue and went to a guest house called Blakeshay Farm just outside Leicester in the Charnwood Forest. We were there from Saturday to Tuesday and had a very happy, but in retrospect sad, weekend amongst the springtime daffodils and the hosts of hikers. We talked and walked a lot and kept out of the farm as far as possible. We went to church in Newtown Linford on the Sunday.

It was really such a short weekend in which to ready ourselves for Arthur's departure to the front in Europe with all the uncertainty of not knowing when we might see each other again.

Arthur went to Stratford to see his parents on the 12th and 13th but otherwise we spent a normal busy family time at the flat preparing to move on the 19th. The move itself went well and on 20th April Arthur was to travel by train to Market Rasen in Lincolnshire on the way to embarkation.

Christopher and I went to the station and helped Arthur with his kitbag as he boarded the train. With tears in my eyes, and holding our two-year-old son so very tightly, I watched him go.

CHAPTER FORTY-ONE

I knew that Arthur was to be posted to Italy. He travelled first to Market Rasen in Lincolnshire and from there to Liverpool where his regiment embarked for Naples. He was disembarkation officer and on arrival had some weeks of training before moving to the front.

From reading the newspapers we knew that Italy was proving to be an extraordinarily tough campaign. There had been landings at Salerno in southern Italy in September 1943 and the Allied forces had faced a German army determined to prevent the Allied advance up the Italian peninsula. Landings at Anzio in January 1944 had reinforced the Allied forces and in May the fiercely fought battle at Cassino had finally achieved an Allied victory.

Almost immediately thereafter, on 4th June 1944, there was general rejoicing at the news that Rome had fallen to the Allies. The reports of this were just coming in when we first heard that Arthur's regiment had landed in Italy. In parallel with this the huge Allied invasion force, the Second Front, started to move on 6th June so within a few days of the success in Rome we knew of the massive D-Day landings in northern France. Understandably it was the Normandy landings which tended to dominate the news and it was not easy to follow what was happening in Italy.

The first letter arrived from Arthur and although it was censored he was able to comment on seeing the poverty of Naples, and then tell us that he had been into Rome pursuing the retreating Germans through the outskirts. His letter told me that the enemy had left the city largely intact. He said that he was now preparing for action and about to move further north.

Almost immediately afterwards there was a second letter to say that Arthur had dysentery and was in hospital, with the likelihood that he would be there for a week. Then there was a third letter, this time saying that he was well again and was going back towards the front line. It was difficult to tell from the newspapers where the front line was: by 20th June it appeared to have reached Perugia and on 24th June I read that heavy fighting had continued both day and night in Chiusi. I could find these in the atlas. It seemed that good progress was being made up the coast, but I then read that the fighting was particularly difficult in the area round Lake Trasimeno where gains were 'slow and gradual'.

The trouble was that letters were so delayed one could never really be up to date; in the meantime the newspapers and radio were full of descriptions of D-day and what was happening in northern France and there was much less news about the Italian campaign. I continued to scour the press for any information on what was happening. There was further mention of advances and losses which worried me but gave insufficient detail to be helpful. I understood that the Germans had now fallen back to a defence line south of Florence and I hoped that the next letter would give me some clue as to where Arthur might be.

Domestic life with Christopher had to go on and I had settled into our new existence in Morland Avenue, enjoying my mother's company and helping her in supporting my father who was always tired from his work and constant commuting to Nottingham.

It was 9th July, two months after Arthur had left England, and I had finished putting Christopher to bed for his morning sleep. I had gone down to the kitchen which overlooked the road and out of the window I suddenly saw the postboy pedalling his bicycle up the slight hill. My heart thumped as I saw him – postboys carried telegrams, and telegrams were so often harbingers of bad news. I watched as he cycled on towards our end of the cul-de-sac, checking the house numbers as he went. I willed him to go past our gate but as I saw him brake and dismount, leaning his bicycle against our front gate, I was already moving, hand to my mouth, opening the front door, seeing the War Office marking on the outside of the envelope that he thrust into my hands.

I felt empty as I opened the envelope and made out the meaning of the words.

MRS M V MITCHELL 23 MORLAND AVENUE
STONEYGATE LEICESTER
DEEPLY REGRET TO INFORM YOU OF REPORT DATED 9TH JULY 1944 RECEIVED FROM CENTRAL MEDITERRANEAN AREA THAT LT. A.F.M.MITCHELL, ROYAL WARWICKSHIRE REGT. HAS BEEN KILLED IN ACTION. THE ARMY COUNCIL DESIRE TO OFFER YOU THEIR SINCERE SYMPATHY.
UNDER SECRETARY OF STATE FOR WAR.

I was completely numb. I couldn't cry. I remember saying to myself that I must think of my mother, I mustn't break down. Father was in Nottingham and our telephone was out of action. Wordlessly I passed the letter to my mother who had just come down the stairs into the hall. She started to sob, she held me in her arms for a long time and then, leaving me sitting at the kitchen table, went next door to telephone father and also Arthur's parents in Stratford, whilst I was left like a numbed zombie with my godmother who was staying with us.

I remember so well going to Christopher's bedroom that evening whilst he was asleep and sitting on his bed as if in a dream, thinking he would never know his father now, nor would the baby. I just sat there wondering what was going to happen to us. Then there was the misery of thinking of Granny Mitchell and Grandfather Mitchell having lost their beloved only son, and of my wretched parents having to cope with me and Christopher and the baby to come. Oh God – what misery, and what a waste of a good life and a good man. *Damn* the war and the end of all our dreams.

Naturally everyone was very kind and life had to go on. Christopher didn't understand and I was very busy with him and the worry of the coming baby who was actively making his presence felt. Christopher was very forward with his talking and as I pushed him in his pram people would stop and talk to us. He was very fond of saying, 'My

Daddy's in Ikiki' (Italy) and I didn't know what to say.

Mother was very busy with both of us and father was in Nottingham all day and some nights as well. And so the days went by until 28th August when I went into labour and was taken to St Francis Nursing Home less than a mile down the road from Morland Avenue. I was admitted at about 11 p.m. that night, was given an injection and had a lovely sleep. I always remember that sleep as I was racked with tension and the anguish of losing Arthur.

I woke up and went into labour about 1 p.m. and my son – I should say our son – David was born at 4.45 p.m. It was all very easy and peaceful by comparison with Christopher's birth and by 6.30 p.m. I was having supper and being visited by my parents and showing David off to them. Although David weighed in at nine-and-a-half pounds it all seemed remarkably easy after the time I had had with Christopher.

If only Arthur had been there to share the joy, and joy it was. Although to begin with I was disappointed it wasn't a girl as we had both been sure that it would be, I have never ceased to be glad that 'it' was a boy. A boy was meant and a boy was needed.

God took two men from our family, Stuart and Arthur, but returned two to take their places.

CHAPTER FORTY-TWO

It was a considerable time before Arthur's personal effects came through. In the meantime the formal letter of condolence came from Buckingham Palace. It read:

The Queen and I offer you our heartfelt sympathy in your great sorrow. We pray that your country's gratitude for a life so nobly given in its service may bring you some measure of consolation.

George R

Amongst Arthur's belongings were two letters, one addressed to me and the other to Christopher. Christopher's letter was kept in its sealed envelope until he was able to open it on his sixteenth birthday. He then passed it on to his brother David who was not allowed to read it until he reached the same age.

The text of the letter from Arthur to me was as follows:

Somewhere in Italy. 3.6.44

My own darling

If you ever come to read this letter it will mean that the worst has happened and that I shall not be coming back to you.

Don't grieve too much my dear. I know that at first you will be terribly upset, but try to make the best of a bad job and remake your life as best you can. My great consolation, when thinking of what may happen, is that you have Christopher and, I hope, our second child, to comfort you and carry on the family life which I had so looked forward to enjoying with you all.

You have made me a very happy man since we were married; they have been years than which no man could wish for better, in spite of the time which I have had to spend away from you. And I do most humbly thank you for the happiness which you have given me. I have tried to repay my debt by giving

213

you all the love that I have – and that love is a very deep and sacred one to me.

I'm afraid that I shall have died a poor man and that you will not find it easy to keep yourself and the children (and to educate them) on what little I leave, but I hope that things won't be too bad for you. My great wish is that you should have a happy life and all that God may provide to make it so, please remember that. In course of time I hope that you will find someone to take my place, always provided that he will, for certain, make you happy. If such a thing should come to pass, he will indeed be lucky to have you for a wife.

In your sorrow, be comforted by the thought that I have lived a happy life, I have done my best throughout its 33 years; and I shall have died doing what I could for you in this horrible war, without fear of the future.

All my thoughts are with you now and will be with you in the hereafter (if there is such a thing). May God bless you, my darling wife, and look after you always.

With all my love – and I think you know how much I mean by that.
Yours
Arthur

One thing always sticks in my memory in respect of the period after David was born. I wrote to the Pensions Department of the War Office to inform them of the birth of another child on 29th August and to say that I should now be due an additional allowance of fifteen shillings per week. The reply from the War Office shook me, as I could never have imagined that anybody could think that David might not be Arthur's son, but they told me that 'enquiries and investigations' would have to be made before the allowance could be paid! Fortunately the army authorities were able to confirm that Arthur had been on leave at the likely time of conception so, eventually, I had a letter from the Ministry of Pensions agreeing an allowance for David as a war orphan and backdating his allowance.

David was christened by an old family friend, the Reverend Arnold Lee, at St Mary's in Knighton on 24th November 1944. Louise was his godmother but neither of his godfathers was able to be present.

I was not looking forward to Christmas that year. The deaths of Arthur and Stuart cast their pall over us all. We had no hope of any poultry for our Christmas dinner for everything was in short supply. Then on 22nd December we were offered a goose by our friends the Gees and with great relief we accepted thankfully. On 23rd December our next-door neighbours arrived on the doorstep with a turkey that they had somehow procured, knowing nothing about our goose. Then on 24th December our friend Barbara Castle, thinking we had nothing, also offered us a turkey! We refused the last but were still able to have the goose on the 24th and the turkey on Christmas Day and yet only the three of us plus Christopher to eat it all. I still don't know how we did it.

The war proceeded with all its awfulness and home front shortages. Things were not going well in Europe, the Battle of the Bulge was happening as the Germans made a last-ditch stand to push the Allies back. Early 1945 saw the V-1 and V-2 flying bombs and the 'doodlebugs'. It was a terrible time for Londoners and those living in Kent and Surrey. It must have been almost worse than the Blitz for those in the south-east as the bombs came over day and night and there seemed to be no defence against their power. It was said that all you heard of these extraordinary rockets, launched far away on the European coast, was a buzzing whine; if it cut out overhead you were likely to be unlucky and had to throw yourself under any form of protection as the bomb dived down. The V-2s were much bigger and more silent, left huge craters and did terrible damage.

At last in the early spring the Allies broke through and attacked the rocket launching sites, and the flying bomb menace was over. Then came news of the advance of the Allies on Berlin. Suddenly the war in Europe was over.

The end of the war should stand out and be etched on my memory as a great event, but strangely, but perhaps not surprisingly, I don't remember any great joy. It had cost us so much as a family.

We had no one to come back.

CHAPTER FORTY-THREE

My mother was not someone to let an occasion for a party pass by, so at her insistence we agreed to celebrate the end of hostilities and asked all our friends in the Avenue to come round and join us. I can't remember much about it but there is a photograph of a group of us toasting the end of the war in Europe. It didn't make much difference to our lifestyle. Rationing and shortages were to be with us for several more years.

The war in the Far East continued but of course there were no more blackout curtains, the car was put back on the road and a degree of normality resumed. My father was able to finish his job in Nottingham and moved his office to Leicester in the Ministry of Health medical examination centre at 53 London Road. That was a great relief but he still had to make regular visits to Northampton, Burton-upon-Trent, Bedford and Peterborough to carry out medical examinations at the centres there. Sometimes my mother would go with my father and on one occasion he fitted in a visit to Wisbech Grammar School where his father had been headmaster.

Grandfather's old retainers, called the Collishaws, had a smallholding near Wisbech and my father and mother would bring back eggs and strawberries – unbelievable luxuries. At the time we were still rationed to one egg per week. Little things like that stand out in one's memory. Another was getting food parcels from Arthur's aunts in Australia: that was always a wonderful event with things like dried fruit, raisins and sultanas, food that we hadn't seen in years. The parcels were like gold and seemed to transform mealtimes for weeks – it seems difficult to believe it now.

One cloud arose on the horizon, namely that the owners of our rented house at 23 Morland Avenue wanted it back. Fortunately, some relatives of theirs owned a rented house in Shirley Road which was only a very short distance away. We had hoped to take over the tenancy but the relatives decided that they wanted to sell, and to my father's dismay there was no alternative but for him to raise the money to buy the house outright. In common with many of his generation he had never owned a house in his life, he had always rented and he had never had any capital. However, by now his parents' estate was being sorted out so there was some help there. Amidst his protestations of doom, gloom and potential bankruptcy, which we all took with a large pinch of salt, my father agreed to buy the house and everything was put in motion. Then at the end of July the General Election took place and we were all dumbfounded to find that Churchill was out and the Labour Party and Attlee in. My father's doom and gloom intensified!

In early August my mother took to her bed with a temperature and generally in a poor state. In the midst of all this the news came of the atom bombs being dropped on Japan followed by the Japanese surrender. There was natural and great rejoicing in the country at the end of the war, but my memories of this time seem very blank: thinking back I suppose it was partly the sadness that we had gone through and partly worry over my mother's illness.

Then my mother's condition worsened and coincided with the start of one of her depressive illnesses. Life became very tense and difficult all round. She was put on phenobarbiturates and was not quite normal as a result: she seemed even more depressed than usual and was rather difficult. I was naturally (but selfishly) concerned with the effect this might have on Christopher and David, although the latter was too young to notice.

Mother was very much up and down in health terms and at the end of September we had a nurse in to help look after her. On 5th October two of my father's medical colleagues, one being the superintendent of Leicester's mental hospital, consulted together and as a result it was decided that mother should be moved to St Andrews in Northampton the very next day. It was an awful situation, mother had not been told of the decision but she must have sensed something since that evening she seemed strangely much better and she begged me not to let 'them' send her away. Of course she knew that she was suffering mentally but I felt an utter traitor knowing she was to be taken away the next morning.

When morning came, after a sleepless night for me, mother was drugged with morphine and taken by ambulance to St Andrews.

I felt very much to blame, fearing that it was my failure to cope with the children that had precipitated her condition – of course, with the benefit of hindsight this was not true, but at the time I felt dreadfully responsible.

Then, the very next morning, the telephone rang and we were told that mother had died during the night.

It was quite terrible. We were all stunned and my horrified father was completely devastated. I was totally overwhelmed, but Christopher and David were in the middle of breakfast with David in particular demanding attention. So, once again in our misery we collected ourselves together and tried to pick up the pieces again. My father went off to St Andrews and I took Christopher down the road to play with a friend. On the way back a neighbour called out of the window, 'How's your mother?' I was so bemused, I couldn't think whether to say 'She's dead' or 'She has died' but I got it out somehow.

Morland Avenue was only a short cul-de-sac and everyone was very shocked to hear of this latest tragedy in our family. My mother was so well liked and such a lovely character. I loved her dearly and to lose her at the very time when I most relied on her support to cope with the deaths of Arthur and Stuart was very hard to bear.

The funeral was terrible, crude and rushed through at the crematorium. We should have had a church service but were so traumatized that we did not think through the arrangements, which probably demonstrates the momentary failure of my father's usual iron control. From that moment onwards and for the next twenty years he was always to wear a black tie by way of mourning.

And yet, on life had to go again. My father in his single-minded way would not be seen to be yielding to grief. He went to work as normal the next day and in addition announced that he saw no alternative to his going through with the purchase of 7 Shirley Road the following week. We had to sell a lot of furniture and good things to move, as we had inherited my grandparents' possessions from Highfield Street and had too much to fit into the new house.

The great move took place on 1st January 1946: widower father, widowed daughter and two fatherless children beginning their new life together, a life which was to last for the next twenty-two years.

BOOK TWO

2nd Lieutenant S.V. Poyser R.E.

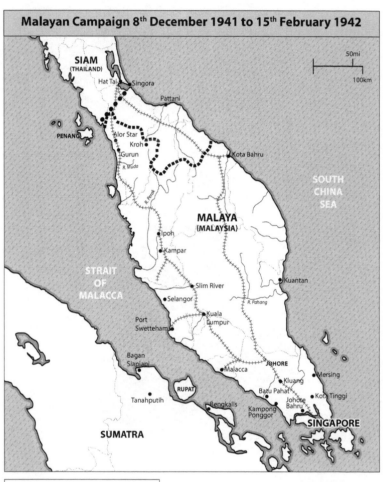

Malayan Campaign 8th December 1941 to 15th February 1942

SIAM
(THAILAND)

Hat Tai ·Singora

Pattani

PENANG

·Alor Star

·Kroh

·Gurun

R. Muda

·Kota Bahru

R. Perak

SOUTH
CHINA
SEA

MALAYA
(MALAYSIA)

·Ipoh

·Kampar

STRAIT
OF
MALACCA

·Slim River

·Kuantan

·Selangor

R. Pahang

Kuala
Lumpur

Port
Swetteham

Bagan
Siapiani

JOHORE

·Malacca

·Kluang

·Mersing

Tanahputih

RUPAT

Bengkalis

Batu Pahat·

Johore
Bahru

·Kota Tinggi

Kampong
Ponggor

SINGAPORE

SUMATRA

50mi
100km

■■■■■■■ Boundary Line

●●●●●● Planned 'Operation Matador' Line

CHAPTER ONE

I never had a father.

That is not to say that my father's blood does not run in my veins, nor that I have not sought in life to atone for his loss of my upbringing and mine of his paternal love and support.

Arthur Farndell Martin Mitchell was killed in action, as the expression goes, in June 1944. I, David Vernon Martin Mitchell, was *en ventre ma mere* at the time, *ventre* being womb and the Gallic precision of the reference emanating from my subsequent life as a lawyer. The prefix Martin was derived from my paternal grandfather Dr Charles Martin Mitchell who is said to have once hyphenated his name. I am not clear whether there was a serious intention that subsequent generations would reassume that pretension, but in deference to that possibility my daughters were given Martin as their third name. They report that they did not find the device helpful to their early life in school playgrounds. My brother Christopher followed suit, but since he too fathered only daughters the expectation of a plethora of double-barrelled descendants has gone.

It will already be apparent that Christopher is my older brother. To most of the world he is Chris, but despite his encouragement I have never been able to bring myself to use that shortening of his name. My usage has caused some of our mutual friends to revert to his full name, to my brother's silent disapproval. He had just passed his second birthday when father was killed and likes to believe that some recollection remains. In his sixtieth year he asked mother what father was really like, and she wrote:

Arthur was not a noisy extrovert like my brother Stuart, but he was very sociable and got on well with all sorts. He belonged to Kings Norton rugby club and enjoyed his tennis and golf well before we became friends. Arthur enjoyed reading, but more the classics, and doing crosswords though he used to read Whitakers Almanac. He was a patient sort of chap, liked his car and enjoyed messing around with it. He got on well with all his mates and enjoyed a beer with them often at the Clarendon pub. Stuart once said in a letter that 'old Arthur is a damn good bloke and has a heart of gold, I've never known him bad tempered and he's a much better character than your big brother ...' To close I would say he was honest and strong, clean minded and straightforward and that was his wish for you to both have in your minds as you read his final letter following your growing up to the age of 16.

The final letter to which she refers was kept locked in the big safe that lived in the garage at Shirley Road where we were brought up by our mother and grandfather. After the death of my father and of my mother's mother my grandfather entered into an arrangement whereby my mother would act as his housekeeper and he would provide for us all.

This worked well: we lived in tolerable comfort, if frugally, at number 7 Shirley Road in a good suburb of Leicester; my grandfather went about his work as Medical Officer for Health and my mother cycled to the General Hospital where she worked as a physiotherapist, for which her training at Bedford Physical Training College had qualified her.

My mother was required by my grandfather to keep a detailed account of her financial expenditure; only a proportion of her total spending would be reimbursed and it was necessary for her to work to keep us boys in the modest manner to which we were accustomed. The detached and stuccoed house had large gardens to the front and rear and there were no trees of significance that were not climbed, nor warlike games that were not played, within those grounds. My brother was allowed to occupy the master bedroom with a bay window overlooking the front garden and the road beyond. This became the gathering point for our friends and for our boys' version of the Famous Five, which in our more extreme youth often split into two factions each of which would make blood-curdling threats against the other before mother called us all in for our tea.

In later years the room housed our record collection, and the required Dansette record player, together with the equipment for such of my brother's enthusiasms as were in vogue. A full set of weight-lifting barbells was one of the final acquisitions to accompany our later teenage years.

My bedroom opened off my brother's, two steps down gaining access to a narrow room with metal-framed windows at either end and a sloping ceiling under which my simple bed was placed. Insulation was non-existent, the room was directly over the garage and the only source of winter heat was a two-bar electric fire. We left the door open at night, and devised a system of signals for when mother or grandfather approached with the risk of our lights-out dialogue being interrupted. Christopher delighted in telling ghost stories in the hope that I would be frightened, and was not above creeping into my room and uttering moans from under a sheet to add to the atmosphere. Since it was customary for me to read *Swallows and Amazons* or the like by torchlight beneath the covers, which partly accounts for my extreme short sight, it was rare that I was intimidated. In later years I was often required to remain imprisoned in my room whilst my brother was entertaining a girlfriend, my only escape route being out of the rear window on to the flat roof beyond and descent via the edge of the glass roof over the backyard. With hindsight it is perhaps surprising that I survived.

To return to the final letter: it was customary for those away at war to write letters to be read by their loved ones in the event of death. My father was no exception and his letter to my mother, which I was shown in my early twenties, was poignant. My mother decreed that his letter to Christopher should be read by each of us since he knew that another child was on the way. It seems that I was to be called Alison had my chromosomes so dictated – and I remain grateful that I was born a boy.

Mother recalls that we were allowed to read the letter on our respective sixteenth birthdays. My recollection had always been that it was not until we were eighteen, but there would have been little logic in that anniversary since twenty-one was still the age of majority in those days, so she is probably right.

The letter, dated 29th May 1944, was written almost exactly a month before father's death. It was headed:

Somewhere in Italy

and started with the words:

If you ever come to read this letter, it will mean that the worst has happened and that I shall not have returned home from the war. It is a sad thing for both of us …

I am sitting outside the Mess at a Base Camp in Italy, from where I am due to go into the line at any moment, to do my share of the fighting which has been forced upon so many peace-loving people like myself.

Having now reached grandparental status I can only begin to imagine how strange it must have been for any father of a two-year-old boy to seek to encapsulate a lifetime's advice into a single letter which would not be read until many years later. We learn fatherhood by experience, an opportunity denied to those losing their lives in such conflicts, so to seek to anticipate what guidance will be valuable must be extraordinarily difficult.

In any event Christopher did not share his earlier knowledge of the contents with me but I am sure that we both, at our separate readings nearly three years apart, felt the raw sadness of the emotion of those distant words.

For me it was an individual rite of passage setting out infinite wisdom, from a face I had never seen, speaking with a voice I had never heard.

I recall that on occasions I was asked whether I missed my father. It is perhaps less painful to miss what one has never known, and I do not think I was qualified to answer the question until I had children of my own. It was only then that I knew the depth of the love my father would have had for me, and to appreciate its certain reciprocation.

I was a voracious reader as a boy, and much of the post-war literary diet involved prisoners of war. The Colditz story and other writings fed my favourite fantasy, which was that my father had been captured and would one day return home. The detail now blurs but I seem to recall that I invented some remote Stalag where news of the liberation had not yet been heard. In my early days at boarding school I would imagine the summons to the headmaster's study – and the welcome that my resurrected parent would give me, hopefully coupled with some pride at my achievements in his absence. Whether or not this imaginary anticipation caused me to study harder, or behave better, I am uncertain.

I only remember one occasion when I cried publicly for my loss. I must have been about twelve since it was when I was a monitor at Christ's Hospital Prep School, which lofty status I reached in the year before entering the upper school. The whole school, including the prep school, ate in the huge dining hall overlooked by the vast fifty-yard-long painting by Antonio Verrio, and we precocious prep school monitors had the good fortune to sit on a dais in one of the two bays framed by the stained glass windows overlooking the quadrangle. It must have been July because that morning I had received a letter from my mother in which she had for the first time set out to me the circumstances of my father's death, which I now know was in that month of 1944. Her letter described how he had been advancing down a village street when he was machine-gunned by one of a group of partisans concealed nearby. I had a compulsion to share the news and read out the passage to a fellow monitor and friend, I recall his name was Sills. In the process of the reading I must have put the machine-gunning words into action which caused me to start a fit of laughter in which he joined. My laughs then degenerated into sobs, to his discomfort and my great embarrassment.

What I now know was missing from my childhood was the witnessing of ordinary marital intimacy. My mother was the only woman in a household of men: even our Cairn terrier was male. Christopher and I would dutifully kiss both our mother and, in earlier years, our grandfather, the latter being an abrasively scratchy experience in view of his moustache. Mother would embrace us, and kiss her father, but those latter often perfunctory peckings defined the limits of any outward display of love. It was a loving household, but to grow up without visual third-party experience of embracing, handholding and similar signs of affection led to my finding it awkward to make overt displays in such matters. Even now my mother will complain that I do not return her hugs with sufficient enthusiasm, failing to appreciate, understandably, that this was a small if significant consequence of my upbringing.

I should conclude this comment on my early life by saying that my grandfather Vernon Poyser was a philatelist of some importance. One of his interests was in postmarks, and in later days after the war he would extend this to the printing techniques that allowed sorting machines to position and identify the letters. Stamps were his principal hobby, and of an evening at Shirley Road a brown baize cloth would be spread over an extended gate-leg table in the drawing room and a child-sapping concentrated silence would envelop the evening. Woe betide us boys if we sought to disturb the process. As we grew older we were drawn into the activity ourselves and even now have our more modest collections tucked away for posterity. My collection of Great Britain sports its obligatory penny black, not of the highest quality, and contains references to such esoteric and long-forgotten details as the printer of each stamp. Canada was another of my chosen countries, whilst Christopher's collection majored in Australia; each of us was proud of our particular choice and suitably disdainful of the other.

I even joined the Philatelic Society at school, and recall my mortification when my thematic entry of 'The Queen's Head on Stamps' failed to win first prize in the annual competition – on the ruling that the descriptions were written up in pencil. Grandfather had always written his multitudinous entries in pencil and I could not have contemplated any alternative. Prior to his death he decided to sell his forty-seven-album collection, housed in its specially built cabinet, in order to ensure that its true value could be properly realized. Serried ranks of grey-suited valuers travelled to Leicester to pore over such joys as the entire album of penny blacks and, less enthusiastically, the peculiarity of sixty pages of 'Postage Due' triangles. The total amount raised was considerable, although it would no doubt appear modest by today's inflated figures. The sale of the collection enabled the proceeds to be invested for what my undemonstrative but caring grandfather could see would be my mother's precarious financial future.

It is unsurprising therefore that letters from my deceased uncle Stuart to my grandfather, or indeed from any other family member or friend who might have ventured abroad, made routine reference to the posting of letters.

Of course, it was mother who was the principal figure in our lives but I know it was not until later years that we fully appreciated the huge amount she had done for us. I suppose this is typical and that from the perspective of children growing through their formative years there is little comparison to make until the child reaches maturity and advances towards an age similar to the age the parent was then. As those adult years have advanced, the great sacrifices that she made and the debt that we owe her have come into context.

I ought also to say that my grandfather's influence cannot be underestimated. Having lost son and wife in short order, he had to shed an entire generation to become the father figure to two small boys. From his bench in the unheated garage he produced a wooden fort with a working drawbridge, a fire station complete with pole for toy firemen to descend to their fire engine and other delights of that nature. For the garden he commissioned an angular wooden swing upon which one could variously fit a traditional swing or a trapeze, or slot in climbing bars. This green-painted construction formed the focus of our 'gang' gatherings. His beloved lawn – an inconvenient bell shape bordered with flowers on one side – became a cricket pitch, croquet lawn and even short tennis court. Metal poles slotted into the ground so that high nets could be hung to contain the ball, although our wayward shots still flew into the adjoining gardens. He coached us in cricket and many other sports: a high-jump frame with adjustable bar assisted our competitions; a 'bumble-puppy' post (an early form of swingball) boasted a corded and drilled tennis ball which would on occasions detach itself and fly away to distant gardens; and we and our friends became skilled in 'golf' croquet and even bowls.

Grandfather, whom we called 'Grandy', was often stern, always restrained, constantly active: but supportive at all times. His tolerance, particularly when Christopher and I started to cut our beer-drinking teeth, giggling home from the nearby tennis club bar and hiccupping our goodnights, must have been sorely tested – but I cannot recall any outburst of (justifiable) anger or ill temper.

Mother determined that her sons should, if at all possible, have a boarding school education. I believe that her thinking was that this would in some way balance out any disadvantage we might have from being brought up by what would today be termed a single mother. The self-sacrifice on her part was considerable, resulting in my leaving home for school in Sussex at the age of ten and Christopher going to Epsom College in Surrey at thirteen. There was only one free bursary available at Epsom: having father, grandfather and uncle as former pupils might have suggested that a second place could have been found but it was not to be, so mother had to consider other options for me. Fee paying was out of the question – we had no money. A solicitor friend of my mother's, Gerard Haxby, to whom I was eventually destined to become articled as a trainee solicitor myself, used his influence with a former Lord Mayor of London with whom he had been at university. This resulted in an introduction to Christ's Hospital, the Bluecoat school, and after very many months of letter writing to potential benefactors my mother succeeded in gaining me a place at that wonderful establishment where, clad in knee breeches and yellow socks, I was to be for seven years from the age of ten onwards.

Money was short and mother would save up to visit me once a term. I was not allowed out overnight so she would stay in modest accommodation in the nearby town of Horsham and visit me on the Saturday and again on the Sunday, before the long train journey back to Leicester on Sunday night. During term-time telephone contact was only allowed in cases of emergency so all communications were by letter; in the early homesick terms the twice-weekly letters from home were my lifeline.

At least mother now had more time for herself. She played tennis and badminton and started golf. As the years passed she would add county caps in all three sports to the county appearances she had already made at hockey and cricket. She joined The Leicestershire Golf Club and quickly lowered her handicap and began to win prizes. The club was regarded as rather 'posh', most of the lady members having their own cars and some even drivers. I would love to have witnessed my sporting mother bicycling up Guilford Road hill to our house with a newly presented club silver trophy wedged into the basket on the front of the handlebars.

For me: school and then into law and the life of a solicitor; for Christopher: entrepreneurial business and great success out of hard work; each of us happily into marriage and children, although his marred by the death of both his wife and his elder daughter to cancer.

Our lives were built on the stability of the upbringing achieved by our mother despite her various handicaps: hereditary deafness dogging her communications; a non-malignant cancerous growth encroaching on an eyelid and taking an eye; loss of taste and smell blunting her enjoyment; and loss of balance destabilizing her gait. Throughout it all, supported by grandfather until his death in 1967, she remained the figurehead of the family – leading the story onwards to the other side of the world.

CHAPTER TWO

My researches into Stuart's wartime exploits naturally concentrated on those extraordinary eight weeks between the Japanese invading Malaya in early December 1941 and the Allied forces' surrender at Singapore in mid-February 1942. Interested readers may appreciate the following summary of what I believe Stuart's movements to have been, putting the dramatic descriptions in his two December 1941 letters into some context. Other readers may prefer to move on to Book Three.

The statistics are stark. The Japanese army, using only three divisions, conquered Malaya and Singapore in just eight weeks.

The Allied 'Order of Battle' on 8th December 1941 – the formal battle instructions for when the invasion started and war with Japan commenced – showed the Allied strength at about 80,000 men. Within this number was the 11th Indian Division, in which Stuart's small 3rd Field Company was included. There was the 6th Indian Infantry Brigade, in which the 2nd Battalion East Surrey Regiment was the major element; the 15th Indian Infantry Brigade, in which the 1st Battalion Leicestershire Regiment was the major force; the 28th Indian Infantry Brigade; the HQ Malaya Command Reserve; and the Krohcol HQ force.

In simplistic terms a battalion consists of around 1,000 men and a brigade usually contains three battalions. Two entire brigades were decimated in a series of battles from the battle of Jitra through to the Allies' penultimate stand at Kampar. The East Surrey Regiment and the Leicestershire Regiment – the Tigers – bore the brunt of the early fighting and were both so diminished by casualties that their survivors joined forces at Kampar to become the 'British Battalion' which combined force went on to distinguish itself as the campaign worked south to its early and tragic conclusion. Stuart and his 3rd Field Company fought alongside these troops, using their specialist skills where possible, but otherwise fighting as ordinary infantry.

In all a total of five brigades were virtually annihilated and casualties in the Malayan retreat, omitting the very large additional forces in the Singapore Island battle, numbered 25,000 men including 8,000 prisoners.

So what was behind the Japanese invasion? Earlier aggression had given them a large presence in China, and a build up of occupation along the remaining Chinese coastline towards Hong Kong. Crucially, the Vichy Government of France had also allowed the Japanese into French Indo-China.

Japan particularly needed oil and steel, rubber and tin. Protracted talks with the Americans had failed to produce any guarantee of such supplies. Malaya produced nearly half the world's rubber and almost a third of its tin. Consequently, during the long negotiations with America, Japan had built up and trained its troops, expanded its aircraft and armour and planned its strategy for the future. Many of its troops were battle hardened from the campaign in China: they knew how to fight. Japan remained careful to conceal its ambitions to dominate the entire Pacific arena, for which purpose it would have to nullify the American forces and eliminate the British presence in Malaya, particularly its control of the key island of Singapore.

The scale and timing of the attacks was extraordinary. The American fleet was attacked at Pearl Harbor at 7.55 a.m. on 7th December 1941. Scarcely an hour later Japanese aircraft struck Hong Kong without warning whilst, at the same time, the Japanese 38th Division advanced towards Hong Kong across the border from China. As this was happening the Japanese invasion fleet was nearing the eastern seaboard of Malaya precisely where their attack had been anticipated. Also on 8th December there was a surprise Japanese air attack against British airfields in both Malaya and Singapore.

Singapore was impregnable from the sea but needed to be protected from the north which meant holding at least the southern part of Malaya. Operation Matador was designed to prevent Japanese forces from landing in the north at Singora and Patani and at the least to enable the Allied forces to take up position in Thailand, thereby to hold and delay in a strong defensive position such Japanese forces as might get ashore. So why was this operation not launched?

The main reason seems to lie in a combination of political and military indecision. Implementation of Matador involved the Allied forces striking north into allegedly neutral Thailand. The powers-that-be persuaded themselves that Japan might attempt a feint – pretend to send an invasion force and then turn back – triggering an over-reaction by the Allied forces moving into Thailand.

So it was that early on 6th December reports came in from two Australian-manned Hudson aircraft that they had sighted two Japanese convoys numbering around seventy ships. That was the moment at which Matador could have been launched, but the military decision-makers were undecided and so sent out more search aircraft. To be fair Major-General Murray-Lyon, the GOC of the 11th Indian Division, was told to be ready to operate Matador at short notice, hence Stuart and his colleagues being assembled and the whole operation made ready for immediate action. A separate Catalina sighting occurred, as reported in the newspapers. However, Allied indecision for those thirty crucial hours enabled the Japanese fleet convoys to advance under the umbrella of bad weather without further sightings. Tragically, it is now known that one further and key Catalina search aircraft had later again succeeded in locating the invasion fleet, but had then been promptly shot down by the Japanese escorting aircraft.

Whilst the Japanese were planning their first landings at Singora and Patani their spies had also told them of the heavy defences described by Stuart at Kota Bharu, which was in Allied territory. The importance of Kota Bharu was its proximity to two neighbouring aerodromes which, if captured, would provide Japanese air cover for continuing invasion operations. The Japanese decided therefore that with no evidence of an immediate threat from the British fleet a simultaneous invasion at that third site should be attempted.

At Kota Bharu the invading force suffered substantial losses as the troops who managed to get ashore bunched up behind the barbed wire entanglements. British fighters and torpedo bombers added to the casualties of the invading force. However, after six hours or more of intensive fighting the Japanese had established a foothold which they were able to exploit despite substantial losses. Crucially the Australian station commander at Kota Bharu airfield then misinterpreted what was happening and evacuated the base, tragically leaving the runways intact for Japanese operations.

The failure to implement Matador meant that the main Japanese landings further north in Thailand itself at Singora and Patani, the very places which the Allies had predicted, were virtually unopposed. What was worse was that sympathizers and fifth columnists had infiltrated the airstrips in those areas and prepared them for Japanese aircraft to land and form a base for their Zero fighters. In comparatively few hours the enemy had managed to land 12,000 men, fully equipped, together with five tanks, nearly 400 vehicles and a large number of bicycles – which some companies of infantry would later put to great use.

The Chiefs of Staff had previously promised to reinforce the RAF in Malaya but this had never happened. 336 aircraft had been expected to arrive by the end of 1941. Instead most of these had been diverted elsewhere in the war theatre, mainly to North Africa. The modest air force in Malaya was largely out of date and although RAF pilots had been assured that their aircraft were more than a match for those of the Japanese, the first encounter with a Zero proved this to be a false premiss. The Zeros quickly demonstrated phenomenal rates of climb and manoeuvrability: the British and Australian aircraft were simply outclassed. This, taken with the tactical errors in airfield support, meant that by the end of the first day British air strength in northern Malaya had been reduced by over half – from 110 operational aircraft to only 50.

CHAPTER THREE

The rain-sodden 11th Indian Division had been standing by to launch Matador since the afternoon of 6th December; by the morning of the 8th time had run out, the option of attempting to deny the Japanese their landing being no longer open. The cancellation of the operation was to the huge anger and demoralization of the troops.

A history of the Sappers by Lieutenant Colonel Muir contains the following passages:

On 8th December 1941 the Japanese flood broke loose and their soldiers poured into every creek and every island of the East. A Japanese air attack was made on the airfield at Kota Bharu on the east coast and 3rd Field Company were ordered south to prepare a demolition belt, but not before a foray was made over the Thailand border to delay any Japanese advance. A road column set out, also an armoured train, keeping in touch with the road column by wireless. To guard against derailing and booby traps, Lieutenant Poyser of 3rd Field Company went with the train, lying on the front of the leading truck inspecting the line as the train proceeded and signaling back to the driver.

The armoured train consisted of two armoured trucks and an armoured engine. The engine had a gallant crew who appeared to have two ambitions: killing Japs and getting more whisky; and two dislikes: moving south and drinking water. The train crossed the frontier at 1900 hours and advanced slowly with Lieutenant Poyser RE on the front of it scanning the rails carefully for mines or derailers by the light of an electric torch. After two hours a 200 foot girder bridge was reached and the Sappers immediately got to work. Almost at once a number of vehicle lights were seen moving south on the road which was about three quarters of a mile from the railway. At midnight the bridge was ready for demolition. The charges went up with a roar which must have been clearly audible on the main road along which lorries were still travelling; but the bridge was only partly demolished and Lieut. Poyser was not satisfied. Work was therefore resumed and it was not until a second lot of charges completely demolished the bridge that the withdrawal was ordered, which was carried out without interference.

To add to the tactical disasters on land and in the air the naval force known as 'Z', largely comprising the mighty battleships *Repulse* and *Prince of Wales*, was not dispatched from Singapore to engage the invasion fleet until late in the day on 8th December. By this time most of the Japanese troops were coming ashore. If only the decision to send force Z had been taken earlier the arrival of the battleships might have been expected to wreak enormous damage amongst the invasion fleet. Also, their large guns could have caused havoc amongst the invading forces as they attempted to land.

Admiral Phillips, in charge of force Z, was actually heading for Singora when his force was sighted by a Japanese submarine which promptly called in an air strike from airfields in Indo-China. The planes failed to find the ships but Phillips is understood to have suspected that there had been a submarine sighting, and being without fighter cover from the air decided to return to Singapore. However, being then given reports (later found to be false) of a Japanese landing at Kuantan, midway down the coast towards Singapore, he decided that his enormous sea power would be more valuable there. Catastrophically, in order to maintain wireless silence and thereby avoid giving away his position, Phillips failed to notify Singapore of the change of plan. One school of thought suggests that Phillips did not seek air support because he believed none was available. In any event, for whatever reason Singapore did nothing to send out fighter cover.

The Japanese dispatched thirty bombers and fifty torpedo bombers from Indo-China in an attempt to seek out and destroy the British ships. Initially they failed to locate them and were about to turn for home when the cloud cover broke and they saw the unprotected ships and escorts below them.

Repulse was the first to be hit, but skilled handling enabled her to avoid the next wave of attackers and she turned to try to help *Prince of Wales* which had now also been severely damaged. In the absence of any air cover the outcome was inevitable. Hit by torpedoes time and again, *Repulse* sank first and then finally *Prince of Wales* turned turtle and sank also. Phillips went down with his ship. Two of the world's greatest battleships had been destroyed in just a few short hours.

The immediate task on land was to delay the Japanese. We know that Stuart on his armoured train with his accompanying engineers succeeded with some limited demolition but the speed of the Japanese advance was too much for them.

The overall strategy was defence: the British troops were not intended to fight a battle of annihilation. It was not even the plan that they should defend to the last man, simply that they should form part of the long-range defence of Singapore and only if the defence lines failed would they need to retreat to Singapore Island itself where they would eventually be needed to defend the aerodromes.

The strength of the Japanese forces was first seen at Asun, north of Jitra, where they overran the first line of British forces dug in there. This was the first shock defeat of the defending army. As the enemy forces drove into Malaya they constantly surprised the British by their ability to penetrate the dense, tangled jungle. It had been assumed by the Allied forces that it would be relatively easy to stop the advance by blocking all the main jungle roads and trails. To their dismay the Japanese troops proved to be well trained in jungle warfare and they moved rapidly through areas that the British regarded as impassable, often working their way round to encircle the defenders. Additionally, as explained previously, to the surprise of the Allies the Japanese had landed a number of light tanks.

The first major stand had always been planned to be at Jitra about six miles south of the Thai frontier and ten miles north of the British airfield at Alor Star. What was to be called the Jitra line was no less than thirty-five miles long. The importance of Jitra was that it was the only prepared defensive position and the only static concentration of British troops between there and Johore state, 450 road miles to the south. The line contained the Leicestershire Regiment and the East Surreys and included two brigades of the 11th Indian Division, including Stuart's 3rd Field Company commanded by his friend Major Beattie.

Although Stuart and his teams had done much valuable work Jitra had not been fully prepared, since it had been anticipated that Matador would have sufficiently delayed the advance to enable final preparation work on the outpost positions to be carried out. The site was waterlogged and last-minute barbed wire barriers and anti-tank mines had to be laid in the frantic few days before the evening of 11th December as the Japanese approached. The troops involved were working against time in bogs of paddy fields, rain and mud. Stuart was by now able to help direct the defensive works.

The Jitra battle itself was complex and occupied the night of the 11th and the whole day of 12th December. Military planners had estimated that a division of men might hold the Jitra line for around three months: in the event it was cut through by the advance Japanese force in little more than twenty-four hours.

Stuart was first involved in demolition work: the 3rd Field Company's main duties were to delay the enemy by carrying out demolitions to the railway and roads. Tragedy had struck earlier in the day when one of Stuart's sapper colleagues thought that the Japanese advance had started and blew a crucial bridge without authorization. The premature demolition proved to be rather too successful and the remaining structure was traversable only on foot and with much difficulty. Two forward companies were trapped on the wrong side and, crucially, this included seven anti-tank guns. Captain Teasdel reckoned that rapid repairs could be effected to save the crucially important armaments but the speed of the Japanese advance meant that the repair was not able to be carried out in time.

As the Allied forces were forced back and the integrity of the defence line deteriorated, Stuart's 3rd Field Company found themselves deployed as infantry alongside the East Surreys. The situation went from bad to worse and eventually Murray-Lyon had no alternative but to order withdrawal of the whole division to the south of Alor Star, a distance of some fifteen miles, preparatory to the occupation of a more permanent fall-back position at Gurun, thirty miles further south. The retreat was more easily said than done: some of the Jitra positions were overrun already, and at many points along the line there were troops fighting for survival rather than being ready for a strategic withdrawal.

The Leicesters, taking the brunt of the fighting, started the battle of Jitra with 23 officers and 625 men and finished with just 7 officers and 150 men.

The speed of the withdrawal meant that in many areas there was no alternative to a running fight. Some groups were cut off and had to try to make their way through the jungle in the hope that they would be able to catch up with the retreating forces – if they survived. This was almost certainly the time when Stuart's last letter reports that he had marched for 'forty-eight hours without stopping'.

The RAF at Alor Star requested permission to destroy not only their runways but additionally a vast amount of equipment in order to avoid it falling into enemy hands. They attempted the destruction themselves but when Stuart arrived to see what help could be given, he and his colleagues were appalled at the trivial damage that had been done to the runways and to the equipment, arms, bombs and ammunition – which had been largely left intact. The sappers did the best they could in the little time available, but the setting alight of the hangars and petrol tanks, visible to the troops in their battle line, was damaging to morale.

A key requirement was to demolish the bridge at Alor Star itself; Stuart and his team planted demolition charges but they only destroyed part of the structure. As this happened the armoured train, in which he had ridden only days before, arrived on the far side. Lieutenant Burns of 3rd Field Company decided that the act of driving the train over the bridge would bring it down, but after they had set the train going and jumped off the bridge remained intact and the unmanned train set off southwards. Burns managed to stop the train and the bridge was eventually brought down with anti-tank mines.

CHAPTER FOUR

After the rout at Asun, the catastrophe of Jitra and the loss of Alor Star the next major delaying action was attempted by the 11th Division at Gurun. The position was suitable for defence, being astride the road and the railway running between the slopes of Kedah Peak and the jungle to the east, but it needed reinforcing. Whilst the Jitra battle had been raging civilian labour had been hired to construct defences at Gurun, but the hired men had evaporated upon the news of the British retreat. In consequence the exhausted troops of the division reaching Gurun on 13th and 14th December had to erect defence works themselves. Some of them had scarcely eaten since the battle for Jitra started on 11th December.

The battle of Gurun was fought on 14th and 15th January. Almost as soon as they had dug into their positions the defenders suddenly found Japanese tanks in front of them. Once more Stuart was forced to fight as infantry alongside the exhausted troops but a Japanese night attack destroyed many of the defences and Brigade HQ was annihilated. Gurun was lost.

During the night of 15th December and the morning of the 16th the remnants of the 11th Indian Division crossed the Muda River hoping for a short respite in Province Wellesley.

Stuart was among the sappers who had successfully demolished the handsome new bridge at Bumbong Lima opened only a few months previously, and was now detailed to destroy the old timber bridge. It appeared impervious to gelignite and gun cotton but when it eventually gave way and the sappers were congratulated, their commander was heard to say, 'I wish to God I could build something for a change.'

In a little more than four days the 11th Division had retreated seventy miles. It was decimated; the survivors were almost out on their feet, badly short of food, with torn clothing drenched and filthy, sodden boots. Most had sores on their feet and leeches were commonplace. There had been heavy losses of crucial weapons, equipment and vehicles.

By 17th December the remnants of the division had been pushed further south, leaving Penang exposed. It was decided to regroup at Ipoh and to merge the shattered remnants of the Leicester and East Surrey Regiments into one force. This would be called the British Battalion and consist of two Leicestershire and two East Surrey companies and a mixed-battalion HQ company.

A few precious days were found and further reorganizations took place including the amalgamation of the 6th and 15th Indian Brigades, necessitated by their substantial losses. It was during one of these days of comparative rest for the 11th Division that Stuart was able to write his first letter home since the invasion – it was Christmas Day.

The troops fell back from Ipoh towards Kampar where perhaps the bloodiest battle of all was to be fought. Stuart's 3rd Field Company was again responsible for demolitions along the roads about Ipoh, whilst the 43rd Field Company 'scorched the earth' on the way, attempting to deny the invading army supplies and support.

Kampar itself was roughly halfway between Penang and Kuala Lumpur and the position was thought to be the strongest in Malaya, more open than the mountainous jungles of northern Malaya and suitable for light artillery in which the British still considered they had superiority. The main road and railway ran past a steep jungle-clad hill, nine miles by six, rising to 4,000 feet with a road on either side. This strategic site was to be occupied by the newly formed British Battalion.

The stand at Kampar lasted from 30th December to 2nd January. Throughout the three days of heavy fighting every effort of the Japanese to force a passage was frustrated by continuous losses. Inevitably the brunt of the attack was borne by the British Battalion which suffered heavy casualties but inflicted huge losses on the enemy.

On the third day of the battle the appearance of a large force of Japanese reinforcements led to the British Battalion's withdrawal. Stuart had been pressed into infantry during the Kampar stand but once withdrawal started he was redeployed into demolition work to try to slow the enemy advance.

Kampar having been lost, now the Slim River confrontation was to take place. This was perhaps the most decisive engagement of the campaign but it goes without saying that the British troops were not at their best. They had retreated over a distance of 176 miles with only two or three days' rest in over three weeks. They had just fought the action at Kampar, one of the fiercest battles recorded, and had almost won. When they were not fighting, always it seemed against superior numbers, they had been retreating. Coupled with all this was the menace from the air, with constant strafing and bombing and apparently complete domination of the skies by the enemy.

Stuart's 3rd Field Company, still led by Major Beattie, was employed on anti-tank measures and preparation for demolition of the Trolak Bridge and a bridge on the Tilau road between the trunk road and the railway. Additionally they were employed in planting fifty booby traps, mostly on the railway, and assisting the infantry in the erection of Dannert wire.

After initial probing attacks on 5th and 6th January, the Japanese changed tactics in the early hours of 7th January. They formed up a column of tanks interspersed with infantry. Enemy engineering sections moved ahead dismantling some of the tank obstacles and the whole column then advanced with overwhelming force.

One Gurkha defending battalion disintegrated and the enemy armour cut through nineteen miles of the 11th Indian Division territory. Ideally the bridges over the Slim River would have been destroyed to prevent the advance but there had been no warning of such a sudden armoured breakthrough. The lack of telephone cable to inform those at the rear of the approach of the tanks caused a disastrous lack of communication which proved to be a major factor.

Again Stuart was heavily involved. To quote from a history of the battle:

Lieut. Poyser of 3rd Field Company, reported to Brigade HQ: 'There's a furious battle going on about half a mile ahead. For heaven's sake let's have permission to block the road.'

Stuart's efforts were now concentrated on roadblocks rather than bridge demolition. By the time the decision to blow the key bridges had finally been taken the first explosive charge had failed and the Japanese tanks were arriving.

The enemy continued to advance and cause further destruction in the retreating British lines – and as a result two brigades of the 11th Division simply ceased to exist as fighting forces. The battle of Slim River was over.

The survivors tried to regroup, and struck out into the jungle, struggling south to try to join up with the retreating British force. Many succeeded but many did not.

There was no alternative to the Allied forces starting the long retreat towards the bottom of the peninsula at Johore. A tactical decision had been made to fall back and then to seek to hold the Japanese north of Johore. It was expected that reinforcements would arrive in the shape of the 18th British Division and it was hoped that the Japanese might be driven back. Additionally it was understood that Australian reinforcements were ready to be landed: perhaps with these increased Allied numbers the Japanese could finally be forced on to the defensive.

CHAPTER FIVE

The depleted 11th Division had been attempting to hold the western end of a defensive line, ninety miles across, from one side of the southern part of Malaya to the other. The idea was to allow the planned reinforcements to reach Singapore by sea, and in fact 7,000 men from the 44th Indian Brigade and nearly 2,000 Australians were successfully landed. However, the Indians were raw and untrained and there was a suggestion, probably unfair, that this was also true of the Australians, one brigadier being quoted as saying 'they were so undisciplined as to be a liability to their own side'.

Since the 11th Indian Division had taken the worst of the battering it was agreed that there should be a leapfrogging strategy to take advantage of the latest defensive line. They would move south of the line and rest in southern Johore. Thus on 13th January the 11th Indian Division duly passed through the bottleneck of the defence line at Tampin and then withdrew to the Coronation Rubber Estate in Kluang-Rengam, a short distance from Johore. This was the planned rest area which they reached on 14th January and where it was hoped the exhausted troops could have some ten days of rest.

Stuart's last dramatic letter was written from the rest area on 15th January. He was obviously bursting to tell his story but it is perhaps remarkable that he had the enthusiasm to put pen to paper so quickly after the huge activity of the last month. It had been planned that the first three days of the ten days' respite would be spent giving the men complete rest; they would then have three days of light work and then four days of training before proceeding to the jungle to reinforce or replace the forces manning the defence line.

Sadly, only the following day the intended few precious days of recuperation were brought to an abrupt end by the actions of the Japanese who had made a number of landings behind the defence line, the major one being on the west coast at Batu Pahat. This was potentially disastrous to holding the line and the entire fall-back strategy so no alternative was found to the exhausted 11th Indian Division being ordered back into action in order to try to hold Batu Pahat and the west coast road. They were taken by lorries to the scene of conflict where Stuart's 3rd Field Company, of which he had now been promoted to second in command, set about preparing roadblocks and booby traps in Batu Pahat town.

Fighting continued over the next week. Again the defensive line was breached and there was alarming news of the Japanese forces killing wounded Allied prisoners. As the scale of the enemy advance became clear the fear of further losses persuaded General Wavell, now in supreme command, to order the final withdrawal to Johore immediately.

This was all very well in theory but around one thousand men of the British Battalion were trapped at Senggarang. Yet further Japanese landings at Batu Pahat had cut them off and they were unable to escape because of tidal swamps. The stranded men began to trek through the swamps of mangroves and eventually reached the Sungai Bata River. They were joined there by other troops including the remnants of the 15th Indian Brigade together with Stuart and the other survivors of his 3rd Field Company.

It was decided that the only place from which this seemingly abandoned group could be evacuated was the village at Kampong Ponggor. Three local boats were commandeered and set off in the hope that at least one might manage to contact the naval authorities at the southern end of the Johore west coast. In the meantime, on the night of 27th January, the small abandoned force crossed the Sungai Bata swamp on a bridge that Stuart and his fellow sappers had constructed from small sampang boats and started the long trek to Kampong Ponggor. It was a slow process but the men, now numbering about 1,500 in all, reached the village at dawn on 28th January.

One of the three boats that had been sent out managed to make landfall further down the coast and was able to report the whereabouts of the missing troops. Naval Command was contacted and some five hours later Lt. Commander Victor Clarke, who had survived the sinking of the *Repulse*, rowed ashore to the mudflats of Ponggor from a small gunboat, greeting the first of the survivors with the words 'Dr Livingstone, I presume?'

The marooned men were given food and medical supplies whilst Clarke returned to base to organize a rescue. HMS *Dragonfly* and HMS *Scorpion* were the main naval ships leading the operation over the nights of 29th, 30th and 31st January. It had to be done at night and during the two long days in between there was a real risk of the rest of the men being discovered by either enemy spotter planes or Japanese infantry passing along the roadway only a thousand yards away.

The Times of 6th February described this Malayan 'Dunkirk' as follows:

British gunboats and patrol vessels, manned by navy personnel, towed a fleet of small launches, sampans, dinghies and other small craft by night to the scene of the evacuation. Because of the shallowness of the water it was impossible for the larger vessels to go closer inshore. Small craft were paddled and poled up creeks and swamps, collected soldiers, and took them out to larger vessels.

It was in this way that Stuart and his fellows sailed around the west coast of Singapore Island and were brought into Keppel Harbour; it was touch and go because as this was happening the last of the retreating troops came across the causeway from Johore and into the north of Singapore Island. The evacuation was complete when, at eight in the morning of 31st January, the pipers of the Argylls played the last men across the narrow passage to the island, and the causeway was then breached to prevent Japanese advances. Malaya had been lost; now only Singapore remained.

The 'fortress' of Singapore was an island with a coastal perimeter of seventy miles and the harsh reality was that much of the south and west coasts were devoid of any adequate defences. When the last of the troops had passed over the causeway the population of the island, swollen from its usual 550,000, stood at close to a million people.

Whilst there were ample supplies of rations the water supply was vulnerable. In short the island was no fortress, it was in effect an undefended tropical island with a coast indented with creeks and mangrove swamps similar to those that the enemy had proved capable of exploiting on the mainland.

From 31st January to 7th February there were constant air attacks and artillery bombardments. The Japanese particularly concentrated their shelling on the long-suffering 11th Indian Division which had now been re-equipped and moved to the north-west. All the other sappers in the 11th Indian Division were fully employed on demolitions in the Naval Base area but it had been Stuart's hard-pressed 3rd Field Company that was again deployed as infantry, leaving him to be once more involved in hand-to-hand fighting.

The Japanese simulated an attack in the north-east which proved to be a diversion. It quickly became clear that the feared major landing by the Japanese was indeed to be in the north-west very close to where Stuart was now positioned.

On 8th February the bombardment increased in intensity and by midnight the Japanese had landed on the north-west coastal area which was occupied by the 22nd Australian Brigade. This was completely overrun. *The Times* reported landings on a ten mile front and counter-attack by the defenders regaining some ground. The fighting was intense over the next few days with incessant attacks by Japanese dive bombers.

On 11th February Stuart's company was detailed to hold the south-west sector of Tenga airfield on the east of the road between Neesoon and the Naval Base.

Brigadier Steedman's 1944 letter describes how, at 9 a.m. on 12th February 1942 and only four days before Singapore surrendered, Stuart was killed.

Would that his father had known the detail of his exploits over those last eight weeks of his life.

He would have been very proud.

BOOK THREE

Ann in her late teenage years

CHAPTER ONE

I do not remember my father. I was told that he had held me in his arms after I was born, and that he used to play with me in that first year of my life before he joined the Indian army in 1940. Mary would boast of her recollection of his playing with her: she had five years of his affections, both before and after his six months' leave in 1937. She would have been three when he came back to Assam and six when he left for the army, and at that time I was only just beginning to walk, so although I pretended that her memories were more wishful than real that was only because I was jealous that she had known him.

When I was old enough to understand Mama would tell me that my father was a great man, and as a treat she would sometimes walk us the five kilometre journey down the track to the middle of the Pengaree tea estate and show us the huge thatched bungalow in which he had lived. When she first did this she explained that he had joined the army and was going to fight a war, but these were words that meant nothing to me. I was impressed by the house on the estate, and I think I would have been pleased if I had known then that our little leaf-thatched mud house, or busti, had been built on land provided by him, but he was too distant a concept for me to concern myself with at that age.

In those days there were no bedtime stories, for neither my mother nor my sister could read. I remember I had to go to bed earlier than Mary, though the charpai where we slept wasn't a bed but a rough bamboo frame with string laced across and just strong enough for two small children. There was another larger charpai for our mother and her sister where they would curl up between us and the doorway of our busti, the sacking across the entrance being let down at night. I suppose they slept there to give us some protection if animals should venture inside. I do not remember any such incursion, but the feral noises of the jungle were a constant background to the night.

Our little house was built out of bamboo plastered with dried cow dung, the roof being of palm leaves or toko paat and the floor plastered with mud. There were no chairs to sit on, save for some small wooden flat stools or pinas, but we children were well used to squatting on the floor.

My earliest memories were of helping Mary and the other village children catch the tiny fish that swam in the rivulets and puddles that surrounded the little circle of huts in the rainy season. Mud must have been a constant accompaniment but a small child was not conscious of such impediment and I recall only the jumping up and down excitement of our occasional tiny catch and my pride when Mary allowed me to carry the water-filled pot in which the small fish lived out their last hours.

There were six Hindi-speaking families in the village, and eight Singpho families. The Singpho tribe were proud of their reputation as the first to farm tea in Assam; their origins were in Burma. The Singpho houses were called chung houses, having their floor as a platform or chung of bamboo built at least nine feet from the ground. I was terrified of climbing the stairs since the split bamboo which was spliced together to make the chung made crunching sounds that frightened me, but Mary and I were frequent visitors, not least because they cooked a special rice called toopala bhat which I loved. The headman of the village, the Gaon Bura, was a loyal Singpho and ensured that their tribal customs were followed. The women were renowned as expert weavers and most of the houses had looms in the sheltered area underneath the first floor where the wives produced coloured cloths using dyes from the roots of trees. The Singphos were allowed more than one wife so there were plenty of women to do the weaving. Each house stood in its own land fenced to keep in the animals.

My favourite meal was boiled rice with dal or lentils accompanied by a chutney called dhamia patta made of coriander leaf, but I also liked to have our daily rice cooked in a sticky sauce mixed with coconut and molasses. Mama called this bora choul. She was proud when we were able to have fish with our bhat or boiled rice. I also loved ghol which was skimmed curd mixed with water, salt and sugar. Mama cooked on a fire built on the ground and we fetched water from the nearest hand pump.

My great delight was to go shopping with Mama. The nearest little shop was a shack just short of the river which crossed the track to Pengaree estate. In the dry season the river was quite shallow and my mother could carry me across it, clambering down the sandy river bank and wading through the fast running water with her sari hitched around her waist and me on her hip. When the water was higher Dhrin Babu, the shopkeeper, would carry over a grown-up person for four annas, or use his dugout boat to ferry each passenger across the river for eight annas. The shop itself was more a stall than a building, but we could buy spices and oils, soaps and cloths and a few utensils. I would plead to be allowed to carry the straw bag holding the shopping but Mary would usually take over after a few yards.

When Mary was six, which was the year my father left, she was allowed to help one of the other local girls look after our cow and sometimes the few other cows in the area. I called our cow Boogoo; it had been bought for Mama by my father and as I grew older I was allowed to help to milk it. The milk was very important in our little village and my mother was generous in allowing others to share it. I remember that at one time a baby belonging to a family who lived in the Lines close to the Pengaree estate fell ill and the doctor said that milk was needed regularly. Rather than their having to fetch the milk every day, Mama simply allowed them to have our cow live with them for the time it took the baby to recover, although it meant that we ourselves went short. Despite her generosity I now know that some of the other villagers were envious that a single mother with only her sister sharing the house had the riches of a busti to herself, and a valuable cow, on land that she had been given.

Our greatest treat was to be allowed to look at the book of photographs that Mama would show us when we could persuade her to do so. I can now see that she longed to remind herself of the pictures and her apparent resistance to our clamouring for them was artificial. The book was a battered half-empty photograph album containing only three pages of black and white prints. The scenes were of my father's relatives and friends in family gatherings. There were pictures of my father's parents, and of his sister. My own sister loved to ask 'What was his sister's name?', well knowing that the answer was 'Mary', at which she would preen herself in delight. One of our favourite photographs was of a garden with a winding path leading past a large bench or garden seat to a little house. Mother would tell us she had been told that the house was called a 'summer house' and was not lived in, but simply used as a quiet spot on hot days. It seemed very strange to us that a house of such quality should not be occupied by at least one family and that a seat of such apparent size should be placed outside rather than inside the house.

Uncle Daniel was working in the bungalows on the tea estate and would call to see Mama every week. I was not old enough to understand but Mama would usually seem to be happier after his visits which, looking back, must have been because he was able to pass on such news as he had of my father. The tea plantation was still manned and those planters who remained would have listened to the news on the radio. They would also have had letters from their friends who had joined up. Sometimes a letter would be handed over, and the next day Mama would leave us and go to the tea estate where I believe the office manager would read the letters to her.

Then there came a time when I came home from playing in the stream near the village and found Mama crying. I remember sitting on her knee and asking her what was the matter and her reply, 'Papa is fighting the war'. I suppose I would then have been about three years old, not understanding that in the past year the Japanese invasion of Malaya had changed both the fears and expectations of those who lived in our part of the world and that the fate of those from Assam who had joined up was in the balance. Uncle Daniel was a regular visitor on almost every day that week and the weeks following, and my mother was not herself, clearly distracted and often tearful, uninterested in all our games and our friends.

I remember that one day Mary herself was looking solemn. I

asked her what was the matter and she said she had overheard Daniel saying that our father's army had lost to the enemy. From that time onwards Mama seemed to lose her sparkle. Our life continued as before, but we would often find her in tears and there were many family discussions from which Mary and I were excluded. Grandfather was now nearly blind, and we would help to lead him around and look after him as best we could. Mary and I played with the other children in the village, speaking in the local language of Sadri.

I must have been a difficult child: I recall many fights with other children and I fear that I may have been the main culprit. The reason was that Mary and I had the disadvantage of our lighter skin, and this singled us out as being different. I now know that there were a number of planters' children in the area, but at that time Mary and I were the only ones in our immediate community, and caste differences were important. This meant that we were often called names, and as I did not understand why I would hit out in response.

It was a humid evening about a year later when Mama sat down with the two of us and finally took us into her confidence. I must have been four years old but only remember that I had been out all day helping Mary with the village cattle and that we had just guided them back from the grazing land into the safety of their night-time shelter. We were hot but happy. We stopped chattering and quietened down when we saw that Mama had been crying. Carefully she laid down the book of photographs which she had been holding and put her arms around us. She told us that there had been a big battle and that the British army, of which our father's regiment was part, had lost and that many men had been captured. For many months she had known that our father was missing and she had hoped to hear that he was held by the enemy and would come home one day. Now she had heard that he had died in the fighting. She said that he had been a very brave man.

I had kept to myself my childish vision that one day my father, resplendent in uniform, would walk into the village and take us back to live in the big bungalow on the tea estate. As I now held on to my tearful mother and sister those little dreams vanished. The evening merged into lamentation with my aunt and my grandmother joining with Mama in shrouding their faces with their saris and swaying together in the merging of their grief.

It is only when I look back that I realize the anguish that my mother had been suffering. My father had been missing for over a year and she had feared the worst. She knew that she was ineligible for the death benefits and the company pension that would have been hers had there been a formal marriage. Most of the money that had been left for her had already gone, and now his death meant that she was alone and unable to provide for her children.

Little did we know what further tragedy was to follow.

CHAPTER TWO

The photograph album in its tin box was kept separately from a leather box into which Mary and I had never looked. We both knew that it contained papers because we had seen Mama take out the box when she thought we were asleep, carefully unlock it with a key that she kept around her neck and turn the pages over as if she was reading them. The box was kept in a hollow in the ground, deep in the hut and close to the back wall, and was covered with sand with a chipped bowl on top to complete its concealment. One day, perhaps a month after the news of our father's death, Mary and I were on our way back from looking after the village cows, for which Mary was to be paid a small coin, when we heard shouts and a high wailing. We ran to our hut to find Mama being held by neighbours as she thrashed her arms and legs and cried out. She put out her arms and clutched us to her but we were able neither to console her nor to stop her constant keening wail. She kept pointing to the back of the hut and we saw that a hole had been cut in the bamboo wall; when we were able to escape her arms and go inside we found that the place in which the leather box had been hidden was now uncovered and empty.

I was still too young to understand, but in later years Mama explained to me that the box had contained details of my father's address in England, his parents' and sister's names, and letters from him asking them to provide support for her and her children if anything happened to him. He had told Mama that this was her protection if he did not return from the war since without this proof he feared that any claims to his parenthood might be denied. Her distress and despair at the theft of the box can be imagined. She was now truly alone with no means of providing education or financial help for me or Mary.

Also, being illiterate, she had no knowledge of any more precise identity save through the tea estate manager, who was unlikely to be sympathetic to the release of any information.

In the days and weeks that followed I would hear Mama sobbing in the night. During the day she would often be in tears. Friends came and went but she remained inconsolable. I know that she would often go to Pengaree to the tea estate and she later told me that Daniel helped her in conversations with the management although she was not able to speak to the estate manager directly. Perhaps it is unsurprising that nothing was done: the tea company would hardly have wished to contact unsuspecting families in England to say that illegitimate children of their beloved but now deceased offspring were seeking help. My father must have realized this and left the letters and papers to support such an approach if needed, although he must have been apprehensive as to the reaction of his own parents if contact were ever made.

Although my mother's family were Hindus, as were all the Adivasi tribe, when she had been with my father he had explained the Christian religion to her and after we were born he had taught her to say prayers with us. Although we spoke Sahdri in the village at home we knew a lot of Hindi and we had been taught some English by our uncle Daniel so that we could say our prayers in English. Mama had used English with my father so she could make herself understood when it was necessary.

The Pengaree tea estate had a small chapel and those who worked on the estate were encouraged to use it. Many of the estate workers had come from Ranchi, well outside Assam, and were Catholics and this was their main place of worship. The chapel had no altar and no pews, it was simply a wooden house standing beside the track on the edge of the estate, but it was somewhere to congregate and there was a Catholic priest who visited on rare occasions. When I was much older Mama explained that she would often go there at this time of terrible uncertainty in order to think what she should do. For herself she had neither fears nor great ambition, but for us she wanted education and a foothold in the world. She knew that the other village children would remain illiterate and live out their simple lives in such employment as they might find on the estates. For us she sought a wider future.

It was the rainy season. We would shelter in the busti and make up names for the sound of the rain. Yesterday it was a tiger: roaring through the jungle and crashing on to the flimsy thatch of the roof. Today it was a water buffalo: heavy and steady, beating out a constant rhythm and turning the flattened earth into mud. Out of the steam of the mist came a figure carrying an umbrella: Daniel, always the one to adopt the trappings of the planters. We watched him tread urgently through the shallows of yellow mud.

'Monglee, Monglee, the priest is on the estate, come quickly!'

'What is a priest?' I asked Mary as Mama, her best shawl over her head and Daniel's free arm around her waist, vanished down the track towards Pengaree.

'Someone who prays all the time.'

I knew about prayers: from an early age Mama would make us kneel down each night to ask God to bring Papa back safely from the war; now we prayed for his soul and for what Mary called our salvation, before we would move on to pray for our families. I sat and listened to the buffalo rain and waited.

It was a long time before Mama returned. Now there was a larger umbrella carried by a fat man wearing black cloth. He made a funny squeaky panting sound and his eyes looked a bit like a frog, but I didn't dare to giggle as we were made to sit on the earth in the middle of the hut as Mama made chai.

I heard the word 'school' and then 'Gauhati'.

'So far!'

Mama seemed to be protesting but I lost interest and went back to tying a small piece of raffia string between my fingers as if it was a spider's web.

CHAPTER THREE

Mary had been told not to tell me what was being planned. She was old enough to have understood what Father Bernard, as she called him, was saying. She knew that he had agreed to recommend that the two of us be taken in by a convent school located in somewhere called Gauhati. She only knew that it was a long way away, but she had never been further than Digboi, which was nearly a full day's walk down the mud road used by the tea estate lorries. She knew that Tinsukia town was twice as far away, so she thought in her own mind that it would be about that distance.

We were often hungry. One day we came home to find Mama handing over her best sari to a neighbour. That was the week that a large container of rice found its way into our hut. Looking back she would always be sewing or stitching and otherwise helping others in our village and I can now remember friends bringing food when they came to visit us, and assume this was by way of recompense. I carried on with my happy childhood but would later recall what must have been weeks of preparation.

Particularly the day we sold the cow: riding with my beloved Boogoo in the back of a company truck and trying to keep out of the way of her hooves; the long journey to the cattle market, sleeping with my head in Mama's lap for most of the way. The first part of the journey was down the jungle road to Digboi, where we had been before and where I had been shown the big railway engines, but then the truck went on a bigger and much busier road to the distant town of Tinsukia, passing through Makum Junction on the way.

Daniel rode in the cab of the lorry with the driver; when we reached our destination it was he who conducted the talks with the men in the cattle market, and it was he who finally lead Boogoo away as I buried my head and cried. Then the shopping, the huge open space with the market and the people and the stalls and the noise. And such noise, lorries and cars on the road, the roaring of steam engines as they battered along their tracks. It was so different from our small hamlet and even the bustle of the tea estate. I held tightly to Mary's hand.

We were each bought a dress, mine a red check and Mary's a lemon yellow with red flowers. I had never had a proper dress and when the shopkeeper held up the big shiny glass and I saw this complete little girl I was shy and covered my face. I had only seen my face in the little cracked glass in the hut. And there were shoes – brown with bright buckles and straps for Mary and little black shoes for me – 'naughty boy shoes' as Mama called them. We bought some pants, which I was quite unused to wearing, and little socks and then Mama said she would spend no more money. She and Daniel had argued during the day about what to buy and I could see her worried face as she tried to bring down the price of each item, remonstrating with the arm-waving shopkeepers, but without evident satisfaction when she was successful.

Then there was the long journey back to the village. We spent a night in a hut belonging to a friend of Daniel's, but I remember only that I was tired and I curled up to sleep once we had eaten our simple meal. It was still the rainy season, and the truck slid and spun its wheels on the yellow mud of the track running between the dark greens of the invading vegetation. I tried to talk to Mary but she was very quiet and I can now understand how she must have been feeling about the separation that was to come.

CHAPTER FOUR

Whilst St Mary's Convent School in Gauhati was less than 400 miles from Pengaree, it could hardly have been more remote than the great capital of Delhi itself as far as my mother was concerned. Neither she nor her parents had ever travelled further than Dibrugah, some fifty miles away, and even that journey had only been made twice by Monglee. She later told me that she still remembered how relieved she had been to return to the simple peace of her village. Certainly she had herself seen the mighty Brahmaputra River, and knew that what seemed to her to be its great width – the far bank barely visible in the distance – was much, much greater as it made its journey to the west. She had been told that Gauhati was close to the Brahmaputra but did not know how far down river it might be. In the simple village school she had once seen a map of the whole of India and had been able to put her small finger on where Assam stood almost separated from the rest. She had also been told that many of the rules and regulations of which both her father and Stuart had complained were administered in Gauhati and that it was much larger than Dibrugah itself.

What I now know Mama could not comprehend was how far Mary and I would have to travel. How could she accept in her mind, as she stared into the darkness of the hut each sleepless night, the still uncertain length of time that she would be separated from us? The cost of the journey to the school was very large – how could she raise funds for us to return for the one holiday each year which she had been told we would be allowed? How could we, and how would she, manage for a year or more apart?

Oblivious to what was happening I lived the giggles and tears of my young life as before. Then came a day when I returned home from the fields to find a cloth parcel with my new clothes and shoes all wrapped up inside. Mary had a parcel too and I could see that Mama was upset. She drew us both to her, sitting me on her knee, and started to talk about her wanting us to go to school. She said that the school was a long way away and that we were to set out tomorrow. She would travel with us as far as Makum Junction but we were then going to go on a train, and Mary would look after me. Travelling with us would be Mansuk Mura, a senior servant of the Pengaree estate who had been to Gauhati and had also travelled on a railway train. He had told Mama that he knew the procedure to be followed.

There was some good news as far as I was concerned. I had a friend called Aileen, and she was to come to the same school with us. Aileen and I were friends most of the time. Some of the time she gave herself airs and graces and I was angry with her, but she was close to my age, and like me she had a lighter skin, so we sometimes fought as a pair together when the other children tried to call us names. Aileen lived in another village with her mother who was also from the Adivasi tribe. Her mother had helped with the cleaning duties at the big house of the manager, Duncan Cummings. I only knew that he was said to be a very important person and Aileen said he was her father. I did not really understand this. I knew that the manager had an English wife who wore beautiful dresses and big hats, and I had once been with Aileen when the manager's wife had turned her head away when we tried to say hello as she walked past us. Anyway, I was pleased that Aileen was going to come to our new school but still did not comprehend what was going to happen.

Mary asked how long we would be at school and when we would come home. She must have sensed from Mama's attempt at a reassuring reply that it might be a long time and she started to cry. I began to sob too and my last memory of that moment was of the three of us holding each other very tightly as the tears flowed.

Later that day all our neighbours came round to wish us well, and then my grandfather and grandmother arrived to share a meal with us. They made a fuss of us and grandfather gave me a small boat that he had carved as a present for the journey. It had a tiny mast with a leaf woven to it as a sail and it was in a small box he had made out of wood to keep it safe.

Early the next morning we set out down the path to the Pengaree estate. Daniel carried the two bundles of clothes and a further parcel of food for the journey. Mama and her sister held our hands tightly. Dhrin Babu did not need to use his boat, he carried Mary and me, one on each arm, and the others all waded across the stream. When Mama tried to give him money he waved her away and patted each of us on the head. Our grandparents and even the headman of the village with all our other friends had come to say goodbye, walking with us to the banks of the stream and waving as we passed between the green walls of the jungle till we reached the estate. There a truck was waiting and we were individually introduced to Mansuk Mura, a kindly and solemn man wearing a red turban and the jacket of a respected chowkidar with the name 'Pengaree T.E.' stitched on to it. Aileen was there with her mother, and Mary and I were dismayed to find that she had a proper trunk with lots of clothes in it. Our small tightly tied packages suddenly seemed very small. She was wearing a dress which she said was 'to travel in' but it was as nice a dress as the only one that I had, and I felt sad.

Mama continued to hold us to her during the jolting passage to the railway station at Makum Junction. She helped us up on to the train and stared intently through the window of the carriage as we were all settled down next to the glass, sitting side by side and holding hands, with chowkidar Mansuk Mura on the far side. I could see that her eyes were wet. For perhaps ten minutes she stood there, bravely trying to smile and gesticulating as the clouds of steam began to hide the platform from view. Then, as a loud whistle from the engine frightened me, I buried my head in Mary's lap, and the train noisily wheezed its way slowly away from the station. Mama waved and waved as we moved out into the sunlight.

The journey took two days. I cannot remember the detail. It was exciting to see out of the windows and to wave at the people in the fields who looked up as the train went by. There were little treats such as the opening up of our food parcel and taking out the different packages which Mansuk Mura explained were labelled for each separate meal. There was a family in the carriage who were very kind to us, and although their children were much older they did their best to keep us interested and shared some of their food with us. Then at the end of the first long day we came to a big town and spent the night at a lodging house before changing trains and moving on in the morning.

Mary tried to keep both Aileen and me amused and to invent games to keep us happy. She suddenly seemed rather grown up: she would even tell us off if we became too noisy, rather as Mama would have done if she had been there. I do not think that I particularly missed my mother during the journey, there was too much to see and do, but by the end of the second day when we were all tired I remember crying for her and that Mary tried to comfort me.

At last we reached Gauhati. It was a very large station, with many platforms and milling people, much larger than the many other stations we had passed through in those two days. Mansuk Mura had already insisted that we tidy ourselves up and put on our dresses and shoes. Mary had helped me and Aileen to get ready in the last hour before the train reached the end of its journey and as the carriages sighed to a halt we were led out on to the platform while our escort looked anxiously up and down. He ushered us towards the crowds at the front of the train and it was then that I saw a tall figure in white who was gesturing in our direction.

I now know that Sister Teresa was an Italian nun, although as far as I was concerned at the time she spoke Hindi, but in a funny way. I was shy and hid as best I could behind Mary, but the Sister seemed friendly and took us all through the station hall to a jeep outside. The driver helped Mansuk Mura with Aileen's trunk and our two small bundles of possessions and I saw some papers pass between him and Sister Teresa. We had become quite fond of our escort during the long journey, and when he bent down to say goodbye all three of us held on to him and kissed him. He stood waving as the car pulled away, our last contact with our families disappearing in the swirling dust of the station yard.

CHAPTER FIVE

The jeep bumped through the outskirts of the town, weaving through the dry potholes and evading the multitude of animals, bicycles, cars and thronging people going about their business amongst the stalls and eating shacks lining the roadside. The driver sounded his horn as he turned towards a building standing behind high iron railings. Mary suddenly read out loud the words 'Saint Mary's Convent' from the big blue board which stood beside the metal gates. At the sound of the engine the two gates swung open and we swept in and around the circular driveway to stop in front of the main building.

The convent school was run by nuns belonging to the Salesian Order of Don Bosco. Most of them were Italians including Sister Clotelde, the Mother Superior. The Italian nuns spoke little English and were in charge of the boarding house. There were also some Indian nuns who knew English and looked after most of the teaching duties. Some outside teachers came in too, mainly to help with the day pupils from the surrounding area. Mary and I were to find that there were around fifty fellow boarders, most from poor Indian families in the surrounding villages, and including some ten of us Anglo-Indian girls. We ten were fortunate to have our separate dormitory within the boarding house, and a small boxroom with pigeon-holes for our clothes.

We had arrived in the late afternoon and as we were led through the main school building which fronted on to the driveway we were overwhelmed by the sound of more than fifty children playing in the walled compound at the back. The back of the building opened on to a wide verandah which formed one side of a central courtyard area flanked by the buildings that comprised the rest of the school, the whole rear section being surrounded by a high wall.

As the sister escorted us through the courtyard area towards the boarding house there came waves of excited chatter as most of the children ran over to look at the new arrivals.

'What is your name? Where are you from? How old are you?'

I was frightened and kept a tight hold of Mary's hand, trying to hide my head in her side. Aileen was a little bolder and called out her name but that only produced laughter when someone said, 'What sort of a name is that!'

She stayed silent until we entered the cool shade of the bungalow building that was to be our home. This was a square thatched building forming one side of the courtyard. On the opposite side was the chapel, and the building linking the two was where the nuns lived and Mother Superior had her office.

Dominating the courtyard, and facing away from the verandah in front of which it stood, was a life-sized statue of the Blessed Virgin.

It was Sister Mary Mascarinas who escorted us: she worked in the school office and was Indian, speaking Hindi and good English. She was small and unfriendly and I did not like her. We were shown into the small room that was to be our dormitory: there were no beds but neatly folded blankets on the swept earthen floor. In the little room next door we were shown which our cubby holes were to be. Mine was number three. Mary carefully repeated this to me until she was satisfied that I remembered the number – I could go from one to ten so three was good. I put my bundle of possessions into the wooden rack and watched Mary and Aileen, eight and ten respectively, do likewise. Aileen's trunk had been carried in by now and Sister Mary's eyebrows went up as it was unlocked and the various clothes were unpacked and squeezed into the compact space of cubby hole number ten. We were then taken off to meet the Mother Superior in her office.

To me Sister Clotelde seemed old and very tall. I suppose she would have been about fifty years old and from my small height looking upwards I could see her long aquiline nose which looked rather like the beak of the Pengaree village rooster. Save for her bony hands she seemed to be totally covered in black cloth, which even surrounded her rather fierce face. I cannot recall that I ever knew the colour of her hair. The Mother Superior's office was at the back of the compound, overlooking the rear wall of the school, and the late afternoon sun angled in across her shoulders as she sat with her back to the single window.

'You are Mary and Ann from Pengaree and your father worked on the tea estate until he joined the army but he has now been killed; you are ten and five years old respectively. And you are Aileen, just six years old, from Digboi and your father was also on the tea estate there and is now in the army also.'

It seemed to be a statement rather than a question, but Mary as our spokesman nodded her head.

'You are privileged to be here. It is thanks to Father Bernard of Digboi that you have been admitted. You will behave yourselves perfectly, and try to be a credit to our school. I will introduce you to the school at morning assembly.'

Not a smile nor expression of kindness crossed the Mother Superior's face as she waved her hand as a signal to Sister Mary to remove us from her presence. I held my sister's hand more tightly.

CHAPTER SIX

Aileen and I were the youngest of the boarders and it was only the boarders who were in the school that afternoon since the day scholars, as they were called, went home at 3 p.m. The time for the boarders to play their own games had just come to an end and they now had half an hour in the study room before evening prayers. One of the bigger girls, Angela, who was about fourteen, was chosen to show the three of us around the school and to explain the procedures. She walked us round the various buildings including the classrooms which were in the main block between the front verandah facing the circular drive and the rear verandah facing the courtyard. The study room was one of these but the others were empty so we were able to explore them. She also showed us the small chapel where the nuns worshipped, too small for the whole school who, she told us, assembled on or in front of the verandah. As she explained this there came the loud ringing of the school bell at which all the other boarding children ran out of the study room in our direction: it was time for evening prayers.

I was pleased that the prayers were said in Hindi. All the sisters lined up on the verandah and we sat on the earth of the courtyard in front of them, standing up or kneeling when required. The Mother Superior was not there that evening, and it seemed that she usually only appeared for morning assembly. The other sisters were all lined up: Sister Carolina; Sister Teresa who was in charge of the kitchen so to become one of my favourites; Sister Ernestina who was in charge of games; Sister Rose and Sister Mary who were both Hindi as was Sister Angela; and another kitchen sister called Sister Anne. They were all looking at us three new arrivals as we tried to follow what was going on. I was always the last to kneel down or stand up or cross myself and I could see Sister Mary's sorrowful shaking of her head as she watched my flustered efforts to copy the others.

I was so hungry. We had finished the last of our food the previous evening, and although Mansuk Mura had brought us some chai and some rice at one of the stops on the train, this had been quite early that morning. As the prayers finished we all trooped into our boarders' house and I saw that there was a dining room that I had not seen previously. There we all sat on long benches and Mary managed to find some space for me on one side of her and for Aileen on the other side. Immediately the other girls opposite and around us started to fire questions to find out our names and where we were from. I said little, but Mary did the best that she could and within a short while we were so pleased to find plates of rice and vegetable curry being passed around. It was quite good and I wolfed it down.

As far as I could tell most of the other girls – excluding the ten of us who were Anglo-Indian– were from poor families from local villages which were too far away for them to be able to travel to school each day. They ranged in age from my five years to fifteen years. In reality Aileen and I were too young to be admitted but it seemed that an exception had been made because Mary had been allowed in, and it was felt that if her young sister was to come then someone of a similar age was necessary too. We Anglo-Indians were separated out in the dormitory; we had a section to ourselves and simply took this for granted because in India there were always caste differences and it was not unusual for such lines to be drawn. The ten of us tended to stay together a good deal of the time; this did not mean that we all got on well or particularly liked each other, but I suppose we recognized the distinction of our little community.

So now the evening meal was over and we had to wash our plates and spoons in a big sink. There was a little time for us to go outside to the courtyard; it was a warm evening and some of the girls gathered together to sing and dance and the rest sat around and talked. I was very tired and tried to curl up to sleep but Mary said I shouldn't, so I sat beside her yawning until the bell went again and we all went back to the verandah in front of the big statue of Our Lady. Now the

Mother Superior came out and gave us a little talk, I was too tired to know what she was saying but managed to kneel down for more prayers, led by the girl who had showed us round earlier.

At last the prayers were over and a queue formed. Mary whispered that it was to go to the toilet. I followed her when our turn came and then we went into the dormitory where I was longing to be allowed to go to sleep. To my dismay, once the blankets had been unfolded we had to kneel down again and each of the girls recited three times what they called the Hail Mary: I did not yet know that this was to be the central repetition of my life from then onwards. Finally we were allowed to lie down, and as I fell asleep I heard Mary, curled up beside me, give a little sob and murmur 'Goodnight Mama, I miss you.'

CHAPTER SEVEN

As village children, unused to electricity, it was commonplace for us to wake up at first light, although Mama would always need to shake me hard to persuade me to leave the warmth of my blanket. Being used to an early start I was not surprised that our new routine at the convent started with the insistent ringing of the 5.30 a.m. bell at which we would all have to rush through our morning ablutions in order to be ready to line up for the morning Mass which started at 6 a.m. This was held in the chapel, where there was room for the boarders but not for the day scholars who would not start school until 8 a.m. The Mass was said by a priest from the Don Bosco Order and was conducted in Latin which I did not understand. However, the prayers were in English for our benefit. Mass would take half an hour and the Father would then go off to the parlour for coffee whilst the boarders performed their appointed cleaning and tidying tasks.

In the beginning, being small, Aileen and I were given light work such as dusting the classrooms or picking up litter around the compound. Those who were naughty had to clean the toilets and the drains and take out the bins. On that first morning Sister Mary told Aileen and me to dust the pews in the chapel, and Mary was given a similar task in the office, but I could tell that there was some resentment amongst the others at our being given such easy duties. We were told that these would be our jobs for the rest of that week; it was now Wednesday, and I was happy that this was a good start. Breakfast came at 7 a.m.: every day it was overcooked porridge made out of rice but watered down and heavily salted – it was not nice. After breakfast we had a short time to tidy ourselves and our dormitories before going off to the classrooms to fit in an hour's work before assembly at 9 a.m.

I wanted to play rather than study. Some of the teaching sisters told me to draw things, which I enjoyed, but most of them wanted me to practise my reading and writing, which I had hardly started. I joined the bottom group, in which there were some big children who were not very bright, and we went back to looking at letters and numbers, as Daniel had shown me at home. It was slow progress and I was easily distracted.

Assembly was in the courtyard in front of the verandah. We all had to stand up straight and sing the British National Anthem 'God Save the King'. I had not heard this before so it took me some time to know the words but once I had got used to them I used to enjoy the simple rhythm and hearing my high small voice merging with the others. Looking back, I am not sure what logic there was in Italian and Indian nuns joining together in encouraging this distant king 'long to reign over us' and I recall that in later years at the school the anthem was changed to 'Jana Gana Mana' which was perhaps more appropriate. Anyway, Mary reminded me that our father had fought in the British army so I continued to deliver the daily chorus with great enthusiasm until the change was made.

Sometimes the Mother Superior would speak to us at morning assembly. On our first day she waited until prayers had been said before saying 'Yesterday we were joined by three new boarders: Mary and her sister Ann, and Aileen. They will all stand up so that you know who they are. They will join us at this school to the glory of our Blessed Lady.'

Mary had to drag me to my feet and I stood blushing with my knuckles in my mouth until the chatter died down and we were able to slide back down into the rows of other children.

Back to our classrooms for over two hours' more work without a break – not easy for an energetic five-year-old and by the time of the 12 noon lunch break I was very restless and being told off for inattention. Lunch was quite good. We boarders went back to our own dining room and the day scholars ate their own packed lunch, or tiffin as it was always called, whilst we tucked into hot rice and vegetable curry.

Now the terrible boredom of another two hours in the classroom before formal school finished for the day at three o'clock when the day scholars poured out of the gates to go home. We had half an hour of cleaning and some little gardening jobs and then a lovely hour from four till five when we could play our own games. After that we had to go to the study room for an hour before reverting to the routine of evening prayers, dinner, singing and dancing, night prayers and finally bed.

I was very homesick and cried a lot. The long journey had made me realize just how far away from Mama we had travelled. I missed her desperately, I missed the daily contact with the rest of the family and village, I missed my pets and the carefree life I had led. Mary tried to be both mother and sister to me but I could tell how hard she was finding it to both comfort me and answer all the questions I would constantly ask. I was at an age when I would ask 'why?' most of the time, but not at an age when I could appreciate that Mary did not have the answers. Each night I would hear her sobbing under her blanket, but each day she would try to keep me cheerful and amused.

Mary started to make some friends amongst the others in our dormitory; her best friend was Angela. I too found a new friend. This was Agnes, who was only six months older than me and had reddish hair. This was a great rarity, even amongst Anglo-Indians, and some of the other girls would make fun of it which upset her. On the second day we were there two girls were pulling her hair, pretending it was not real and would come off, and she was crying so I tugged the hair of her attackers and we all got into a fight on the floor. Unfortunately the noise attracted Sister Mary, who was furious and blamed me for starting the fight. Her logic seemed to be that I was new and there would not have been any disturbance if I had not brought my subversive influence into the school. She caught hold of me by my ear which hurt and dragged me into the centre of the room. Then she lifted up my dress and slapped my bottom four or five times until I was howling. As she stormed out of the room Mary rushed over to try to comfort me but it was some time before my cries subsided.

The result of this, the first of many fights, was that Agnes became my friend and the other girls became a little wary of me – which gave me a certain notoriety amongst my peers, even if that exposed me as a target to the nuns.

CHAPTER EIGHT

There was a sick room for those in the school with occasional illness. I was not conscious of any great level of sickness, certainly not on a regular basis save for routine coughs and colds, but Agnes said that every few months there would be a stomach sickness that would cause the sisters to warn everyone to be careful to wash their hands and clothes more often. I never gave any thought to such matters – I had always been healthy. I remained so when, two months after our arrival, a bout of illness like this came to the school. The word 'dysentery' was overheard being used by some of the nuns and the older girls looked it up in the dictionary. The few who caught it spent a lot of time going backwards and forwards to the toilets, and as the little sick room quickly became inadequate for the sufferers one of the classrooms was converted to a sick room. I went in there once to visit one of Agnes' friends and it was very smelly and we came out holding our noses and giggling. Neither of us caught the infection and those in the school who did so seemed to make a recovery within two or three days. There was an elderly doctor who came in every day and the sisters acted as nurses, and at every assembly the Mother Superior would remind us of the need to wash our hands and be hygienic.

When the illness had almost run its course, and the school was beginning to return to normal, Mary fell ill. She seemed very pale one day and that night she asked to be accompanied to the toilet during the night, which was what we always had to do, and then she was ill the next morning. Sister Teresa came to look at her and ordered that she be transferred to the temporary sick room. I was lost without her support and although Agnes and Aileen tried to help I missed Mary's arm round me and her making sure that I was always in the right place at the right time.

I went to see Mary in the sick room. By then she was the only patient and one of the sisters was able to look after her needs all the time. She was sleeping when I visited but woke up when I held her hand and smiled at me. She looked rather thin. The next day the doctor came again and when he had visited Mary he went to see the Mother Superior and seemed to be there for a long time. I asked Sister Teresa if I could go and see my sister again, and she said no. Later that afternoon we all heard a noise and looked out of the classroom window to see a horse-drawn carriage draw up at the front of the school and two of the sisters carrying blankets into it. Sister Teresa came into the classroom and I was allowed to go out with her as Mary was carried into the back of the carriage, all wrapped up in sheets with only her face peeping out.

'Where is she going?' I cried, and was told that she was going to the Gauhati Civil Hospital in the town so she could be made better.

I called out to Mary and waved at her but I do not think she saw me. Sister Teresa held me tightly by the hand as the doors of the carriage were closed and the two horses were led off.

I was very upset. I cried in the classroom during the rest of the afternoon and despite Agnes' and Aileen's best efforts I would not join in the games. By the early evening I had cheered up a bit and the sisters kept a close eye on me. My favourite, Sister Teresa, came and sat with me for a few moments when I went to bed beside the folded blanket where Mary would normally be sleeping.

The next day, Tuesday, at prayers in the morning and in the evening there was a prayer for Mary's swift recovery. The same thing happened on Wednesday and I was so lonely without my sister that I asked the sisters if I might go to visit her in the hospital. They said they would ask the Mother Superior and on the Thursday I was allowed to go with Sister Teresa to the hospital. This was on the other side of the town and we went in a small carriage and climbed the stairs to the third floor and walked down a long corridor to a big dormitory which the sister said was called a ward. Halfway down the row of beds I could make out Mary's face above the blankets and I shook myself free of Sister Teresa and ran over. Mary seemed so thin and white but she smiled when she saw me and I held her hand and kissed her. Her face was quite cold. She tried to say something and I put my ear close to her mouth and heard, 'I hope you are being a good girl, little sister?'

I chattered to her for as long as I was allowed; I told her what I had been drawing in class and that I missed her at night. After about half an hour the nurse who was in charge of the ward came over and said that Mary was tired and we should not stay any longer. I tried not to cry and kissed my sister goodbye and was taken down the ward holding Sister Teresa's hand. At the door I turned to wave but I could not see Mary waving back.

Mary died the next day. I did not know what had happened save that the doctor came to the school and went straight in to see the Mother Superior. Then, when we were playing just before lunch we saw all the sisters go into the Mother Superior's office and come out ten minutes later. Sister Teresa looked around and when she saw me she asked me to go with her whilst the other sisters gathered the day scholars and the boarders together at the other end of the courtyard. I was taken into the Mother Superior's office which was the first time I had been there since we had arrived at the school ten weeks before. This time she seemed less fierce and asked me to go round her desk and stand beside her chair. She then asked me what I knew of heaven and when I tried to explain she said that my sister Mary had gone there.

It is a long time ago, but I remember crying and that Sister Teresa tried to comfort me. I had seen dead animals: one of the village cows had died just before we left, and the killing of chickens was an everyday event. Somehow I had an image of Mary lying motionless like the cow in the field. I was led outside and Agnes and Aileen were waiting with Sister Mary, obviously having been told to look after me. I could see that Aileen had been crying too. They tried to get me to play in their games but my head was spinning and all I could think was that I was not going to see my big sister ever again. I sat on the ground in a corner and sobbed.

Prayers were said that evening for 'our departed sister Mary' and

I cried again. At bedtime I again saw Mary's folded bedclothes and flung myself on them. Sister Teresa crouched beside me and stroked the tears from my face until I fell asleep.

CHAPTER NINE

I did not know then that in hot countries burials were held as soon as possible, usually the next day. At assembly the next morning the Mother Superior announced that Mary had died. She said that the classes would be bigger that day because a number of the sisters would be attending the funeral. I had already been taken in hand by Sister Teresa who had helped me into my special dress and my naughty boy shoes and had helped me brush my hair and put a ribbon in it. Aileen and Agnes were allowed to come with me and we all rode in a black car with Sisters Teresa and Maria and there was another car with the Mother Superior and some of the other sisters in front. They were all wearing their white habits that were normally only worn on Sundays and Holy Days. It was still early in the morning as we travelled through Gauhati to the Christian Cemetery at Uzanbazar. Then we all went into the little church for a service but I was too stunned by everything that had happened to take in any detail; but I do remember the small coffin that was carried in and put at the front by the altar. I kept looking at it and trying to imagine that Mary was lying in it. I do not think that I cried during the ceremony. Afterwards we went outside, following the coffin, and it was taken towards a hole in the ground beside which there was a heap of dry earth.

Before the hole was filled up by the workmen standing nearby Sister Maria gave me a small posy of flowers and told me to place them on the coffin and say a prayer. I put my head against her long white habit and would not go. Gently she persuaded me to go forward, holding my hand most of the way – I put the flowers on the coffin which was then lowered into the hole. I did not say a prayer but only, under my breath, 'Please come back Mary'. As I stood there, starting to cry, Sister Maria came and led me back to the others.

The rest of the day was a blur – I suppose that I was tired after the events of the last few days, and too unhappy to be able to do more than sit and cry. Agnes and Aileen tried to include me in games but they did not know what to say and when we returned to the school I found that all the other children would simply stop talking and pull long faces when I came by.

I kept saying to myself, 'Please come back Mary' and I longed for the night-time when I could lie down and be alone.

When we finally went to the dormitory that night, and I came back from the toilet ready to lie down, I was willing Mary to be back with me. When I suddenly saw a figure in a lemon yellow dress with red flowers lying on her blanket my heart leaped and I called out, 'Mary, Mary, Mary!' and ran to her. As I got there, Mary's friend Angela, wearing Mary's dress, jumped up and she and the others all laughed. I stopped in mid-stride and with a howl threw myself at Angela and tried to punch her again and again. Sisters Teresa and Mary came rushing in and took in what had happened. Sister Teresa took me in her arms whilst Angela was taken out of the room by Sister Mary. It was a long time before I could be persuaded to lie down, racked by long-drawn-out sobs. Whilst I was lying there a tearful Angela was brought back in, no longer wearing Mary's dress, and she said she was sorry. I kept my face hidden and eventually slept out of exhaustion.

CHAPTER TEN

There was no Mary to shake me in the morning as I tried to burrow under my blankets to avoid the ringing of the bell. There was no Mary to look for my clean clothes. There was no Mary to help me wash and to check that I was properly dressed. I tried to live through each day until I could crawl back into the safety of my bed and escape from the difficult and lonely world of the school.

From that night of the funeral something hardened in my head, and I stopped myself asking 'why', and I tried to cut off that bit of me that wanted to put my head on someone's lap or shoulder. I lived for the night-time when I could be alone with myself and my memories. Angela had come to realize what she had done, and she now went out of her way to be good to me and in some small way to replace Mary's support, but I had turned in on myself and found it difficult to put my trust in others.

I kept fierce hold of Mary's lemon dress and her brown shoes. At first they had been left in her pigeon-hole numbered ten, which is where Angela had found them. On that next day I had taken them and put them in my number three pigeon-hole, tightly bundled. I had even tried on the shiny brown shoes with the bright buckles, but my feet were much too small for them and I could not walk for more than a few steps without tripping over.

Then, on a Sunday two weeks after the funeral, I came out of the chapel to see that Pantoo, one of the Indian boarders who had been sitting behind me, was wearing what looked like the same dress – and I then realized it was actually Mary's dress. I flew at her, but she said that Sister Mary had given her the dress because it was her size. I remember flinging myself at Sister Maria and hammering my fists into her as I shouted that the dress was mine and that Pantoo must take it off.

I was taken away into another room and heard raised voices. After half an hour, and with ill grace, Sister Mary came in with the dress and gave it to me – I clutched it to me and ran back to put it right at the back of my number three pigeon-hole. I think it had been Sister Teresa who insisted that I should have it returned to me. From that time Sister Mary seemed to go out of her way to cause difficulties for me, always blaming me for anything that went wrong and punishing me whenever she could find an excuse.

I loved Sister Teresa. She was in charge of the kitchen where the boarders' food was prepared and she would try to keep a little food on one side for me and Aileen. We would try to creep back into the kitchen after mealtimes and sometimes Sister Teresa would scoop out the marrow from the bones that she had been cooking and quietly feed it to us.

The months passed and the seasons changed. The rainy season came and we held our assemblies on the verandah with the rain sheeting down outside and the courtyard ankle deep in water. Sometimes it was so humid that the classrooms seemed to steam and the nuns' faces were wet with sweat. I soon absorbed the Catholic rituals and obediently said my three Hail Marys each night before bed. In my mind I would substitute my longed-for sister in the prayer and would pretend that I was praying to her rather than our Blessed Lady, but no thunderbolt came to strike me down. The ritual of our life played itself out each week, and as I grew older and gained more independence I settled more into the life of the school.

Weekends were best. We had no school on Saturdays and after breakfast, except in the rainy season, we brought out our blankets and bedding to air them in the sun. We had then to perform a thorough cleaning of all the buildings that we used, removing cobwebs, polishing the brass in the chapel and sweeping and mopping. We took our clothes to the laundry room so that they could be washed, and if they were worn we were taught to darn and sew. I learned how to cut dresses from a pattern, and was given material to try to make up clothes. I was too small at first but Angela helped, and as I became older I got better and learned to use a sewing machine under the strict supervision of Sister Carolina.

After lunch on Saturday we collected the aired bedclothes and also the clothes that had been washed and we went to the dormitory and made our beds very neatly. There was now great excitement in the air because we knew that we would usually be allowed to walk with two of the sisters through the outskirts of the town to the edge of the mighty River Brahmaputra. Our crocodile of children would snake through the streets, drinking in the sights and sounds that surrounded us. Oxen pulling carts, carriages, the occasional donkey, stray sacred cows wandering aimlessly, cars and motorcycle rickshaws – always sounding their horns. Everywhere bicycles: familiar load carriers with a huge variety of goods fastened either to the crossbars or strapped to the backs of the cyclists. Fathers with children perched in front or clinging on behind, wives riding side saddle on the rear grid. Through the narrow streets of the town, holding hands in our neat and ordered column, we chattered and giggled as we drank in the freedom of our surroundings. Then, at last, to the river itself – perhaps more of a great sea than a river, since the other side was too far away to be seen. A long way offshore we could see boats moving along, whilst at the edge of the water a throng of people washed clothes, washed themselves, or just stood in the shallows looking at the surrounding activities.

We were allowed only to walk for a short distance along the concrete pavings that served as a sort of promenade above the high water line. We had to be careful not to be splashed by the enthusiasm of either bathers or clothes-washers, and we were not allowed to take off our shoes and paddle in the waters as we wished. Looking back, I am uncertain whether these occasional Saturday outings were to entertain us, or to enable the accompanying nuns to escape from the confines of the school. Whichever it was, I took comfort in the vision of the world outside, and harboured my daydreams of boarding one of the big steamers that carried passengers along the river and thus fulfilling my desperate wish to be carried back to my mother.

And so the years passed in the everlasting routine of the convent. From the 5.30 a.m. bell to the 6 a.m. Mass; from the daily chores to the 7 a.m. breakfast; from the 8 a.m. start of studies to the 12 noon lunch break; from the 1 p.m. start of afternoon school to the 3 p.m. finish of studies; from the 3.30 p.m. classroom cleaning until the blessed start of 4 p.m. games; from the last hour of study from 5.30 p.m. to 6.30 p.m. prayers; from the 7 p.m. evening meal to the bedtime regime and the concluding three Hail Marys of the constantly repeating day.

I cannot deny that I was seen as a problem child. The hard protective skin that I had forced myself to develop after Mary's death somehow manifested itself in a determination always to be right. With no older sister to moderate my stubbornness I found myself in constant conflict with the sisters. I lost count of the times I was given latrine-cleaning duty as punishment for some offence, and after-school detentions defined my scholastic week.

Part of the problem was the isolation from my mother. Each year there was a six-week holiday when children could return home, provided there were funds for the necessary arrangements to be made. In my case there were no funds, my mother was illiterate and made no arrangements and so each year I had to stay at the school with the sisters and with the handful of other children who were in the same situation. My friend Aileen went home each year, her father being able to afford the train fare and sending one of the tea estate bearers to accompany her. How I longed to go with them and how I sobbed each time Aileen left. Aileen would seek me out as soon as she returned, and tell me that my mother sent her love and good wishes. She would also bring notes that my mother had dictated to one of the letter writers who functioned on the Lines behind the tea estate and in that way I learned of the events of the village and the state of health of my mother's family but these communications only increased my sense of desolation at the enforced separation.

The nuns did try to break the monotony of holidays. Occasionally they would travel to visit other convents and would take pity on me and let me go with them. Not that this meant that I would meet the young company that I craved, but at least I would have a change from the confines of the school. I recall that one such journey was to the north bank of the Brahmaputra when we visited St Joseph's convent at Tezpur. The great excitement for me was that we had to travel on a steamer to cross the vast river. I had seen so little of the outside world and to be able to stand on the deck of what seemed to me to be a huge ship, and to watch the passage of boats and people as we slid through the water, was wonderful. We stayed for a week at Tezpur and I was not allowed out but was able to look forward to the return trip and again to drink in the huge views and to revel in the vision of ordinary people enjoying their lives.

When I was ten, five years after starting at school, I was mentally preparing myself for the usual agony of the start of the school holidays by pretending to be engrossed in a book as Aileen packed her clothes ready for her journey home. Sister Teresa came into the dormitory and told me that the Mother Superior wanted to see me in her study. I feared the worst since I knew that my behaviour in the previous week had been bad; I think it was always worse as the holiday period approached. What deprivation might she visit upon me whilst I stayed at school over the next few weeks I wondered? Most holidays I was given quite an easy time but I began to imagine what extra duties might be imposed to make my life more miserable.

When I entered the study I was astonished to see the smiling face of Mansuk Mura, the chowkidar who had been with us on our original journey from Pengaree and to hear, as if in a dream, the Mother Superior telling me that my mother had sent a return train ticket and that Mansuk was to accompany Aileen and myself to go home for the holidays. I remember I burst into tears and then, on being prompted, quickly ran to pack up my few possessions, and within an hour I found myself in a car heading for the train station.

CHAPTER ELEVEN

I was choked with emotion on the first day of the journey and must have been a poor travelling companion. On the second day, as we neared the station at Makum Junction I became so overcome with the thought of seeing my mother again that I was again in tears. I had never possessed a photograph of my mother and in the intervening five years since she had waved goodbye I had reached the stage where I could no longer bring her features to mind, and I even feared that I might not know her. But as the train pulled into the station I recognized her small figure in a plain brown sari, standing in isolation at the back of the platform. I found later that she had slept on the platform for the past two nights, unsure which train I would be travelling on but determined to be with me on the last stages of the journey to the village.

I threw myself from the train and our hugs were so tight that we were both short of breath as we cried together. 'So like Mary!' were the words my mother kept repeating, as she tried both to hold me at arm's length to look at me and to clutch me to her.

Arm in arm, and constantly talking and interrupting each other, we waited for Mansuk to locate a truck that was travelling to Digboi and on to Pengaree. Eventually one was found, carrying some parts for one of the tea estate engines, so we happily crammed into the cab for the uncomfortable journey. At the estate we said goodbye to Mansuk and then walked the track to the village, passing the old familiar points which I still remembered from so long ago. It was nearly nightfall when we reached the village but some of the older children had met us on the path and word had travelled ahead. All the village had turned out to greet me. I rushed to my now blind grandfather and my grandmother, I ran from relative to friend and back again: it was one of the happiest moments of my life.

The few weeks that I spent in the village that holiday were perfect. Although the elders of the village were conscious that they had said goodbye to two children and only one had returned they were most welcoming and smiling faces surrounded me every day. As for the children, even those who had been less friendly because of our caste differences seemed delighted to have me back. I suppose that in their eyes I had become rather elevated – I could read and write, I was wearing a tidy, if threadbare, dress, and the little urchin girl who had helped her sister tend the cows was no more.

I was eager to find out how the tea estate had fared. Elephants had caused the usual problems, breaking into the area of bushes and trampling or eating the vegetation in their path, and leopards had been lifting pet dogs at night. In turn, I was able to tell my former friends about travelling on a train and sailing on a steamer, and to describe all the detail of life at a boarding school. No doubt an element of exaggeration crept into my dramatic descriptions but I had a ready audience of both young and old and I made the most of my brief time in the sunshine of fame.

As for my mother, she spoiled me in every conceivable way. When the village awoke she would allow me to sleep on and discourage visitors until I had yawned my way out of the hut. Food and refreshments were thrust upon me whenever I seemed to be receptive to consumption. If I seemed tired she would suggest that I should rest and there were no longer any restrictions on places I might wish to go.

Whilst there was sadness when the time came for me to return, I felt much more settled now that I had been reunited with my former life; and when Aileen and I set out with Mansuk for the return journey, I knew that arrangements had been put in place for me to come back each year. Quite how this my mother was going to fund this I was not to know, but I was assured that she would see me the following holiday and for almost the first time I felt that I had a prospect of future happiness.

I suppose I was something of a rebel, but this tended to enhance my popularity and I built many friendships over my years at the convent school. I worked hard at my studies and also at sewing and other domestic task. The sisters would sometimes say that I would make a good wife – and seemed irritated when I laughed at them.

Each year I was able to travel home to Pengaree, Aileen and I sharing our escort. My annual homecoming was now an accepted event, and although I found it difficult to acclimatize to the primitive conditions in our jungle village, having the love of my mother and the support of surrounding relatives and neighbours happily compensated for the harshness of the conditions.

CHAPTER TWELVE

In the third year following my return Aileen told me that her parents were moving from Pengaree to Digboi itself. Digboi was a bustling little town and, being a railway junction, full of activity and life. I envied her that she able to live in the centre of the social activity I longed for, and when she had moved I would drink in the stories she told of the young people she met and went around with.

One major handicap of the move was lack of transport. Aileen's parents' position in the tea company had always guaranteed their use of transport on the occasions of our homecoming. When we reached the railway station my mother and I would ride in a company lorry or jeep with Aileen and whichever of her parents had come to meet her. Once Aileen moved to Digboi this privilege was lost and although we were sometimes fortunate to find a vehicle returning to the estate with a driver happy to take us with him this was not always the case.

The journey from Pengaree was a distance of some eighteen kilometres and the churned-up mud of the track passed through the thick rainforest of the Buridehing Reserve. I well remember the first time there was no lorry and my mother said we would have to walk. We had started out in the morning and the first few kilometres were easy, but by late afternoon I was very tired. Night was falling as we trudged along the last few kilometres of the rutted path, my small bag of possessions from school in my hand. The dank and dripping vegetation of the jungle crowded the roadway, and although there was enough moonlight to see our way I was frightened of the dark and held tightly to my mother's hand. I suppose I must have been about twelve years old and the trumpeting of elephants and other jungle noises terrified me. I was already tired when I started out because of the long trip from Gauhati, and after more than four hours of walking I sat down and refused to go further. Mama tried to persuade me to move, but I cried and would not walk on until she told me that a tiger had been seen over there 'just the other day'. I was petrified and, still sobbing, followed her closely until we finally reached the village, both completely exhausted.

There was little in the way of entertainment during these holidays, although occasionally I was able to go to Digboi and stay with Aileen. During the day I kept busy with village activities and would help Mama plant paddy in the fields: my holidays always coincided with the planting season so I became quite skilled at this back-aching task. We went to bed when the sun went down but in the early evenings I would spend long hours looking at the photograph album of my father's family. This was one of the few possessions that had survived the theft of papers all those years before.

There were only three pages of small black and white photographs. People in white clothes were pictured sitting beside what my mother said was a tennis court. I had seen tennis being played when we passed the club at Doom Dooma one day so I could imagine that quite well. Then there was the picture of my father with a bearded man on his left and an elderly woman on his right – Mama thought those were his grandparents. This must have been right as the next picture showed my father and his own father standing with the same couple. Then there was the picture of the car with three people; my mother said the one in the centre was my father's sister Mary. I spent hours looking at her dress and clothes and trying to imagine what she was like. There was a picture of my father beside the support to a roof over what looked like a verandah – I loved to look at him and to think how he might have held me in his arms when I was very small. Then there were the pictures that I loved of the big garden with the summer house in the background looking one way, and a winding path looking the other way. There was the long wooden bench beside it and you could see the flowers in the garden and imagine how warm and sunny it might have been. In two of the pictures there was a small dog, and my favourite was the one of the dog sitting on its hind legs and begging for food from the woman who bent over him. I often lay awake at night imagining myself sitting on the bench in the garden with the little dog begging for scraps on the lawn in front of me.

I pestered my mother to give me information about my father. Her pronunciation of his first name sounded like Stephen; because she could not write she could not spell out the surname but I knew it began with a P. Her knowledge came from what he had told her over the time they had spent together. She knew his sister was called Mary and was younger than him and that his father was a doctor and his mother had been a nurse. She said she thought his grandfather had been a schoolteacher. Of course she knew a lot about his time on the tea estates, where he had been and what his jobs were and who his friends were, but she never had enough information about his family or life in England to satisfy my constant questions.

Back at the convent I continued to brood about how I could make myself known to my father's family. I thought they would want to know that he had been survived by a daughter. I had talked to Mama about this and she said she thought they might not want to know. I did not understand at first, but she told me to talk to cousin Daniel so I went to see him at the bungalow where he was still the chief bearer. I remember that it was a lovely day, the rainy season had ended, the humidity was low and the sun was shining across the tea bushes stretching into the distance towards the mountains on the horizon.

The planters were out and as a special treat Daniel let me sit on the verandah in the big chair that he said my father had sat in.

Daniel was clear that in the eyes of my father's family I would be seen as an embarrassment. He said that they did not want to know children born outside marriage. He went on to say that the English did not see the Indian people as equals, and that I would be seen as inferior.

I knew all about castes: my life had been spent as an Anglo-Indian, not accepted in our village community as either a European or as a true Indian. I saw the caste system everywhere I went and did not question that some people were born to clean the latrines and perform other lowly tasks. Somehow I had not applied that thinking to the Europeans on the tea estates but as Daniel spoke to me my dream of acceptance by my father's family began to fade.

I cried a lot but Daniel was very caring and eventually I was ready to go home. Before I left, Daniel asked me to assure him that I now understood all the difficulties and the impossibility of making contact. I told him what he wanted to hear, but in my heart I brought back into view the pictures of my father and his family, and the kindness that I knew my father had shown to my mother, and I made myself believe that his family would want to know me.

Daniel had at least been able to give me some more information about my father, gleaned from conversations he had had with him. Most importantly, he was able to write down the name 'Poyser' which Mama had not been able to spell out. Two weeks later, when I was back at the convent in Gauhati, I thought and thought about everything that Daniel had said, but remained determined that I had a chance of making contact if only I had an address. I also knew that without funds the nuns at the convent might eventually make me leave school so it was important that I could demonstrate to them that I was in touch with my father's family. I finally made a plan. The tea company records would list my father's next of kin: my grandfather's name and address would be there, I would write him a letter and he would be certain to make contact.

I put my plan into action the following year when I was fourteen. During the annual holiday, and without telling my mother where I was going, I walked down the track to the Pengaree tea estate and asked if I might have an appointment to see the manager. I was very nervous about going into the company offices but the manager's secretary took pity on me, and after questioning me she said I could come back at ten o'clock the next day. She wanted to know what I wanted, and I just said that I had a question about my father. She knew who I was, and as I would not tell her anything else she decided to give me the precious appointment.

I was outside the office at nine o'clock the following morning and the secretary told me to stay outside as I was too early. At ten o'clock the manager swept up the steps into the office building, not looking at me standing outside. At half past ten the secretary told me

I could come into the office where she worked and gave me a chair to sit on. I was very frightened but at the same time determined and kept repeating what I was going to say to the manager under my breath.

At eleven o'clock the secretary picked up her telephone, listened, and then told me to go into the manager's office. Gingerly I opened the door and saw him sitting behind a big desk working on some papers. The air from the rotating ceiling fan stirred my hair as I was waved to a hard chair in front of the desk and sat down.

'Please sir, I would like to contact my grandfather who is a doctor in England, I know his name is Poyser. I think that the records of my father should show his address.'

There was a long silence as the manager looked at me, his face growing red, and I could sense his anger.

'Your grandfather? Who is your grandfather? Who indeed is your father? I do not know your father. Leave my office and never trouble me again!'

He picked up a little bell from his desk and rang it. As his secretary came into the room he waved his hand, dismissing me and inviting her to escort me out. In an instant I was swept outside and down the steps, tears running down my face as I stood alone outside the office building.

I have so often relived that moment. For over a year I had built up my hopes and in a moment my plan had been broken into pieces. Forlorn and despairing I made my way down the long track to the village. My mother knew something was terribly wrong but I would say nothing. All night I stared into the blackness and wept at the destruction of my dreams.

So it was that I went back to the convent at Gauhati. The nuns knew that I had been planning to try to locate my grandfather and now realized that I had failed. Change was in the air: some of the sisters would not meet my eye and I sensed that something was wrong. For a week nothing was said, but Aileen shared my belief that there was a problem of some sort. Over the last year some of the older nuns had left including the study class sister Sister Brangaza and the office sister Sister Mascarinas. They had moved on within the organization and the newer nuns who had replaced them were much less friendly. I suppose those who had been at the convent in the early days when Mary died had tended to be sympathetic towards me, but all that was now a distant memory for them, and in any event many of those who remembered her had moved on.

It was also the case that the school needed funds, and it had been made clear to me that my mother had spent all that she had and was not able to contribute further. This meant that my upkeep and education was a continued burden on the convent expenses and the new nuns went out of their way to refer to this in little ways.

'Another helping, charity child?'

Comments of this nature were now commonplace but I tried my best to ignore them. I decided in my own mind that they were being difficult because I was a Hindu child, so I determined to be baptized into the Roman Catholic Church.

Immersed as I had been in the Catholic faith since I arrived at the school more than ten years before it was not a difficult path for me to follow. I made an appointment with the Mother Superior to tell her of my decision. She seemed pleased but I was aware that the lack of funding remained a problem and that my public embracing of the faith would not grant me immunity. In any event, I immersed myself in my preparations for the baptism and felt a great sense of security and comfort in the process.

The whole school was present when I joined three other girls in the baptism ceremony in the school chapel. I found it a moving experience and sensed the feeling of shared community that had often been lacking in my childhood. Almost for the first time I felt both happy and popular. It helped that I was now also beginning to excel at games, and as one of the more senior girls I had many friends although these still tended to be those who were from a similar single-parent or orphaned background.

All this made the shock of my next summons to Mother Superior the greater. I found myself standing in front of her desk as she recited what she described as my 'history of disobedience'. She said that it had been decided that a change of school would be of benefit to all concerned. A place had been found for me at a newly established school within the same religious order but closer to where I lived. It was called the Little Flower School and was in the town of Dibrugah. This was much nearer home so would be better in terms of transport cost and convenience.

My life was turned upside down. I had been at Gauhati from such an early age that I had few memories of life elsewhere. All my friendships, built up over so many years, were at Gauhati. I had spent so little of my life at home that the convent school was the centre of my small universe. I had fondly imagined that I could continue my studies, and particularly learn shorthand and typing to try to build a future career. My mind could not accept that I was being told that I was now forced to leave.

I tried so hard to change the Mother Superior's mind. Every argument that I advanced failed to impress. My tears, and there were many of them, seemed to be in vain. Even brave attempts to intervene by Aileen and numbers of my other friends were repulsed. I was to leave the following week.

Later I was to find that Sister Louise Miorelli, the Mother Superior from the Little Flower School in Dibrugah, had regularly attended meetings with the other nuns of the Order when they all met up from time to time. She had listened to the complaints made against me by the nuns at the convent school and, once it became clear that a move was inevitable, volunteered to take me into her school. The final decision had to be made by the Mother Provincial, Sister Catherine Mania, but it was known that she approved of what was planned and so the transfer was put into action.

There I stood in a strange street, holding a small suitcase with the few clothes and possessions that I had in the world and dusty from the long train journey. As I looked up at the imposing doorway of the Little Flower School I seemed to be empty of the tears that I had shed as I said my farewells to all my old school friends. I would have to start all over again in this new and unfamiliar place.

CHAPTER THIRTEEN

There were two consoling factors. The first was that my enthusiasm for games and my abilities in the sporting arena were to give me some useful standing amongst my new fellow pupils. The second was that Sister Louise Miorelli as Mother Superior took an instant liking to me and I to her. She was an Italian nun and a lovely person. When I was taken to her office on arrival, she came round the desk and embraced me, she listened carefully to the history of my life (and I did not know at the time that she had heard most of this from previous meetings of the Order), and she seemed immediately sympathetic to the problems I had encountered.

I had two huge disadvantages at the Little Flower School. The first was that the school had a reputation for academic excellence, and I did not. I suppose I was of reasonable intelligence, but even my greatest friends would agree that I was not clever – and yet cleverness was what the school expected.

The second and greater problem was that the school was intended to cater for the daughters of well-to-do families. I did my best to deflect inevitable curiosity about my background, and to avoid reference to my mud-hutted village history, but schoolgirls are cruel and it was not long before my illegitimacy and impoverished circumstances were generally known. There was some kudos in my father having been an English army officer, but it was clear to my peers that his untimely death meant that I had no prospects of future financial inheritance so this hoped-for lustre soon faded.

There was also the humiliation of having to do cleaning jobs about the school by way of recompense for the fact that my education was subsidized. I did not mind the work itself but having to do it singled me out as of lower status and made life difficult for me.

There was nothing I could do about my social disadvantage save to work at friendships and hope for the best; but with regard to the first problem Sister Louise came to the rescue. She became my mentor, enrolling me in a typing and shorthand school nearby and arranging some extra academic coaching at the local high school to try to help me catch up with the others. I became good at typing but rather struggled with the shorthand because my poor English meant that both basic spelling and grammar were difficult. I persevered and gradually improved, and Sister Louise found me some outside work giving lessons to some of the kindergarten children at a nearby school. This meant that I earned some pocket money which I desperately needed because the other girls had funds given to them by their families, and I had none.

The greatest joy was that Sister Louise introduced me to an elderly retired teacher, an Anglo-Indian woman called Miss Tessie Dixon. She lived in a small house in Dibrugah and invited me to visit her at weekends and occasionally stay overnight. It seemed that Miss Dixon, as I came to address her, had helped Sister Louise obtain a good job with the Assam Railway and Trading Company. This was before Sister Louise became a nun and from that time onwards they had become friends and Sister Louise felt obliged to her. I loved the occasions when I was able to stay the night with Miss Dixon. I had my own little bedroom under the eaves of her house where I could look out on to the little road that ran outside. Privacy was something almost unknown to me, my school life having been spent in dormitories, and to have a room to myself even for a single night was unbelievably good. Miss Dixon would sometimes wake me up with a cup of tea, although usually I would try to look after her rather than the other way about, and I enormously looked forward to my sporadic visits.

Meeting someone who in my eyes seemed close to being a full Englishwoman also reignited my fantasies about locating my roots. I had now persuaded Mama to allow me to keep with me the precious page of photographs of my father's family and I still pored over each one, usually when I had an opportunity to be alone. I loved the picture of the little dog, begging on his hind legs, by the bench beside the winding path in this so black and white English country garden. I would often wonder how my father's sister might dress and talk, and Miss Dixon's demeanour and immaculate manners fuelled my imagination.

A year passed in this way. Although I missed my old friends I had made a few new ones, and I was now able to reach Pengaree much more easily and had been allowed two visits a year which delighted my mother.

Came my fifteenth birthday, some cards from my friends and a message sent to me by my mother and I looked forward to at least another year, or possibly two, improving my shorthand and typing skills before seeking outside employment. The usual leaving age tended to be about seventeen and I felt that I would then have a reasonable chance of a good junior job.

Then one day Sister Louise called me into her study and gave me bad news. She sat me down beside her in the window seat which overlooked the courtyard of the school playground, baking in the summer heat, and told me she was leaving.

I was devastated. The Order for which she worked had decreed that she should move on, and the transfer was to another school many days' travel away. She had no alternative but to follow her instructions and doubted that we would see each other again unless she was able to visit the area. Prior to that moment and for the first time in my life I had felt I had at last achieved a degree of stability but now my mentor and friend was departing. I thought I had grown out of the tears of my childhood but I was inconsolable when, a few short days later, I waved Sister Louise off as her taxi took her to the railway station.

Sister Louise's replacement was everything that her predecessor was not. Sister Margherita was a short and plump Mexican, Spanish speaking and with less ability to communicate than some of the Italian nuns had been at Gauhati. She was totally uninterested in me and rejected the attempts I made to achieve a respectful friendship with her. Not that I was particularly singled out: she seemed aloof from most of the children at the school.

Although saddened by the loss of the personal friendship that had been instrumental in bringing me to the Little Flower School in the first place, I continued to settle in well and enjoyed my extra shorthand and typing studies, although I was not the quickest of learners and continued to find my studies hard work.

After about ten months I sensed that the nuns had started to talk about me. They would suddenly stop conversations when I came within earshot and sometimes I saw them looking at me when they were talking earnestly together. Then came the day when I rounded a corner and almost walked into two of the sisters, and as they started and looked guilty I ran through my mind the sentence that I had interrupted:

'She's young but she'll get used to it.'

I had a friend called Gita and she and I discussed what 'it' might be. I thought perhaps I was going to be given some new demeaning task to perform, but how could my age be relevant if that was the case? So it went on until about a week later I was summoned to the Mother Superior's office.

The only time that such a summons had proved to be good news was on the day I was able to return home from my previous school all those years ago. At the convent school my subsequent and fortunately rare visits to Sister Clotehelde's office had always involved some disciplinary or behavioural issue where the ordinary sisters had felt that a greater punishment than they could impose was necessary. No similar summons had previously been issued at the Little Flower School and it was with considerable trepidation that I closed the door behind me and stood before the dark wood desk with the crucifix standing on it.

'Now, Ann, you have started quite well here at Little Flower School but we have to think of your future. Your mother has no financial support and it would be difficult for a job to be found for you in the village where she lives. Anyway it would not be right for you to spend your days living in the foothills of the jungle and planting rice in the fields. I have been pleased to note your progress in domestic tasks and the sisters tell me of your skills in sewing and cooking. We have discussed your position and I am very pleased to say that a solution has been found.'

I could not work out where the conversation was going or what this solution could be. I knew that some children had left the school at fourteen and I was now fifteen, but I had hoped to stay on for another two years and improve my typing in order to pass my exams in shorthand and typing and become a secretary. I was dismayed at the thought that I might have to stop my studies, quite apart from again having to leave new-found friends.

'You are fortunate to have had an offer of marriage.'

I can only remember that I gave an involuntary cry, my hands to my mouth, and heard her next words in a swirl of panic.

'He is a typist to the Bishop and he works at the Bishop's house in the town. Our enquiries lead us to believe that he is very hardworking and a good man. He is only thirty years of age and in need of a wife and is very impressed with your credentials.'

'No! No! I don't want to be married!'

'Now listen to me, Ann, it would be both ungrateful and unfortunate for you not to accept the offer. I am sure it will work out for the best.'

I could not help myself, I was crying and shouting out and then I remember throwing myself on my knees at the side of the desk.

'Please, you can't make me – please, No!'

Through my tears I could see the Mother Superior's thin lips draw together and heard her say that I was to go outside and think about what she had said and that she would speak to me tomorrow. I must have run from the room because the next thing I remember was being in the dormitory, lying on the bed and wondering what was to become of me. The age of consent in India was twelve, and fourteen was an age at which arranged marriages were not uncommon, but in my wildest imaginings I had never dreamed that the school would propose such a thing for me. Surely they could not really mean it?

Suddenly I thought of Miss Dixon and I managed to sneak out of the school gate to find a shop where they allowed me to use their telephone – Miss Dixon had the luxury of a private telephone so I was able to speak to her. She heard my tearful entreaties for help and said immediately that she would contact some other Anglo-Indian friends that I had met and discuss what could be done. She said she would then contact the school and make such objections as she could.

I lay awake, horror struck at the thought that the sisters were trying to marry me off to a stranger twice my age. As my sleepless night wore on I went over the situation in my mind again and again. I was without qualifications and in the fiercely competitive world of Indian employment this spelled disaster in the job market. A single girl without sponsorship or support was not easily accepted in society and would be at risk. My prospects of a career seemed at an end unless the school would change its mind, indeed the whole course of my life would be changed.

CHAPTER FOURTEEN

I did not sleep that night. The next afternoon I was summoned back to the Mother Superior's office. Standing behind her and to her right, as she sat imperiously at her desk, stood a small man wearing a tight suit, shiny with wear. I was told that this was the man who had proposed marriage.

I refused to look at him – I repeated that I did not wish to be married – I said that I wished to continue with my studies. There was a silence and I was asked if I had anything else to say. I hung my head, determined not to raise my eyes.

'You need not think that your Anglo-Indian friends can help you,' Mother Superior said. 'I am the person who decides these matters, and my decision is final. Again, I ask you to agree to this marriage.'

I could not trust myself to speak, and just shook my head.

I was escorted from the room.

The next day I was back in front of the Mother Superior's desk.

'Ann. You have been disobedient. We have discussed your position. It has been decided that you must leave the school. We can no longer offer you education here. I have here a one-way ticket to Digboi. It is for tomorrow morning. You will be taken to the station after morning assembly.'

I had feared that my refusal would have dire results, but not so soon and not so dramatically. I felt sick with fear at the future but was determined not to show my terror to the sisters. I walked out of the room with as much dignity as I could muster.

The next day, blinking back my tears, I packed up my possessions, said goodbye to Gita and the new friends that I had made and walked out of the gates of the Little Flower School for the last time.

It was only a short distance to Dibrugah station and there by studying the train timetables and speaking to the man in the station office I found that my ticket was valid for travel for three days. I resolved that I would seek protection and advice from Miss Dixon: although she had not been able to prevent my expulsion from the school, she must surely be able to help me in some way. Carrying my heavy case I walked the three kilometres to the house where I had stayed and where I had been so happy. It was dusk. I was terrified that Miss Dixon would be out and hugely relieved when she answered my anxious knock on the door.

I stayed at Miss Dixon's house for two nights. She had to go to work each morning so I simply stayed at home and made myself useful by cleaning and preparing a meal for her return. I had repeated my tearful tale to her the first night but I was exhausted and so no discussion took place. The second evening, after I had cleared the dishes away, we sat at the table and discussed what I should do. To my dismay Miss Dixon said that I must return to Pengaree. She said it was wrong to deceive my mother, and that whilst she would make enquiries herself, she was not sure that she was going to be able to help. In the meantime I must go home and confess what had happened, and hope that some help could be found. She was kind but very firm.

So the third day saw me back studying the timetables at Dibrugah station. After a two-hour wait the train for Tinsukia where I would need to change trains for Digboi pulled in, enveloping my stricken face in steam. I saw no alternative to going back to Pengaree – but what was I to tell Mama?

As the train continued its ponderous journey my brain raced. My mother would be horrified if she knew that I had been evicted from school: all the ten years of separation and sacrifice would be seen to have been wasted. On the other hand I could not see that I could deceive her, I had no means of support and so I would be forced to live at home. Assam was not a place where a single girl of only fifteen could safely live on her own or find accommodation without help. Was I destined to become a village girl and plant paddy in the fields for the rest of my life?

When I reached Digboi I spent many hours trying to find a lift from the station to Pengaree. At last I was fortunate to find a truck returning to the tea estate. I was quiet as the driver tried to make conversation in the noisy cab as we lurched over the broken surface of the road. I thanked him on arrival and soon, having set off on foot down the familiar jungle track, I reached the river which I used to cross on Dhrin Babu's raft of logs, a wooden bridge now enabling me to walk across towards the village. The boatman was still there in case the rains made the bridge impassable and he greeted me happily but I responded in monosyllables to his friendly enquiries as to my health.

Nervously I walked into the village. When I saw Mama my intentions of telling her the truth vanished: I did not have the courage to do so when she was so happy to see me. I blurted out that I was awaiting final examination results and that I had been allowed to return home in the meantime. She took this at face value and bustled about preparing food and sending out messages to friends and relatives inviting them to join in a small feast to greet the return of her successful daughter. I was churning inside, but did my best to answer the many questions and respond to the simple good wishes of the community.

'For how many days are you staying?' Caught up in my deceit I stammered that I would be at home for nearly two weeks. To my relief no one thought to challenge me that this was a strangely long time during the normal term, and the moment passed.

My unexpected homecoming was a source of conversation in the village but this was quickly overtaken by the dramatic events of the following day. I heard a great commotion and went down the track to the main clearing to find out what was happening. I was told that a rogue elephant had been reported in the area. The village houses were flimsy and vulnerable, as were the crops upon which everyone relied. Parties of villagers were being dispatched to guard the edges of the fields in the hope of distracting or frightening off the intruder.

Fortunately our village escaped but the very next day the neighbouring Singpho village was attacked by the elephant which, completely out of control, smashed into the central clearing, trampled three huts and killed one of the village elders. The rogue beast had now retreated into the edge of the forest but could be heard crashing through the trees and it was feared that he would shortly return and wreak further death and destruction.

The Europeans at the Pengaree tea estate had guns, and a deputation had been sent to them but it seemed that the planters were not keen to take on a task that they might have regarded as routine thirty years earlier: a rogue elephant was highly dangerous and they decided that a specialist was needed to cope with such a task. Messages had been sent and help was said to be on its way.

Whilst there was much weeping and lamentation in the next-door village, and much apprehension in ours, the next rumour we heard was the cause of no little excitement and anticipation. It was that a famous and highly skilled hunter, a man known as the Elephant Boy of Tea, was on his way.

It was years later that I heard the full story of the Elephant Boy, so called after the hero of the film in which a child had survived in the jungle, rather like Mowgli in *The Jungle Book*. The story I heard was that a Major-General Sir Arthur Nuttall of the Gurkha Brigade had a grown-up son who had married and was then posted to Assam. He had subsequently become estranged from his wife on her deciding to return to England, leaving their small son Arthur Nuttall, the general's grandson, in his father's care. Unfortunately the father died and the white child or baba was raised by bungalow servants in their jungle village. The boy became an expert in kheda – elephant training – and a talented shikari or elephant handler. After years in the jungle, living as a native boy, he fell ill and was taken into the local estate where he was seen to be white and immediately transferred to the tea estate hospital.

The boy was a child of the jungle village, his friends were elephants and tribesmen and he had neither education nor knowledge of European customs or way of life. Nonetheless the tea estate management decided that it was an unacceptable situation for a white child to be in and therefore arranged that the boy, Arthur, should attend St Paul's School in Darjeeling. It was soon clear that he was a total misfit. Whilst he quickly absorbed the English language and Western culture he did this under protest and exhibited a violent temper. Incident followed incident and eventually he was compelled to leave without finishing his final studies, whereupon he returned to the jungles of the Naga Hills.

Fortunately the rapid expansion of the tea industry meant that contractors for jungle clearance were in great demand. Clearance meant elephants and the wild young man spoke their language. Thus it was that Arthur Nuttall came out of the jungle and was put in charge of the working elephant herd of a major contractor. He was in his element but again his fiery temper was his downfall and he lost that job and became a temporary ticket collector on the railways. Finding out that he was not being paid the proper rate, his violent reaction forced his resignation. Now he started all over again at the very bottom of the tea estate world, as an apprentice at Moran tea estate. 'Nutty' Nuttall, as he came to be known, again flourished, finished his apprenticeship and became a valued, if occasionally troublesome, planter. He was popular with the workers on the estate being fluent in Hindi and Assamese, and was quickly promoted, eventually becoming Acting Superintendent of Moran Tea Company.

During the war the Japanese air force bombing was widespread and their infantry forces moved into the Naga Hills causing many planters to evacuate, including the Superintendent of the Moran Company. Foolishly Arthur Nuttall, as Acting Superintendent, spread the rumour that his senior had run away; when the truth came out yet again Arthur was out of a job. Managing to find work with the Makum Tea Company in 1944 he once more achieved promotion, was transferred to Namdang Tea Company and was billeted in Bogapani.

Here the wheel turned full circle. Arthur was asked to destroy a rogue tusker which was creating havoc at Bogapani railway station. He confronted the animal and instead of shooting it simply talked to it, finally leading it away. It seems he had noticed faint chain marks on the elephant's feet and so reasoned that it was not wild but would understand mahout's language. The myth that he could communicate with wild beasts started then and from that moment his reputation as a master and hunter of elephants was made. So it was that he came to be on the way to Pengaree.

A huge elephant, thickly coated with mud, a houdah on its back with two white people looking out, passed our isolated property and lurched down the narrow track towards the cluster of village houses. I watched the tallest of the two look in my direction. I ran down the path after the elephant and reached the other houses as it knelt and the two men were helped down. They were dressed in khaki and as they stepped out they were greeted by the headman and given directions by the excited villagers. Three of our best hunters or shikars from the village were selected and given ammunition holsters and other equipment to carry including the big elephant gun. I saw that the taller man, who was Arthur Nuttall himself, was handsome in a rugged sort of way. He wore a revolver at his hip and carried a lighter gun. Climbing back into the houdah with the shikars trotting alongside the stalking party set off into the jungle.

It was five hours later, as dusk was falling, when the group returned. News had travelled ahead and we had already heard that they had been greeted and fêted in the neighbouring Singpho village. Our village congratulated them similarly, the native hunters reporting in boastful terms that the elephant had been killed. Long and voluble descriptions of the hunt were being given as the Englishman smiled at the outpouring of thanks, threw away his cigarette and went to climb back into the houdah. Suddenly he saw me and seemed to hesitate. He called over the headman, the Gaon Bura or village elder, and they had a conversation as they looked in my direction. I was nervous and ran back to our house, knowing that the elephant carrying them would soon be passing by.

The next thing I knew was that the elephant had stopped nearby and the Englishman and Gaon Bura were approaching Mama's house. I was being beckoned to join them.

I now know that Arthur Nuttall had noticed me because of my fairer skin and particularly because I was wearing the clothes in which I had returned from the school. I suppose I stood out in this remote and cut-off community and I could understand that he had seen this as unusual. Mama was overcome with excitement as she went to greet the distinguished guest and bustled about to prepare some chai.

The Englishman started to address me in Assamese. To his initial surprise I was able to reply in English and he soon discovered that this was because I had been at a convent school. He asked why I was in the village. It was fortunate that we could talk in English since Mama did not know what was being said. I therefore blurted out the recent events that had led to my being expelled from the Little Flower School. By now it was clear to Mama that I was distressed and that Mr Nuttall was being sympathetic; but instead of telling her the truth I said that I was telling him of my early life and Mary's death, which seemed to satisfy her.

Mr Nuttall said that he would see if he could help, salaamed his thanks to my mother and set off still acknowledging the vocal thanks of the villagers who had followed him down the track and were waiting outside our hut ready to wave him off. For a few hours I was an object of attention and interest but I told everyone that he had just been interested in my schooling and they seemed satisfied. As I curled up in the hut that night I prayed that some miracle might happen.

Four long days passed. I had all but given up hope of any salvation through Mr Nuttall – what could he do anyway? I resolved to tell Mama. I planned to say that I would approach Daniel in the hope that he might at least be able to find me a cleaning or waitressing position perhaps at one of the planters' clubs where I could try to give myself a better, if servile, future than that which awaited me in the village.

'Hunter coming back! Is there another tusker?'

I heard the cries of one of the boys who was running past our house from the direction of the river. The fastest children soon came into view from the village and I watched as a battered and dusty Land Rover forced its own wider route down the track and stopped in front of our hut. The rains had started and as Mr Nuttall strode through the mud towards us the children and other villagers who had arrived scattered to the cover of the surrounding trees from where they could peer out and watch.

'What is the matter? What is happening?' Mama was rushing about, arranging the charpai for the great white hunter to sit down, anxiously looking at my nervous face.

'You are able to return to school.'

Mr Nuttall spoke in English and smiled patiently as my tears overtook my stammered thanks.

'I think you had better tell your mother what has happened.'

Mama's understanding of English was sufficient for her to have understood what had been said without knowing the reason. In a torrent of Assamese I gabbled what had happened, telling her of the ultimatum that I should get married and of my expulsion. I told her how sorry I was that I had not been able to tell her the truth and she just stood there with her hands to her mouth.

Mr Nuttall interrupted to tell me that he had met with the parish priest at Digboi, Father Fosati, and that they had jointly confronted the sisters at the Little Flower School saying that a young girl with incomplete education and no means of support should be helped and not expelled. They had called on the sisters to remember their religious foundation and principles; but I was later to learn that it was only when Arthur Nuttall agreed to pay for the remaining shorthand classes to finish my course that the nuns had relented.

All I cared about was that I was now able to return to school. I did not know how to thank my new-found saviour and was stumbling over the words when he held up a hand, told me to stop and went back to the Land Rover. I watched him lift a large cardboard box out of the back and carefully bring it back to the hut where he solemnly handed it to me.

Inside the box were three dresses which he said had belonged to his daughter Diana and that she no longer needed. There was also a bottle of perfume and, finally, an envelope in which I found the sum of fifty rupees – as much as a sirdar on a tea estate would earn in a full month.

Of course I cried even more. I had never had dresses like this, perfume was not something I had ever contemplated, and the money would not only pay for my ticket back to school but provide pocket money for the foreseeable future. I knelt on the mud floor in thanks to Mr Nuttall but he just lifted me up by the hand, wished me every good fortune and went back through the rain to the Land Rover which soon bumped off through the trees towards Pengaree.

CHAPTER FIFTEEN

Sister Margherita was hardly gracious when I returned to Digboi. Her obvious discomfort no doubt came from her being forced to acknowledge that I seemed to have rather more influence than she had given me credit for. None of the sisters mentioned the circumstances of my earlier departure. It was explained that the shorthand and typing classes were to resume as before and I was able to settle back happily into my life surrounded by my friends.

Even those girls who had previously been disdainful of what they regarded as my lowly status gave me grudging respect. One or two even persuaded themselves to admire my new dresses and looked enviously at the shapely perfume bottle beside my bed in the dormitory. After the huge trauma of those last weeks I found a new lease of life and threw myself into my studies with great enthusiasm. I felt that the future course of my life was now charted out.

I took my final shorthand and typing exams and passed. I was fulfilled and very happy. My friends and I were now at an age when we could move on from the Little Flower School and I was excited to be offered my first job with James Warren & Co. Ltd, a small company in the town. The salary was low at only 150 rupees a month but I felt I would just be able to afford to rent rooms in Dibrugah, although with rent and travelling to and from work there would be very little left over from my salary at the end of each month.

Now I had a stroke of good fortune. A school friend called Maureen, who had left the Little Flower School the previous year, had found a job in the town teaching at a private school and offered to share her rented rooms with me. I was happy to accept. The arrangement seemed ideal: we both went out to work and we could both lead independent social lives but we would have someone to talk to when we came home.

Maureen had family in the area: her father was an officer in the River Steamer & Navigation Company and her parents lived nearby together with her brothers and sisters. We didn't keep servants so did all the housework ourselves. I had become rather expert at cleaning from my time at school but as far as cooking was concerned I was absolutely raw – I had not been allowed in the kitchen at either of the convent schools and at home Mama would do everything. I managed to get by with the help of Maureen and a good Anglo-Indian family as near neighbours but my cooking remained rudimentary and whenever Maureen was out I was quite happy to manage with a loaf of bread and a cup of tea! I did not go back to the house for lunch but would instead carry a snack, or tiffin, and eat this in the company's waiting room. It felt good to know that I was able to be independent and support myself.

My lunchtimes were occasionally sociable. It was company practice that visitors would not normally be seen until after lunch so there were often people sitting in the waiting area until the offices reopened in the afternoon. One day a young Englishman called Tony Clarkson offered to take me out to lunch at the Dibrugah planters' club which was quite a distance from the centre of town. He took me on the back of his scooter and we ate quickly so that he could get me back before the office reopened. Unfortunately I was seen on the scooter by the parish priest, Father Dalsovo, and when I reached my rooms that evening he was waiting for me. He cross-examined me about the man I had been with: it seemed that the Father saw me as a vulnerable convent girl who needed guidance. He said he thought my present accommodation was unsuitable and that I needed to be watched over.

The next week I was sent by Father Dalsovo, clutching his letter of introduction, to visit Mrs Ratna Baruah who lived in a large chung, a bungalow raised on pillars. She was about sixty years of age and had four grown-up and good-looking daughters – Pronoti, Ira, Pakhi and Kuku – all married. She rented out rooms and although she did not have one to spare, since it was the Father who had made the request she allowed me to use a small room that had previously been an office. I was allowed to share her bathroom too, although for that purpose I had to go down the front stairway, walk underneath the bungalow and then climb up the back stairs to the bathroom. I was very sad to leave Maureen but she was comfortably involved with her own family and agreed that I ought to do what the Father had recommended.

I was very happy with Mrs Baruah who took care of me very well. Since her daughters had left home I was some company for her in the evenings and she would often take me out to visit her friends locally. This was good as I did not have any other form of entertainment or a boyfriend.

There were two disturbing incidents. One of the other tenants was an elderly gentleman of about sixty-five years of age with whom I exchanged pleasantries – he was always very polite. One day Mrs Baruah handed me a large parcel and told me that someone had delivered it saying it was from my mother. The wrapping was too good to be from a villager and there was no sender's name. I opened the packet to find a negligee, panties and dressing gown together with a set of make-up and some Cadbury's chocolate. I was frightened since I could not think who would send me such expensive things. Mrs Baruah said the parcel must be from a boyfriend. I told her I did not have a boyfriend and she called me a silly girl and said I had better use it all anyway.

The dressing gown was very useful for my trips to the bathroom, but when I opened the chocolate I found a note saying 'To the beautiful pair of eyes' which made me even more worried. Months passed and I feared that my new admirer would come to the office or even stop me in the street, but nothing happened. My daily routine was to leave my towel and underwear in the bathroom to dry after my evening bath but one day I arrived for my bath early and found them missing. I went back to my room to see if I had left them there and when I returned to the bathroom, empty handed, I was surprised to see the missing items were there. The towel was warm and rather stiff and I scolded the servant boy whom I suspected of using the towel on his ironing board as extra padding. When I threatened to report him to Mrs Baruah he was frightened and suddenly blurted out that the old gentleman used to remove my towel and underwear and take them to his room.

I was disgusted and told Mrs Baruah what had happened, but she would not hear any criticism of her lodger and said that I must be imagining things. Some weeks passed and another parcel arrived. Among the contents was a pink dress with a label marked 'Punjab Tailors' so I went to the shop and found out from the owner that the dress had been bought by the elderly gentleman at the bungalow. Now at last Mrs Baruah accepted that there was a problem and took action, asking him to leave; although she used the excuse that she needed the room for her family since she did not want a confrontation.

The second incident was with another tenant, a pilot officer who lived in the next room. One hot summer night I left the window open with the table fan running. I was disturbed by a noise and saw a shadow on the wall and then a man jumped down from the window and on to my bed. He put his hand over my mouth and told me not to make a noise and ran his hands all over me. I was terrified but managed to break free and scream. Pronoti was staying in the house at the time so I ran along the corridor to her room and woke her up. I said that I suspected I had been attacked by the pilot from the next-door room and although she did not believe me at first she was persuaded to knock on his door. On being challenged he said he had been fast asleep, having returned early from a party and gone to bed. Pronoti asked him why he had gone to bed with his suit on. The next day he too was asked to leave. I think the Baruah family were becoming rather tired of having me as a guest and at the same time I was increasingly aware of how vulnerable I was as a single girl.

My low wages meant that I was limited in what I could do in terms of outings or entertainment and whilst I kept at my job I longed for something more lucrative. Much to my surprise one of the friends I had met through Miss Dixon, a Mr George Bradley, came to see me with good news. It seemed that Mr J. E. Atkins, the labour adviser (who might nowadays be called a personnel manager) of the Assam branch of ABITA, the Indian Tea Association, was looking for a secretary. Mr Bradley had put my name forward. The job was at Dikom, twenty kilometres from Dibrugah, and I was to attend an interview.

In trepidation and wearing my best dress I travelled to Dikom and was interviewed by Mr Atkins himself. The interview did not go at all well. I found it very difficult to read back the shorthand I had nervously noted down, and my typing was full of mistakes and corrections. I was certain I had failed and travelled back to my lodgings in a state of depression. Little did I know that Mr Atkins' wife, who had been a secretary herself, had seen my test paper and persuaded her kindly husband that I would surely improve. The next thing I knew was a telephone call to say that Mr Atkins had decided to employ me on a salary of 450 rupees a month and with transport laid on so that I could commute to and from work by car! I was in raptures.

Mr and Mrs Atkins had no children of their own but they had four dogs, Jimmy, Lofty, Brownie and Buloo. All four grew progressively fond of me and I of them. Lofty, a dachshund, faithfully followed Mr Atkins to and from his office which was within walking distance of the bungalow where they lived, only a stone's throw from the road leading to Digboi.

I was now just twenty-one years old and still rather unworldly. Both Mr and Mrs Atkins became very protective of me and each Monday morning I was required to give my new mentors a brief explanation of how I had spent the weekend. They kept a close interest in my personal life and social activities. As for my work, that gradually improved, but this was only due to the patience of Mr Atkins in putting up with my mistakes. I saw him as my friend, philosopher, guide, teacher and, almost inevitably, a father figure.

As to my real father, I continued to harbour hopes that I might trace his family and learn about my roots. I often discussed my longings with Mr Atkins, and he made the sensible suggestion that I should find out from Mama on my next visit to Pengaree which regiment my father had served in. I could not think why I had not thought of this before and went home with eager anticipation. Sadly, my hopes were dashed when Mama could only tell me that she knew my father had been 'killed in action' but had no knowledge of either his regiment or his rank.

In social terms and outside my working life I expected to be isolated, as many of my breeding were, but it was a small town and fortunately the Anglo-Indian community was active. There were only a few of them but I would meet some of them on Sunday mornings after church and was occasionally invited to have a meal with these new friends.

One day two young handsome men came to the house looking for Mrs Baruah. They were very courteous and when I told them she was out I asked where they had come from. They said they were from the air force and their names were David and Ian; they were both Anglo-Indians. I was rather impressed. Boldly I invited them to my room for a cup of tea and asked if they were pilots and perhaps stationed at the Chabua airfield nearby. The next day Ian came to seem me again looking very sheepish. He told me they were not in the air force but that they worked in tea – they had said they were with the air force since they thought that might make them more attractive to me. David was the one who was said to be very interested in me but in the event it was Ian with whom I kept in touch.

Some evenings I would visit a friend called Jane who was happily married to an Assamese man with two sons. There I met an Englishman called Roy Hooper. He was a big man and twice my age. He was obviously keen on me and I enjoyed his company. He visited me at the bungalow and took me out to meet his other friends in the tea business, hoping to make me more involved in the culture and thereby presumably more enthusiastic about him. We got on very well together, he made me laugh and he was clearly destined to be a powerful and influential man within the Moran Tea Company for whom he worked.

I persuaded myself that I might come to love Roy. Mr and Mrs Atkins were far from convinced – I think they regarded both the age gap and the difference in social status as impossible obstacles – but as usual I was stubborn and did not listen to their advice.

Looking back I think Roy was very much attracted to me but at heart it was partly because he was sorry for me and partly because he was very lonely. After a few months, to my excitement but also apprehension, he asked me to marry him and said he had applied to the company for permission to take a wife. I hesitated and then said yes.

I had a sleepless night trying to imagine what the future would be like; but the following morning Roy came to me in a state of distress and told me that the executives of the company had refused permission. The senior people in the company had already met me socially and I guess that they felt I was not quite the person to be a tea executive's wife. Roy confessed that they had told him to go home on leave, find a wife in England and come back married. He said he did not know what to do, he talked dramatically of leaving the company and marrying me anyway but I was pretty sure that he wasn't really serious about this and I would hate to have seen him give up his job. By now I knew him well enough to be aware that he was fiercely ambitious and that it would be quite wrong for him to throw away his career.

The trouble was that Roy was of an age when he desperately wanted to have a wife. We talked far into the night and the next evening he came round to the bungalow after work and we went for a long walk together. He said that he had decided to follow the advice given by the company and was deeply sorry.

I was upset but deep down I think I had realized that it would not have worked out even if he had been given permission to marry. Mrs Atkins could see my distress and consoled me as did Mrs Baruah, although I do not think that the latter had approved of the proposal anyway. The Atkins made sympathetic noises but I could sense their relief also.

The planter community was very active and there were very few single European or even Anglo-Indian girls in the area. This was understandable: the lights of Delhi and Calcutta were a brighter and more enticing alternative to the isolation of Assam. The other issue was that most of the Indian girls were kept on a short rein by their parents and would tend to socialize within their own social and religious groups and families.

So there I was, young, unattached and by all accounts attractive.

My lighter skin marked me out as different and perhaps even alluring to many Indian men. Whilst I was still a shy convent girl at heart I wanted to make the most of my independence and saw no reason why I should not maximize my advantages. I quickly worked out how to dress for different occasions, had my long brown hair cut into a modern style and soon found myself on almost every planter's guest list and so invited to a series of lively parties. Most of the parties were held at the various planters' clubs, the Panitola Club generally being regarded as the best of these.

I do not think the Atkins' really approved of my new social success but they liked to see me happy and their weekly Monday briefing, when I told them where I had been and whom I had met, seemed to keep them reasonably content. Naturally I was careful to give acceptable descriptions of my activities. Mrs Baruah was generally disapproving of my constant outings but I was popular with her daughters so she put up with me. And so I continued in this way, working hard but happily in my fairly sheltered environment and then going out at least twice a week to the various club nights and parties. Of course I went back to the village to visit Mama and her family as often as I could, and I continued to make enquiries of the planters that I met to see if any of them could help me in my quest for my father's family. But the people I met were of a younger vintage and my questions led nowhere.

Occasionally my childhood friend Aileen would come to see me. She was working as a teacher in a convent at Tezpur and was able to visit during her summer and winter holidays. I looked forward to her visits and we enjoyed reminiscing about school life.

The Christmas after I first met Ian he told me that the manager at his tea company, Alan Morris, was keen to meet me. He therefore invited Aileen and me to his bungalow for Christmas lunch. Alan had a ten-year-old son but his wife had sadly died. We were excited but nervous as we had not been to a formal meal like this before. The day came and a car was sent for us. The garden was the Romai tea estate only about fifteen miles from Dibrugah. We were offered soft drinks and snacks and then called into the dining room. Unfortunately the seating plan was such that I was the first one to be served by the bearer whereas I had been hoping that I would be able to watch how everyone else helped themselves. Neither Aileen nor I had been to a Christmas lunch before or even seen a turkey or such a well-laid table. Each time the bearer came round Aileen and I looked at each other for sympathy and support. When the peas and potatoes came round we both said 'no thank you' as we did not know how to eat the peas with a fork. Alan was concerned thinking we did not like the food, but prior to this we had always had buffet-style meals so this was all very strange to us. I fear we were not good company that day but Alan appeared to want to be with me since he invited me out on subsequent occasions. I liked him very much.

Now my friend Jane's married brother John visited from Canada and we all went off to the Panitola Club to celebrate. During the course of the evening I was looking across the large reception room adjoining the bar when I saw a tall and distinguished-looking Sikh in air force uniform. Our eyes met and he immediately detached himself from the people he was with and came over to introduce himself. He said his name was Mohan Singh. I found him very attractive, he was a senior air force officer and he said his home was in Jullundur in the Punjab but that he was temporarily stationed near Dibrugah. He was twelve years older than me.

We talked all evening and I went home with my head in a daze. The next morning the telephone rang at the office and it was my new-found friend inviting me to an air force party that coming Saturday and offering to pick me up. I was very excited and spent hours dressing myself up for the evening. I cannot remember much of the party itself as I had eyes only for Mohan who in addition to being very handsome was excellent company.

Mohan invited me to other air force parties and before long I was becoming known as his girlfriend. Friends from the tea estates started to invite both of us to their parties knowing that I was going out with him.

Alan Morris did not know of my new relationship with Mohan and invited Aileen and me to join him on a film night at the Panitola Club. Unfortunately Mohan arrived too and greeted me effusively. Alan was at the bar at the time and when he came over he asked me who the air force man was. I told him he was Aileen's boyfriend as I didn't want to hurt anyone. A few minutes later Mohan asked me who Alan was and I told Mohan that Alan was Aileen's boyfriend. Fortunately there was a good understanding between Aileen and myself and she took it well. A short time later she went back to Tezpur at the start of term which meant that when Alan again saw me with Mohan at the Panitola Club he realized that I had a boyfriend and to my great regret I did not see him again. As the news of my relationship spread, Ian's friend David also lost interest in me. Looking back I realize how differently things might have turned out if I had not had eyes only for Mohan.

CHAPTER SIXTEEN

I was in love with Mohan and could not see enough of him. He would invite me to parties and we would stay out progressively later and later. The gate to Mrs Baruah's house was always locked at eleven at night and as she would not let me have a key I would climb over the gate to get back in. One night I tore a pretty dress that got hooked over the gate as I jumped down.

Mr and Mrs Atkins realized what was happening as my Monday morning briefings on the events of the weekend became shorter and less informative. I was hardly going to describe to them the passionate love-making that had now become a feature of my young life. I realized that I was hurting them in not being as communicative as I had been previously, but I was young and single-minded and not ready to listen to their advice.

Equally Mrs Baruah was becoming less friendly, clearly disapproving of my constant outings and late-night returns. Jane tried to counsel me but I now saw Mohan as my confidant and I was foolish enough to feel that I needed no other help.

One evening, after a particularly late return the previous night, Mrs Baruah called me to her sitting room. She was embarrassed but firm: we could not go on in this way; she was giving me notice that she wished me to find alternative accommodation.

I was shocked. I had not anticipated this was going to happen and still could not see that I had done anything wrong. I rang Mohan immediately and he came round. We sat in his car and talked. He said he would find me a house and help with the rent.

The next day he told me he had located a four-roomed house and that he would pay half the rent to make it affordable. He said he recognized that he was responsible for my having to move. Although the house was small it was in a good neighbourhood and I was to discover that my neighbour to the left was a medical college professor, to the right was a judge and to the rear a public prosecutor so I felt I was well protected!

I was tearful and upset to be moving, but the excitement of having a house to myself where I could entertain my lover at will was overwhelming. I bought a few pieces of furniture and found a woman to do part-time work during the day and stay occasional nights.

There was to be another addition to my household. From visiting Mama I knew that she had taken in a boy whose parents had died soon after his birth. They were related to us. He was called John Tanti and was now four years of age but very independent. Mama agreed that John could live with me; the woman I employed would look after him during the day and I would take care of him at night. To complete my new home I bought a dachshund puppy which I called Bimbo. John and Bimbo became good friends and I felt that Bimbo would protect John when I was out.

I was happy in the new house and Mohan visited regularly. I was reasonably friendly with my neighbours although they regarded themselves as of a different class and were unhappy about my single status – girls of my age living alone were rare as it was not considered safe. If I was attacked the police might well take no action. I was seen as vulnerable.

The fear of vulnerability was soon to be justified. It was known that I was fond of dogs and this led to a frightening incident when one night a small puppy was left outside my door. The poor puppy was crying outside and Bimbo was sniffing from the inside when I heard a man's voice telling me to take the puppy in as it was disturbing the area. I called out that it was not my dog and that I was not going to take it in. For over half an hour the voice urged me to open the door but I refused and eventually there was silence. I was terrified and still would not open the door as I was all alone with John and Bimbo. Later I was told by my neighbours that they had heard that the man was a local bad character, he had two other men with him and he was using the puppy as a ruse to make me open the door so that they could rape me.

After some months Mohan was posted to Jorhat which was about a hundred miles from Dibrugah. I was very concerned because it meant that his visits were now less frequent. He would stay with me most weekends but I was alone during the week. When he could not have time off at weekends he would invite me to Jorhat and pay for my transport there and back. I was able to stay at his lodgings in Jorhat. This was fine, we were in love and I was happy, although I was still worried about my weekday isolation.

There were weekends when I would go back to stay with Mama and catch up with the news of the village and family. Her house, standing at the side of the jungle path some way from the other houses, had a large open area of paddy fields at the back leading down to the river.

Mohan knew that I was going home one particular weekend and before he left he had made an odd request. This was that I was to stand in the fields at twelve noon and think of him. He assured me that he would be thinking only of me at that same time of day. This seemed a romantic idea so I went along with it but I felt rather foolish standing in the middle of the paddy fields on a raised path between the rows of rice plants, trying to conjure up thoughts of my loved one. Then I heard a sound which grew louder and I realized that a jet aircraft was flying low over the jungle. I put my hands over my ears – the plane was almost touching the trees and the noise was deafening. I was frightened there might be a crash and looked up, rooted to the ground with fear.

Suddenly I recognized the plane – it was a Vampire with twin tail fins and I knew that Mohan's 45 Squadron flew these small fighter bombers because he had once taken me to the airfield and pointed them out to me. It was then that I realized that the bomb doors of the jet were open. The plane banked steeply as it passed overhead and then came back towards me, and as it flew by for the second time I saw something drop out of the doors. I kept my eyes on this object and it splashed into the paddy about a hundred yards away. The plane banked and flew back over the clearing for a third time, waggling its wings. I waved until it disappeared into the distance and then I ran over to pick up the thickly padded package which had written on the outside in large letters, 'For my lovely Ann'.

I was trembling with relief and pleasure as I tore open the packet to find a large box of chocolates and a love letter. I could just make out Mama standing outside our house on the far side of the paddy and she waited as I came back towards her. Now I had to explain about my new boyfriend!

It was a time of great happiness save for the weekly isolation, but then Mohan announced that we were going to go on holiday and that he was also taking me to meet his parents in the Punjab. I had two weeks' vacation owing to me and I could hardly contain my excitement as the great day of departure approached. First we flew to Delhi: I had not been in an aeroplane before so that was an experience in itself. There we stayed in a hotel which was wonderful: I kept going backwards and forwards into the attached bathroom admiring the fittings, and went again and again on to the balcony marvelling at the view. We went shopping in stores the opulence of which I had never seen before and Mohan bought me a selection of clothes so that I could be shown off to my best advantage. I had a good figure, and on the arm of this thirty-five-year-old dashing air force officer in full uniform I liked to think that we made an impressive couple.

We took the train down to Agra and visited the Taj Mahal. I was admiring the monument from the side of one of the channels of water that run through the gardens when Mohan asked me to sit down with him on one of the stone benches. Suddenly he was asking me to marry him. I could only nod in happiness as he produced a small box and opened it to show me a beautiful diamond ring. I was in heaven.

In a dream I sat in the train holding my fiancé's hand as we travelled back to Delhi. I allowed my imagination to run free as I looked to the future and the position I would have as the wife of a senior officer. Perhaps he would be promoted to squadron commander and beyond. My life seemed complete.

The next day I was taken to the exclusive Delhi Sailing Club where I was introduced to Mohan's sister Molly who made me welcome. Mohan told her of our engagement and she congratulated me. After two days we caught the train to Jullundur and took a taxi to Mohan's parents' house. I liked them very much and they seemed pleased to meet me. I sensed a hesitation when I was introduced by Mohan as his fiancée but assumed that they were simply taken aback because he had not mentioned the engagement to them before. We had a happy two days with them before journeying back to Dibrugah. I had left John and Bimbo with Mama, and as soon as I could I journeyed to Pengaree to collect them and was able to tell her of all the excitements of my trip and break the news that her daughter was now engaged to be married to an air force officer. She seemed very happy.

Back in Dibrugah, still ecstatic after my wonderful holiday, my earlier concerns about security again proved to be justified. Another assault was attempted. An unpleasant local gunda, or hotel owner, broke the lock and chain on my front gate at dead of night and removed the porch light bulb. He shook the door and called out my name. He said who he was and asked me to open the door. I knew that he had a bad reputation – I had always been afraid of him; he was fat and ugly with pockmarks all over his face. I was very scared and whispered to John that he was to call out that I was not at home. John managed to do so, but the man did not believe him and carried on saying that he wanted me to open the door so that he could talk to me. I called out that I did not want to talk to him and would not open the door. I said that if he wanted to speak to me he was to come round in the morning. He then started to swear that he loved me and to say that he thought I was wonderful, that others were not sincere to me and that he would look after me. I knew he had the strength to break down the door and I was ready to run out of the back of the house if he did, but eventually he went away leaving me huddled up in the hallway with John and Bimbo in my arms.

I was very shaken and next day sent a note to say that I could not go to work. Mr Atkins' managing director, George Bradley, came to see me, and when he heard what had happened he reported the incident to the police but nothing came of it. I am sure my neighbours all heard that someone was trying to get into my house and I was distressed that none of them had come to my aid.

All of this illustrates how vulnerable I was as a young single woman living on my own, and how wise Mr and Mrs Atkins were in trying to look after me. I had not told Mohan of the first event and really did not want to tell him what had happened the second time because I knew how angry he would be. It was in vain: when he next visited he could see I was worried and eventually persuaded me to tell him of both incidents. Predictably he was very upset, he insisted on my telling him the full details all over again and was very understanding but very firm. He was adamant that it was not safe for me to live on my own and so I must go and stay with his parents in the Punjab. It would mean giving up my job and my new-found independence.

In my defence I suppose I can only say that I was in love and quite unable to see reason. Mr and Mrs Atkins were desperately worried about my decision and they spent hours trying to persuade me not to go. Jane and my other friends did likewise. Even Aileen, speaking to me by telephone from her school, tried in vain to deter me from leaving. They had to accept that I was engaged but they pointed out that there was no date set for a marriage, Mohan was much older than me and they thought that until I was married I ought to stay put.

CHAPTER SEVENTEEN

Those who know my stubborn character will guess what happened next. I gave up the tenancy on my house, sold the small amount of furniture I had and said a tearful farewell to little John Tanti and my beloved Bimbo. Mama was happy to have them back with her but John had become used to seeing me as his substitute mother and was very upset at my departure. Of course I promised to visit him often, but I knew that travel from the other side of India would be difficult and expensive. Secretly I harboured the thought that when I was a wife and had a child of my own Mohan might allow me to have John to live with us.

So the day dawned for my farewells. Mr and Mrs Atkins had very kindly packed up some little presents and food for my journey, but although I was effusive in my thanks I knew that I was to travel with Mohan so I expected that we would eat well at restaurants and on board the train.

The journey was uneventful, but I was apprehensive at the thought of having to live in a new household where Mohan would only visit when he could have leave of absence. I kept asking him when we could be married, so that we could then live together wherever he was posted, and he would simply reply, 'Be patient, little one, these things take time.'

The house in Jullundur was large and I had a big room to myself and an adjacent bathroom which I shared only with Mohan's younger sister who was still living at home. She was shy with me but friendly. Mohan's father Mohan was a government official and worked long hours and his mother had a busy social life so she tended to leave me to my own devices.

I had felt queasy on the journey to the Punjab but now found that I was increasingly feeling sick each morning. It took only a few days of this for me to realize that I had missed my last period and that I was probably pregnant.

I did not know what to do. I decided to ask Mohan's mother for the name of their family doctor without giving her the reason. She gave me a strange look but provided me with the details, and the next day found me in his surgery. He said that he would ring me with the results of the tests that he had taken but he was almost certain that I was right. Later that day the telephone rang and he gave me the confirmation.

I was dismayed. Although I was engaged I did not want to have the baby out of wedlock and no date had been fixed for the wedding. I rang Mohan and left a message. The border conflict of the Indo-Pakistan war was raging and the air force was in constant demand. I knew that he had very little spare time. Eventually he rang me back and I told him the news: there was a silence over the line for a while before he gave me his congratulations and said how happy he was. I asked when he would be home and he said that he would try to get time off that coming weekend.

I did not tell Mohan's parents who were rather distant towards me that week and I desperately looked forward to Mohan's return. Eventually he arrived and kissed me and said how pleased he was at my news. He took me to my room and perched on the end of the bed as I sat in the armchair in the bay of the window. I asked when we could be married.

'I have a confession to make.'

I could not think what was going to come next.

'I am waiting for my divorce to come through.'

Divorce? But there had been no mention of his being married. It could not be true, he could not be married already. I was completely stunned. I sat there with my hand to my mouth, unable to speak.

'I had meant to tell you. It makes no difference to us, we still love each other and we will be married one day, but these things take time.'

I remember shouting at him, I remember lying on the bed

sobbing, I remember feeling such pain as if my heart would break, I remember my broken questions between the tears and I remember the answers.

Mohan had been married for fourteen years; he had been separated for twelve years. I later found out that he had a reputation as a womanizer and that this had been the reason for his wife seeking a divorce. The fact that the divorce had not been finalized over such a long period seemed to prove that there were complications. Now I knew why his family had been reserved and occasionally distant. Now I realized how utterly I had been betrayed and how foolish I had been.

I stayed in my room for two days. Food was brought up and left outside but I could not eat. I cried most of the time, I had pain in my stomach and feared I might lose the baby but then I would think that this might be the best thing. On the second day the doctor was summoned and he came and stood outside the door. After some persuasion I allowed him in. We discussed my symptoms but otherwise he just talked to me. I told him that I wanted to kill myself and he talked some more. He told me I must eat and drink for the sake of the baby, he said that the new life was important and that I should think of the future.

Mohan had gone back to his base. His mother tried to talk things through with me and persuade me that time would resolve the divorce but I would not be convinced, I did not see that my faith in Mohan could ever be restored.

On the fourth day I decided to return to Assam. I knew the difficulties: it was hard being a young single woman in India; it would be much harder being a young single mother. I was going to be at enormous risk and very alone.

I did not say goodbye to Mohan. I had saved a little money from my previous earnings and also from presents that he had given me. I packed my few possessions and clothes and told his parents that I was leaving. When they saw that I was serious Mohan's father took me to the station in his car and helped me with my suitcase on to the platform, where he left me waiting for the Delhi train.

The journey back to Pengaree took three days. I was still suffering from morning sickness but my state of mind was much worse. I had developed a hard outer shell from my early lonely years at St Mary's Convent School, but the love of the past months had softened me; now I would need to harden my soul and once more learn to survive on my own.

I found a lorry from Digboi to Pengaree and trudged the final kilometres to Mama's house. As I came near Bimbo scented me and rushed to find his mistress, the whole of his hindquarters wagging with joy. John Tanti was playing in the mud outside and squealed with delight when he saw me. Mama took one look at my face and took me in her arms.

CHAPTER EIGHTEEN

If I saw myself as vulnerable as a single young Anglo-Indian girl, it can be imagined how much more at risk I would be as a single pregnant girl and then a single mother. Outside the protection of the village and immediate family I would be regarded as of easy virtue and open to assault. Complaining to the police was not likely to be helpful: in some castes an independent witness had to be found to testify in cases of rape, and the automatic denial by any assailant and his friends would almost certainly result in no action being taken. Furthermore I had neither house nor rooms to go to and without earnings I had no money to pay for accommodation. Even if I found the money, few landladies would be prepared to take in a pregnant girl without a husband.

As I recovered from what I saw as my ordeal in Jullundur, I renewed contact with Jane and with Mr and Mrs Atkins by taking an early train from Digboi to Dibrugah and spending the day visiting each of them before journeying home. They managed to avoid saying 'I told you so' but the unspoken words hung in the air. Their sympathy was real and of comfort but they could not think of any solution to my problem until I was able to work again, which would clearly not be until after the baby was born.

There was nothing for it but to stay in the village. Mama was very happy that I was back at home, although the small property was very crowded with the two of us, John Tanti and of course Bimbo. I helped in the house with cooking and cleaning, I visited my grandparents and other old friends in the village and I did my best to settle into the slow ways of village life. The rains came and the limits of day-to-day existence narrowed with the constant wall of water and resultant mud. Making running repairs to the fabric of the house, trying to prevent the ingress of insects, detaching the leeches to interrupt their daily attack on one's lower limbs – such was the nature of my life during those long months of pregnancy. Sometimes I would take out the pages of photographs and look at them. I even had the idea that there might be vital information on the back, so I carefully peeled off each photograph but found nothing to help me. Sometimes I would think longingly of my house in Dibrugah, my room in Jullundur, even of the luxury of the hotels in Delhi, but to no purpose: I had created this mess and I had to live with it.

It was now 1967 and the time when the baby was due. The village midwife, large and friendly, visited daily and was finally called out one late afternoon when I went into labour. Daniel had said that he could try to have me taken to the Pengaree Tea Estate hospital but I preferred to stay in the village and hope for the best. It was a long and painful labour but by the early morning I was holding my new little girl, whom I had decided to call Anita. She was lovely and I felt exhausted but surprisingly fulfilled, if apprehensive as to what the future held.

Something of a miracle now occurred. Mr Atkins had retired from ABITA but had accepted a part-time position with a firm of lawyers in Dibrugah called Associated Law Advisers. He wrote to me to say that he had managed to secure an offer of a job for me at the firm working for him. It would be at the same salary as before. He and Mrs Atkins had also realized that I would need to earn enough to employ someone to look after Anita and his letter said that he thought he might be able to find me some extra out-of-hours work to supplement my income.

Mama looked after Anita and John whilst I travelled to Dibrugah for the interview. This went reasonably well and the law firm, trusting Mr Atkins' recommendation, confirmed the job offer. As to accommodation, the office chowkidar or manager, a man named Bahadur, told me that he could organize a place for me in a Bengali widow's house. I went to see her – the room was small but I had to start somewhere so I arranged to move in. With Mama's help I found an ayah or nurse for Anita. She was a young teenager called Mimi who came from the next village. She knew very little but seemed keen to learn.

So there I was with Anita, Mimi and John sharing one small room with only outside washing facilities and a pit latrine at the end of the garden for a toilet. This was not very clean; it also backed on to the crematorium and I found it rather frightening to go there after dark. I did not have any furniture so we slept on the floor at night. All I had was a tin box which held my clothes and an empty tea chest which I used as a dressing table in the morning and a dining table during the rest of the day. I stood it on its side and the hollow side served as a storage area. The landlady laid down a lot of restrictions including that no meat or fish was to be cooked in the house and onions were not allowed either.

Each day I would try to dress as tidily as I could after washing myself outside and then go off to work leaving Mimi to look after three-month-old Anita and seven-year-old John. John, although very young, was now used to doing some of the cleaning and usually made himself useful.

Some months went by and I knew that I could not carry on at the widow's house for much longer. Anita was crawling now and needing more space. When I came home from work each evening I started my quest for better accommodation and I would usually take Anita and Mimi with me. I followed up leads that I had heard about, and sometimes people gave me directions to houses that I might try.

The problem was that I was a single unmarried mother of mixed race and not likely to be seen as an acceptable tenant. The first question the house owners would ask was 'Where is your husband and what does he do?' Some were courteous in their refusal and made polite excuses but others were rude and told me to go away or made comments such as 'Who gave you this false information about my house?' There was no doubt too that many of the wives saw me as a potential threat to their husbands. Soon I was in despair and I asked Bahadur to help find a place which would be not too far from work but not too expensive. He did his best but the houses he found were outside my price bracket so it was in vain.

Then one morning when I got to work Bahadur told me the

good news that he had found some rooms in a house. These were much better than the one we were occupying; he said they were fine, I did not need to inspect them and the owner had agreed that I could take possession that evening. He said he would meet me there. I was delighted and was allowed to leave the office slightly early. I packed up our box and tea chest and put them on one cycle rickshaw whilst Anita, John, Mimi and I squeezed into another and off we went in convoy to the new house. Bahadur was waiting, we approached the front door and an elderly lady came out. It was explained that her husband had agreed to let us have the place but the lady said she was sorry, she knew nothing of the arrangement and we would have to leave. Her husband, looking guilty and embarrassed, then came out and tried to argue with her but she was adamant.

I was in despair. It was getting dark, Anita was crying and we were all tired and hungry. The rickshaws had left and there was no way we could return that night, even if the Bengali lady would let us in. Next door was a post office with a verandah running round it. I decided we would have to shelter there for the night and we huddled together and slept as best we could. Bahadur felt very guilty and as his house was nearby he went home and fetched food for us, but he said there was no room for us to stay with him.

It was a terrible night. The next morning I left Anita, John and Mimi on the verandah and went to work as usual. As soon as I got there I told Mr Atkins what had happened. He was very upset and asked why I had not telephoned him. He summoned Bahadur to his office and immediately dispatched him to the last house he had found for me, which I had thought too expensive. Fortunately it was still available, Mr Atkins said he thought I could manage it financially and I agreed to take it. I was able to fetch Anita and the others and move in immediately. Although the rent was rather high it was a nice place with attached bathroom and the owners, who were from a tea planter's family, were very friendly. I was to live there happily for the next five years.

After paying the rent I had little money and as a single mother my social life was very restricted. I was not invited out save by my local friends and Mr Atkins and his wife who took great care of me. He knew that I was hard working and if he saw me with an unhappy face in the morning he always enquired what had gone wrong. One morning I must have been looking worried because he questioned me and heard that Anita had fallen off the bed during the night. 'Do you not have a cot?' was the question, and when I said no he promptly telephoned his close friend Frank Wilson from the Maijan Tea Estate and a cot arrived the very next day.

One Sunday in church I met an overseas medical student. He seemed nice and we started to talk to each other each week. We became friends but then he began to say that he loved me and told me that as soon as he completed his studies he would take me and Anita to live with him. He was in his final year of studies and I had hopes for the relationship, but before long he was doing everything he could to scare Anita – I think he thought that I might abandon her and go with him. So that was the end of that friendship.

I got to know quite a lot of people through the office. Associated Law Advisers tended to deal only with tea garden cases and so a lot of tea planters used to visit with their labour and industrial disputes. One young Sardarji planter whom I had met once or twice in the office told me that he was having a big party and that I was invited. I explained that Anita was small and I did not like to leave her. I guessed that the party would go on late and I thought it better to refuse. He said it would be a good party and mentioned the names of various planters who would be coming. I asked if Mr Atkins would be there and he said that it was only for the young group and quite informal. He then said that I could take my daughter and my ayah, Mimi, who could use the guest room whilst I was there.

I had not been out for such a long time that I decided to accept. I spent a long time getting ready, packed the bottle of milk and other things for Anita and Mimi and waited for the car which he had said he would send for me. I was surprised when the host himself was driving the car and I asked who was at home to greet his guests, but he said he had left a friend at home and I was not to worry about it. His tea estate was Khowang which was about thirty miles away so the journey was long. On reaching his bungalow I could not see any other cars and when we got inside there was no sign of any party arrangements nor were there any bearers to greet us.

I asked what had happened. The young planter told me that there had been a death in his family and the party had been cancelled but he had been anxious not to disappoint me and had therefore thought to bring me along anyway. He told me to relax and brought out drinks. I told Mimi not to go into the guest bedroom but to stay with me: I was not comfortable and had guessed that there was something suspicious about the whole arrangement. My new friend told me that the cook had taken off, he complained that staff could not be relied upon and that it was typical of this to happen just when he needed someone to look after us and cook some food.

He tried to persuade me to relax and have a drink but I was frightened and went to the guest room to collect Anita and her things. He followed me and started chasing me round the bed. I called out to Mimi to help me and told him to stop this nonsense and take us home. When he refused I told him that I would report him to his manager – fortunately I had remembered the manager's name. Again he said that he would not drive me home and told me that I could walk home, knowing that it was too far for me to do so.

I saw no alternative but to set off out of the gate heading through the darkness towards what I hoped was the manager's bungalow, carrying Anita and with Mimi following behind. At this he came up behind us and said he would drive us back to Dibrugah which he did in silence. I was so relieved to get home safely but very disappointed too having been all dressed up and looking forward to going to a party.

Despite these problems of vulnerability I was happy to be in work and surviving in my single-parent role. Anita was growing up as was John, and Mimi was now very good with them. I had had some limited contact with Mohan Singh as at one stage I had threatened to take him to court to provide some maintenance money for Anita. He agreed to provide some finance for a period of time, he did not want rights of access and that was fine by me. The money stopped after a time and I did not pursue it further: I realized that to take him to court would involve him in loss of prestige if the case was successful and perhaps I was too soft to want to do this.

It was now 1972, Anita was nearly five and I had learned a great deal in my work and rebuilt much of my self-confidence. I knew that Mr Atkins, having already retired once, could not continue indefinitely so it was not a great surprise when he told me that he was retiring. I was very sad to hear that he and his wife had decided to leave India and spend their final years in Scotland but I could do no more than wish them every happiness and give them my heartfelt thanks for all they had done for me.

Mr Atkins performed one final act of kindness before he left: he gave me a letter of recommendation to Mr Beattie, the general manager of the famous Assam Railways and Trading Company in Margherita, who at that time needed a general secretary. Mr Atkins knew Mr Beattie well and so it was that I was appointed to this responsible position which now carried executive status. The company controlled not only the railways but also coal mines, tea estates and timber mills. I was very proud and happy to be in this new and senior job.

So I now moved to live in Margherita. I was in respected employment with ample earnings and so was able to take a house for myself and install our family in it. Life was quiet but good. I was even able to bring Bimbo back from Pengaree; he was now rather boisterous but still very happy to be with me.

Until the age of five Anita was able to go to the Ledo Valley Nursery School at the Ledo Club, run by the wives of the company executives. Mimi and John kept the house and I could now have a much more sociable life. I was allowed to join the Margherita Club as one of the very few women members and this gave me some considerable status. Club evenings and club days became the centre of my social activity. I even had a car of my own which I bought through the company car loan scheme.

When Anita reached her fifth birthday I found a place for her in a boarding school some distance away at the Carmel Convent in Digboi. It was a great wrench for me to have her leave home to go away to school at such a young age and inevitably I was reminded of the loneliness I had endured all those years ago. But I felt she needed to go away to school to have the best chance in life and Digboi was nearby so I was readily to hand if any problem occurred. She remained my great joy and I was delighted when she excelled at her school and said how much she enjoyed it; she was able to come home most weekends so we were constantly in touch.

In 1973, a year after I joined the company, the colliery section for which I was then working was nationalized by the central government and I was transferred to a sister concern called the Makum and Namdang Tea Company (India) Limited but working on the same terms as before. By now I was reporting to Mr J. C. Varma, the Group Financial Adviser, who later became a director of the company and moved to their Calcutta office. He was a very good and understanding man to work for.

I had two particular worries. The first was the primitive accommodation in which my mother still lived. The hut was very basic and as she grew older I felt she needed more comfort. I therefore decided to rebuild the original property, converting it into a much more spacious bungalow with proper sanitation and cooking facilities. Most of my leave was spent in Pengaree supervising the building work and making sure that my mother was properly looked after.

The second worry was what to do about Anita's education. I did not want to see Anita moving still further away but the sensible choice was for her to progress from the Carmel Convent to the distant Loreto Convent in Shillong. Shillong was remote, high up in the Megalayha mountains, but it had an excellent reputation and from there she would be able to graduate to the more famous branch of the same school, the well-known Loreto College in Darjeeling. Darjeeling was of course the other great centre for tea production in India and through the tea company I had contacts and links in that area but it was a long way from Assam. I was happy for Anita to be at school there but the distance meant that her visits back to Margherita and Pengaree were less frequent than either I or my fast-growing daughter would have liked.

As the years passed I channelled all the resources I could into Anita's education and saved money by taking my holidays in Pengaree with my mother rather than travelling further afield. My career continued to progress and I became settled in the community and respected in business circles. On occasions I would travel to Calcutta with Mr Varma and so began to build up contacts there.

Life was fulfilling, and very different from the turbulent years of my youth.

CHAPTER NINETEEN

My search for my roots never ceased. Whenever I came into contact with European tea executives or visitors I would ask for any information or for suggestions as to how I could advance my search. None of this came to anything until one day I decided to clear out the old files in my office. Whilst rearranging the papers I came across a circular issued by the commanding Lieutenant Colonel of the Assam Valley Light Horse. Attached to it was a Roll of Honour and to my excitement I saw that on it was the name S. V. Poyser. An address was given as Bokpara, Doom Dooma. I remembered the photographs in which my father was shown in uniform and quickly realized that this must be the uniform of the AVLH and that they would surely have details of his resting place, and possibly even the location of his family.

That evening found me in the Margherita Club showing the entry to the planters there. The most senior ones, whose recollection went back to those early days, told me that the AVLH had ceased to exist. One of them recalled that there had once been a headquarters building in Dibrugah itself but thought that the property had been washed away over twenty years before in the great Bramaputra floods of 1954.

I was bitterly disappointed but at the next opportunity went to Dibrugah and made enquiries there. I drew a blank: there was certainly knowledge that there had been a building and that it was not now there, but no information about the AVLH or what had become of it. There were some who told vague tales of the local exploits of the AVLH and the camps that were held but it was generally understood that the group had disbanded when its members joined a variety of regiments when war was declared.

More years passed. Anita was now nearing graduation from

Darjeeling and was talking of seeking to make a career in Calcutta. Mama was increasingly frail but still in good health overall. John Tanti was now grown up and had returned to the Pengaree community and we enjoyed meeting up when I visited. Mimi was still in my service but Bimbo had sadly wagged his tail for the last time.

I was settled and respected in my community in Margherita, I was equally respected in Pengaree and I made frequent visits to Calcutta. Although I was content with my life, the need to find out about my father and his family still burned within me.

The company was multinational and used to subscribe to the *Daily Telegraph*. The newspaper would first be read by the Superintendent and then be circulated to the five tea gardens within the company before being returned to the Superintendent's office for filing. I used to go through the paper at this filing stage, and would always read through the deaths column. My morbid thinking was that my father's parents might pass away, the name 'Poyser' would appear and this would then give me an address.

One day I chanced on a copy of the *Daily Telegraph* of 16th August 1985. What caught my eye was an article written by General Edward Fursdon who was described as 'Defence Correspondent'. He was writing about a V-J Day anniversary celebration. I had a sudden thought to write to him to see if he had any information about my father's resting place.

I still have my copy of the letter which I addressed to Major General Edward Fursdon on 16th September 1985 'care of' the *Daily Telegraph*, Fleet Street, London:

Dear Sir,

While reading the Daily Telegraph No 40, 483 London, Friday August 16th 1985, I came across your article 'V-J Day marked with Reception at Museum' and this gave me the inspiration of writing to you.

I would appreciate your help in please finding out the burial place of my father, Late S V Poyser. I have been trying for years but without any success. The purpose is just 'sentimental' and perhaps as years keep passing one becomes worse and I wish to pay a visit to his grave someday.

I am enclosing herewith a Photostat copy of a document which I came across in our office. Whatever other papers my mother had in our possession, such as addresses, were lost when I was very young. I do have a lot of photographs of him and his people in England. My grand father was a doctor.

My father was a tea planter and at that time he was working at Bokpara Tea Estate, Doom Dooma Post Office, Assam, India. The company belonged to R G Shaw Wallace & Co Ltd, 4 Bankshall Street, London EC3. My father got killed when I was just a baby of a few months old.

My mother is still alive – she is from the tea garden labour community and is illiterate. I know from her that my father was a wonderful person – and I really wish he was still living.

As for me, I am working as a Confidential Secretary in the above named tea companies' Registered Office, here in Margherita having its London Office at Victoria House, Vernon Place, London.

Sir, any assistance that you can please give me will always be remembered and do forgive me for the inconvenience caused to you.

With kind regards,
Yours sincerely
(Ann Poyser)

Much to my surprise, only two weeks later I had a short written acknowledgement dated 1st October. General Fursdon said that he had received my letter and would see what he could do to help. He explained that he had written to one of his friends in the Indian Army Association who would be familiar with the AVLH and might provide some 'clues' for him to follow up.

Only a week later an envelope arrived marked 'Indian Army Association'. I tore it open and found a letter dated 9th October from Lieutenant Colonel Mains. At first I found it difficult to take in what it was saying but read it with growing excitement:

Dear Miss Poyser

General Fursdon has passed me your letter of 16 September 1985. I have contacted the Commonwealth War Graves Commission and they have produced the following information.

'Lieutenant Stuart Vernon Poyser No 145287, Royal Engineers, seconded to Field Company No 3, King George V's Own Bengal Sappers *and Miners; died 12 February 1942 aged 30. Son of Arthur Vernon and Millicent Mary Poyser of Leicester'*

No 3 Field Company, KCV's Own Bengal Sappers and Miners was part of the 11th Indian Division which fought the Japanese from the Siam Border to Singapore Island. I see that your father died (on active service) three days before the surrender. His name is recorded on Column 38 of the Singapore War Memorial. This means that he has no known grave, otherwise the CGWC would have given me the Cemetery and plot number. I presume that he was buried before the surrender, but in the confusion the details of his burial place were not recorded, and were not found when the British retook Singapore. His name should be in the 'Book of Remembrance of Officers of the Commonwealth' in the Royal Memorial Chapel in the Royal Military Academy, Sandhurst. I will check, as I live very close and might be able to get a photograph of the relevant page.

You will be interested to know that I know Assam well; I was Chief Intelligence Security Officer for Assam, with HQ at Gauhati July 1942 to October 1943 and later when I was Chief Security Officer 14th Army, Assam was my 'ilaqua'.

Is your mother a Gurkah or hill woman; if so give her a special 'namaskar' from me and a 'Jai Gorakh'.

With kind regards

A A Mains

Chairman

Late 9th Gurkha Rifles, Indian Army

I was overwhelmed. For forty years I had longed to know where and how my father had died and to have details of his family. I had even mistaken his first name all those years, believing him to have been called Stephen. Now I knew where he had been killed, where he had been fighting and, more importantly, the names of his parents whose photographs were so familiar to me.

When I was able to compose myself I rang Anita's school and told her the news, I rang my other close friends and, back at work the next morning, I spent a contented hour showing the letter to everyone I knew. They were all very happy for me as they knew that I had been searching for information all my life.

It was Friday and the very next morning I set off for Pengaree in my car. Mama was surprised to see me as I was not due to visit for another week. I sat her down in the newly refurbished bungalow and read out my letter to General Fursden followed by Colonel Mains' reply. My mother cried, partly with the news and partly because of my joyful reaction. When we had both calmed down she asked me what I was going to do next. I said that I would have to see whether my father's family could now be traced. She said she knew this was what I was going to say, but I must be careful and above all I must not be disappointed if I found them but they did not wish to know of our existence.

I understood what she was saying. Many years had passed and I had read and seen what had happened as India moved to independence in 1948 and had gradually distanced itself from the former Empire. Many were the articles and books about Anglo-Indians and the difficulty not only of assimilation but of acceptance. I well knew that news of a previously unknown grandchild might be unwelcome, always assuming that my grandparents were still alive. Nonetheless I was determined to try to make contact, and the names Arthur Vernon and Millicent Mary kept turning over in my mind.

The next day I wrote back to Colonel Mains:

Dear Colonel Mains

I write to express my sincere and grateful thanks for your letter of 9th October and for all the trouble that you have so kindly taken to send the information about my father.

You will perhaps be interested to learn that from the age of about 13 I have been trying to obtain information about my father and to get in touch with his people but never succeeded perhaps because I did not know where to turn. Your letter has given me such joy that to express it is difficult. Prior to receiving your letter I did not even know what the initials S V stood for; I thought that my father's names were Stephen Vincent Poyser and always imagined him to be from Birmingham as some of his photographs that I have with me have a Birmingham Studio's markings.

My mother often talks about my father's sister whose name was Mary. She and my father were the only ones in the family and according to my mother (I am not sure of this), my paternal grandfather was a doctor. My mother has always spoken very well about them.

My mother is a Tribal (originally from Ranchi). She is living about 25 kms away from Margherita and the place is known as Pengaree, near Digboi (the famous oil town). My father had bought this plot of land for her when he was a tea planter in Pengaree Tea Estate. I mentioned to my mother about the correspondence exchanged between us and she was so grateful to know that so much trouble and pains were taken on her behalf and has asked me to convey to you her personal thanks, gratitude and good wishes.

I shall eagerly await any further details that you may be able to furnish regarding my father and would like you to know that I shall treasure the information you have so far given me.

Yours sincerely

CHAPTER TWENTY

I was still unsure how to proceed. How would I make enquiries in Leicester – it was so far away and I knew no one. I talked the problem through with my friends and whilst I was still thinking what to do next I was notified by the district post office that a bulky envelope had arrived marked for my attention. I rushed to collect it and found it was from General Fursdon and contained many photographs of the Kranji War Cemetery in Singapore. The letter opened:

December 7th 1985

Dear Ann (if I may)

Before I even left for the Far East Pilgrimage Tour, I had made up my mind that somehow I was going to trace and find your father's name in the Kranji Commonwealth War Graves Commission Cemetery, so that I could write and tell you I had found and seen it.

I went up there early in the morning of the day before the Memorial Service was to be held out at Kranji on Sunday November 10th, which was attended by the Duke of Kent and the Secretary of State for Defence, Mr Michael Heseltine – plus many diplomatic representatives of the Commonwealth.

I went up the day before, so that I had time to fulfill my mission. I soon found your father's name in the Book of Record. The entry reads:

'Lt Stuart Vernon Poyser (145287) RE, Seconded to 3 Field Company K G V O's Sappers and Miners. Died 12 February 1942. Aged 30. Son of Arthur Vernon Poyser and Millicent Mary Poyser of Leicester. Column 38'

I then went to find your father's name on column 38. I now send seven amateur photographs which I took for you, so that you can have a visual record of your father's Memorial.

The letter went on to describe the position from which each photograph was taken and then read:

I hope I may have now helped you, in my own small way, to settle part of something deep down inside you. Perhaps, I hope, you can now say – like one of the war widows did to me that first early morning out at Kranji –

'It's as if a veil has been lifted inside me – I now know where he is after all these years'. I hope so.

If it is difficult for you, please do not answer – I will understand. If you do please to my home not to the office address at the top of this letter.

Yours sincerely

Edward Fursdon

The kindness that both General Fursdon and Colonel Mains had shown was overwhelming. I did not know how to thank them. I wrote back to General Fursdon immediately and again journeyed to see Mama and read the letter to her and showed her all the photographs. She was very tearful at the sadness of seeing the Memorial but at the same time so happy to know that my long quest for information had been satisfied in such a manner. Whether or not my father's family could be located was another matter, but at least I now had the news that I had awaited for such a long time.

Shortly after General Fursdon's letter and photographs reached me the Chairman of the Makum Company, John Guthrie, visited our offices at Margerhita. It was a small community and my immediate superior Naloo Dutt happened to tell him of my recent success in tracing my father's memorial. To my surprise Mr Guthrie was very interested and asked me to sit down in the office he was using and explain what had happened and show him the letters I had received. When he had looked at them he said he would like to help by making some personal enquiries when he returned to London. He asked whether he might borrow some of my papers and in particular take copies of some of the photographs that I so treasured. Of course I was happy to agree but understood when he said that the task might be difficult.

As we moved into 1986 there was no news from John Guthrie and I began to give up hope. I realized that he had other business to conduct and enquiries would take a long time but I constantly hoped for some positive news. Then we had a visit from a Mr Moore who came to see me in the office and told me that John Guthrie had asked him to help, that he would be returning to London within a few weeks and would concentrate on making enquiries once he arrived.

It was in fact early 1987 when I heard further news. Mr Moore wrote to say that he had managed to trace the former address in Leicester of my grandfather, Arthur Vernon Poyser. Unfortunately the house had been sold and the new occupants knew only that Dr Poyser had died and it was thought that his wife had died many years before. The letter went on to say that further enquiries were being made to see if other members of the family could be located, and that if I could produce my birth certificate and some other formal information this would all help by way of identity if the investigations proved successful.

I was in turmoil. I appreciated that my grandparents would be old and I had feared that one or other might have died but to have come this far and to find that both were dead was distressing. Still, I gathered all the papers I could find to link me with my father, including the remaining precious photographs, and sent them off. I was very worried because I did not have a birth certificate but I wrote a letter to say that I might be able to obtain a certificate of baptism from Gauhati – I hoped that would be sufficient.

Having posted my letter to England and my request for a baptism certificate to Gauhati I waited in an agony of anticipation. So many months had passed since the photographs of Kranji Cemetery had arrived and I feared that the line of enquiry might have dried up. Then, only three weeks later, I received a further letter from Mr Moore containing the auspicious words:

Please do not concern yourself with any further documentation. You will be delighted to know that I have been in touch with your father's sister, a Mrs Mary V Mitchell (nee Poyser) and have discussed your situation with one of her sons. I understand that Mrs Mitchell is in the process of writing a long letter to you which she hopes to dispatch this week. No doubt you will receive this in the near future and I hope you will find it of tremendous comfort. I am pleased to have been of some help.

I read the letter over and over again. At last I had found my father's family. Over forty years of searching had finally reached a conclusion.

I managed to get through to Shillong on the telephone and told an excited Anita that our dreams had at last come true and that my father's sister, my aunt – I had an aunt! – was writing a letter. I drove to Pengaree to share the news with Mama. She was overwhelmed to hear that the sister of whom Stuart had so often spoken was writing to me. Her fears that I would be rejected appeared to be unjustified; and Mary was the name that Stuart had chosen for my sister all those years before.

I wrote back to Mr Moore:

… I am so very happy that I keep reading the letter because its like a dream to me – I can't believe that such a wonder has happened – I really cannot find words to express my feelings and gratitude for what you have done …

I found it hard to sleep that week. Everyone at the office knew what had happened, I must have been useless at my work but no one complained and they all rejoiced with me when the letter finally arrived. A handwritten envelope postmarked 'Leicester – England' and within it:

Dear Ann,

No doubt this letter will surprise you.

Last week I had a phone call from Mr Moore of the Company you work for, to say that my brother Stuart had a daughter!

Since then I have seen copies of all the correspondence of the last few years that you had undertaken to try to trace your father's family. I fully realize the difficult life you must have had and your feelings for your father and also that you would like to find his family. Naturally it has been a shock and surprise to me.

From your correspondence and all the letters you have written I fully realize that you are Stuart's daughter and acknowledge that fact and I'm glad, Ann, that he has left something of himself behind and wonder whether you resemble him?

My brother wrote to his parents every week for ten years and I have five years of those letters (1937-42) kept by my father who was very proud of his son. I nearly destroyed them last year so it seems fate that I didn't.

348

As the letters of condolence to my parents from his commanding officer said: 'he had no officer who excelled your son in gallantry, energy and efficiency – he was always in the thick of things – his fund of humour and amusing descriptions of his adventures were a tonic to us all.'

Stuart was a fine man and a father of whom to be proud. He had great courage and a wonderful sense of humour and was very popular.

With kindest regards from your 'Aunt' Mary (Mitchell)
I look forward to hearing from you soon.

CHAPTER TWENTY-ONE

The last twenty-four hours would live on in Ann's memory. She had flown before, as had Anita, but only on local flights between Assam and Calcutta and never in a large jet aircraft. They had taken the train from Calcutta to Delhi the previous day and stayed overnight with Ann's good friend Soom Bhatt. Ann did not tell her host that she had not slept, lying awake with her mind whirling as she contemplated the journey she was making. Soom had taken them to Delhi airport early that morning for the Russian Aeroflot flight to London Heathrow via Moscow. This had been the cheapest flight that could be found.

To Ann and Anita the plane was huge, Anita huddled next to the window as Ann sat in the centre seat constantly worrying about the arrangements. Would she manage the stop in Moscow, did they need to change planes? Would all the signs be in Russian? Would the flight onwards be delayed, and if so would the arrangements for meeting them still happen? Would the immigration people let them into the country, was the sponsorship letter, tightly folded in her purse, sufficient? What would they do if they were not met? Would she and Anita be made welcome?

The plane rattled and crashed in the turbulence. The plastic-packaged food was strange and although Anita ate most of hers, Ann was not hungry. Anita was young enough to take the journey in her stride and she chattered on as Ann felt her nervousness increase. At Moscow they had disembarked for an hour, and by following the other ongoing passengers Ann had been relieved to find that the boarding for the final leg was straightforward. Now they flew over Europe and Ann heard from the announcements, mercifully in both

English and Russian, that they were preparing for the descent into Heathrow.

Ann had not cried when she was questioned for so long by the passport officials. Why was an Asian woman and her daughter being sponsored to stay by an English solicitor from Leicester? Was it credible that she was related to this Leicester family? Was Anita her daughter? What guarantee was there that they would wish to return to India? It had taken an hour before they were finally allowed to proceed.

Ann had not cried when Christopher and his brother David waved at the two small Indian women as they emerged into the milling Arrivals area. The two tall men had greeted them with kisses and taken their luggage to the waiting car.

Ann had not cried when the car drew up after the long motorway journey through the unfamiliar landscape. There she had first seen her aunt Mary, standing waiting for the car outside her bungalow. She had not cried when Mary had helped her out of the car and hugged her. The final stage of Ann's forty-year search for her family was now complete, and as she sat in her aunt's sitting room quietly drinking in the atmosphere and watching Anita talking excitedly to her new relatives she began finally to relax.

They went into the garden for photographs to be taken. Mary stood tall with her arms around Ann and Anita. Suddenly Ann saw the long white bench standing under a tree on the far side of the garden. Her hands went to her mouth.

'The seat, look at the seat!'

Ann heard Mary's voice, as if in the distance, explaining:

'That bench came from my father's house — it used to stand on the path leading to the summer house.'

The scene was burnt into Ann's memory from the torn page of the album of her childhood dreams: the bench standing beside the winding path and the summer house in the background. Remembering the long hours spent poring over the pictures; remembering as a small child sitting on the earth floor of her mother's hut; remembering as a young girl carefully removing each picture in quest of clues to her father's name; remembering her long years of isolation – carrying the page of faded photographs wherever she travelled; remembering the pain of her long search.

Now at last she could grasp the reality of the reconciliation that her mother had said would never happen. The end of her journey.

And Ann cried.

EPILOGUE

Ann was made redundant when the Makum Company was taken over by another group which decided to reduce the size of its Margherita office. She resolved to set up her own tea estate. Using her redundancy money and additional savings she managed to purchase further land adjacent to the property in Pengaree provided by her father for her mother's busti. She cleared and planted the land which now flourishes as a small self-sufficient plantation named the PoyserBari Tea Estate. The leaf is processed at the nearby Pengaree estate and the quality of their Assam tea is such that it is supplied to Harrods in London and other retailers. Ann has also built a substantial house in Digboi at which she takes guests, travelling from there to supervise the management of the estate. She has visited her aunt and family in Leicester on a number of occasions and particularly enjoys looking through the family photograph albums and other memorabilia.

In 1989, two years after Ann and Anita first visited Leicester, Anita became engaged to a doctor from Calcutta. David and his wife travelled to India and were principal guests at the wedding, at the reception at the Bengal Club meeting many of the friends that had helped Ann over the years. Anita and her husband now have two children and have visited Leicester with them. Ann journeys from Assam to visit her aunt at regular intervals.

Mary Mitchell, in her 99th year as at September 2013, has an apartment in a residential home in Leicester, supported by her sons Christopher and David and their families who live nearby. She enjoys exchanging letters, emails and photographs with Ann and Anita and her family.

Monglee contracted cancer but survived until 1995, long enough to meet Christopher's daughter Sallie who travelled to Assam in that year – the first member of the Leicester family to visit Pengaree and the PoyserBari estate. In 2004 Christopher's stepdaughter Sarah was visiting Ann when they encountered Michael Palin during the filming of his 'Himalaya' travel series. Page 203 of the *Himalaya* book describes Ann's story and shows a photograph of Ann and Sarah, talking to Michael Palin, in a train near Digboi.

Mary with Ann and Anita at their first meeting.

BIBLIOGRAPHY

Unpublished collection of letters written by Stuart Poyser 1935-1942

Unpublished letters, diaries, photographs – variously by Vernon Poyser, Mary Mitchell, Arthur Mitchell, General Fursden, L. Moore, Brigadier Steedman and others

Unpublished writings (series of exercise books) by Mary Mitchell giving her life and family histories 1915 – 2011

Unpublished writings and notes by Ann Poyser giving her life and history 1939-2011

'A Tea Planter's Life in Assam' by George M Barker – Calcutta: Thacker Spink & Co 1884

'Assam Planter' by A R Ramsden – John Gifford Ltd, Charing Cross Road, London WC2 1945

'Assam Shikari' by Frank Nicholls – Tonson Publishing House, NZ 1970

'The Chota Sahib' by Harry Williams – ISBN 0-95-357990-5 – Harry Williams, Norwich 1999

'The Assam Railways and Trading Company Ltd – Centenary Volume 1881-1991' Pearson Surita for A R & T India Limited, Calcutta 1991

'Through Fifty Years – a History of the Surma Valley Light Horse' by W H S Wood – Assam Revie Publishing Co, Calcutta 1930

'The Story of the Assam Railways and Trading Company Limited 1881-1951' – Harley Publishing Company 1951 (V13390 – British Library)

'Tangyes Limited – a Hundred Years of Engineering Craftmanship' by

Rachel E Waterhouse – Smethwick, London 1957

'Handbook of Castes and Tribes on Tea Plantations of Assam' V25372 – British Library

'Blitz over Britain' by Edwin Webb & John Duncan – ISBN 0-946771-89-8 Spellmount Ltd, Tunbridge Wells, Kent 1990

'Wartime Britain' by Juliet Gardner ISBN 0-7553-1028-4 Headline Book Publishing, London NW1 2004

'Asiatic Land Battles: Expansion of Japan in Asia' by T N Dupuy – Edmund Ward (Publishers) Ltd, London EC2 1965

'Singapore Burning' by Colin Smith – ISBN 0-670-91341-3 Penguin Books Ltd, London WC2 2005

'Singapore 1942' by Alan Warren – ISBN 981-05-6680-8 Hambledon Continuum, London SE1 2002

'Singapore 1941-2' by Louis Allen – Davis Poynter Ltd, London WC2 1977

'The British Battalion, Malaya 1941-2' by Chye Kooi Loong – (private publication)

Box of hand-typed records of Malayan Campaign by Leicester Tigers Regiment (private collection)

'King George V's Own Bengal Sappers and Miners Association, Unit Records 1939-1947' IRW 1966, a, 1297

'Brief History of the Bengal Sappers and Miners. August 1939 to July 1946' printed in Roorkee in 1947 – British Library

'The Bengal Sappers 1803 to 2003' by General Sir George Cooper and Major David Alexander – British Library

Times Newspaper reports December 1941 – February 1942 – microfiches from British Library